Global Terrorism: An Overview

Global Terrorism: An Overview

Chester Alexis C. Buama

SOCIETY Publishing

www.societypublishing.com

Global Terrorism: An Overview

Chester Alexis C. Buama

Society Publishing

2010 Winston Park Drive,

2nd Floor

Oakville, ON L6H 5R7

Canada

www.societypublishing.com

Tel: 001-289-291-7705
001-905-616-2116
Fax: 001-289-291-7601
Email: orders@arclereducation.com

ISBN: 978-1-77361-129-7 (Hardcover)

ABOUT THE AUTHOR

CHESTER ALEXIS C. BUAMA

Chester Alexis C. Buama, is a college instructor at Laguna State Polytechnic University College of Arts and Sciences where he served as its College Research Coordinator, University Publication Adviser (Unit Head), Bay Breeze Group of Publications and Coordinator of Curriculum, Instruction Quality Assurance. He is also a member of local and international organizations: he is a senior Member of the Royal Institute of Educators, Singapore, Reading Association of the Philippines, and International English Learners Training Institute. He was a Philippine Youth Ambassador to ASEAN countries and Japan which was sponsored by the Cabinet Office of Japan (Office of the Prime Minister) and Office of the President of the Philippines in 2010. He has a Master's degree in Management major in Public Administration a. He was conferred a Doctorate Degree in Philosophy major in Public Administration, h.c. in 2016. At present he is teaching Principles of Management and Organization, Good Governance and Social Responsibility, Business Communication, Macro and Micro Economics and Philippine History and Constitution. Moreover, he has actively participated in the Civic Activities of the Global Cooperation Society International, Philippine National Chapter and is often invited as resource speaker in various journalism and leadership seminars in Laguna.

TABLE OF CONTENTS

Preface ... *ix*

Chapter 1 **An Extensive Historical Overview of Terrorism and Related Issues ... 1**

Definition of Global Terrorism ... 1

Historical Roots of Terrorism ... 9

Politics, Ideologies and Strategies of Both Contemporary and Older Terrorist Groups ... 18

Chapter 2 **Survey of Terrorism Today ... 33**

Introduction ... 33

Recent Attacks ... 46

Any Hope For The Future? Is Terrorism Getting Worse? ... 50

Trends In The Global Terrorism Index Over The Last 10 Years. ... 61

Chapter 3 **The Law on Terrorism ... 65**

Introduction ... 65

Terrorism-Related Laws ... 66

Legal Issues ... 77

Court Cases ... 78

Chapter 4 **Terrorism Funding ... 81**

Criminal Activities As A Source Of Fund To Terrorist ... 81

Narcotics Industry ... 83

Business Abuse Legally ... 84

Community To Strengthen Countermeasures ... 85

Myths Associated With Raising Funds To Support Terrorism ... 86

Paramilitarism ... 88

Terrorism, Organized Crime And Business ... 89

Chapter 5 **Chronological Survey of Major Terrorist Attacks, Evidence and Other Relevant Events ... 101**

Military Failure ... 116

Chapter 6	**Terrorism. Ideas of The Left and Right**	**125**
	Introduction	125
	Dissatisfaction From The Left: Ideology And Beliefs	127
	Right Wing Dissatisfaction: Marxism And Minorities	131
Chapter 7	**Counter Terrorism**	**137**
	Introduction	137
	Techniques of Combating Terrorism	138
	A Review of the Un Global Strategy Against Terrorism	140
	Weapons of Mass Destruction and Mass Casualties	145
Chapter 8	**Aspects of Natural Psychological Warfare: What Measures Must be Taken to Respond and Curb?**	**153**
	Emerging Threats From Ammunitions of Mass Demolition	153
	The Heritage of The Cold War	154
	Emerging Household Risk	154
	Synthetic Weapons of Psychological Oppression	155
	Natural Weapons of Mass Devastation by Fear Based Oppressors	156
	Reasons For Control and Response Planning	158
	Media Piano and Power Hypothesis	159
	No Production, is The NPT In Emergency?	160
Chapter 9	**Argument For Terrorism**	**163**
	Moral Yardstick	163
	Religious Test	164
	Conclusion	173
Chapter 10	**Brief Histories of Terrorist Groups and Biographies of Leaders of Global Terrorist Groups**	**175**
	Introduction	175
	The Terrorist Leader	176
	Terrorist Groups	200
	Organization / Leadership	227
	References	**231**
	Index	**237**

PREFACE

The recent terrorist attacks in different parts of the world have necessitated people to crawl the internet to look for information and answers relating to terrorism activities. Terrorism dates back to the 18th century and it advances day by day. Terrorist organizations have also flourished and despite measure to counter their growth, they seem invincible due to their large networks and nefarious methods of operation

This book looks into various aspects of terrorism including an extensive historical overview of terrorism and related issues: definition of global terrorism, historic roots of terrorism politics, ideologies and strategies of both contemporary and older terrorist groups, terrorism today, recent attacks, trends in the Global Terrorism Index over the last 10 years. The law on terrorism, the relationship between terrorism and other forms of violence and political change, chronological survey of major terrorist attacks, trials, and other relevant events; ideas of the Left and Right, counter terrorism, justification of terrorism, brief biographies of leaders of terrorist groups and predictions and analysis on the future of global terrorism.

The Book is meant to give the reader an insight into the development of history, so as to understand the terrorist mind, motivations, arguments, backgrounds and why some places are better targets of terrorist activities than others.

Writing this book has been an insightful journey that has helped shaped my perspective on terrorism. I have come to understand why the response against terrorism is as worldwide as well as it has become.

There is a lot of information out there regarding terrorism, a lot of which is not factual. To get the real facts I had to go through an intensive research on the subject from reliable information sources.

The book is divided into related sections for ease of reading and referencing. You can read the section that is most relevant to you.

However, I would recommend reading the whole book so as to have a holistic understanding of global terrorism and related issues.

1 AN EXTENSIVE HISTORICAL OVERVIEW OF TERRORISM AND RELATED ISSUES

DEFINITION OF GLOBAL TERRORISM

Overview

Terrorism as a subject has overwhelmed the world with the attention given to it. Toward the end of the year 2001, Osama bin Laden, the world's leading terrorist icon, launched an attack of the United States, a symbol of power, giving new meaning to the word "global terrorism." It was an attack that was aimed at challenging the dominant power and clearly sent a message across the world that the view of terrorism from the West is not the same way it is seen in other parts of the world.

Prior to this attack terrorism was and is still a problem and in the global news channel, the audience has been receiving a dose of terrorism from different parts of the world. After the attack came the politics of terror that has led to the overbearing fear of what terror can do to any nation, regardless of its military might or position in the fight against terror. In trying to look at terrorist activities in the past decades and comparing them with what we have today makes one wonder why with the improvement in social order why such savagery is becoming more and more sophisticated.

A simple definition of terror can as well be said to be the alternative acts to modern civility on how humans relate and associate with one another in its most simple terms; terror has stood as the stark alternative to civility in social relations from the time of humankind's earliest recorded reflections. (**Thomas Hobbes**, 1608) in one of his treatise, defines terrorism as "Out of civil states, there is always war of every one against everyone the nature of war, consists not in actual fighting; but in the known disposition thereto and which is worst of all, continual fear and danger of violent death; the life of man [Sic], solitary, poor, nasty, brutish, and short." Hobbes highlighted the fact that terror and forced violence are inherent and to some extent very hard to distinguish whether such 'normal' tactics or human activities are used as a form of strategy or violence.

Modern research on the topic of terrorism has been known to fail due to the extremes that lie in the unstructured ideals of terrorism. The concept of trying to understand terrorism has been made difficult because of the need for researchers to look at the broad limits and angles that do not lead to a conclusive answer to what terror should be or these factors do not lie within the matrix of defining terrorism, on the same note some of the areas of study in this subject present a narrow view of any serious researcher can use to define what terror is. We cannot also throw away the angle of complexity that cannot be analyzed systematically.

Most of these concepts of terrorism are the political lineage that terrorism takes on a global landscape. When this is the case defining terrorism borders in between trying to rationalize an act of terror between civil and uncivil acts of violence, this willed to terms like necessary and unnecessary terror depending on which side of the divide one decides to use. The definition is further complicated by the fact that some acts of terror committed by nations in the name of liberation which further defines a terrorist as a political opponent for political gain and effect. This is the same way the term "communist" was used to gain political mileage in the cold war era.

Bruce Hoffman's book, *Inside Terrorism* (Columbia University Press, 1998), gives a broad view of terrorism, stated that it is a deliberate act aimed at creating and exploiting people's fears through acts of violence in the primary focus of achieving political change. His definition at least tries to create a clear demarcation between terrorism and criminal activities or violence. In his definition he gives the definition more personified characteristics by insinuating the altruistic nature of the cause of terrorism for political change.

We can as well say that terrorism are acts of a criminal nature and become more effective when Orthodox means of violence are meted on its victims. There are so many similarities in the following that a person who studies terror as a subject cannot ignore.

- Terrorism
- State repression
- Organized crime
- War

After the Nuremberg trials towards the end of World War II in 1945, the criminalization of the use of arbitrary violence at the time of war took effect. This is the time State repression, or "acts of state terror," became an interesting subject to look at such a time and the international community saw the need to step in. Another scholar who offers us another broad perspective on the definition of terror,

Caleb Carr, (Random House, 2002), looks at both terrorism and modern warfare as acts of terror, at the same time, he offered a clear distinction by saying that warfare is a deliberate act upon innocent civilians to end their dream of affiliating themselves with a particular political choice, leader, or policies. He further states that terror is fashioned in an unrestrained manner to portray violence to interfere with the will of an individual or a group of people to offer resistance or seek justice in a way that seems logical to them. Such acts according to him are driven by controlled fear of unspecified consequences.

Both **Hoffman and Carr** dwell more on the psychological effects terror, but looking deep into their definitions they differ on the use of terror for the quest for power. Hoffman talks about the need to use terror to have a new political dispensation, while Carr speaks about the use of high powered state resources to cause terror and put in place a new center of authority to facilitate conquest. In the book, *Transaction Book* **(Schmid and Jongman**, 1988) gives us a more complex definition in an attempt to give a broader perspective on the terrorism. The definition they have is far too broad and complex to be used in a systematic research. They defined terrorism as a repeated violence aimed at creating fear and anxiety either done by an individual, group or government agencies for both criminal and political reasons. In their definition, the human casualties are normally picked at random or selectively chosen with the aim of sending a particular message to the survivors. The form of communication of acts of terror involves the use of manipulation and fear mongering among the target population.

Both **Schmid** and **Jongman's** definition includes a common factor: the state and non-state agencies as the primary actors. Their inclusion has widened the political aspect of terrorism recognizing its activities as a reiteration or an immediate response to the acts of brutality.

The most difficult point that we have today is the different attempts to define terrorism being lost in the global claim that terror is a necessary political act. The fact that terror is redefined to include the political aspect is an indication that it's becoming generally accepted for states to use terrorism to peruse or achieve a common goal. Theoretically, when perusing such goals the actors are supposed to be rational in their approach which in many cases rationality does not help an actor achieve his or her final objective. Carr continues to argue that such strategies must be seen as an irrational form to be classified as acts of terror. He tells us that terror can never be rational, but it is counterproductive when used to gain political scores.

This appears to be the center of the argument that the issue of violence (terrorism) in the context of the human and systemic development presents terrorism is an unsolvable problem

In many countries that have suffered most in the hands of terrorists, being identified as one bears consequences that vary from country to country. Some will have the creation of special courts for prosecution, circumventing the legal system to make the suspect stay longer without trial for "interrogation" and the restriction of basic freedoms and human rights. Terrorism in such countries has led to the ratification of the modern day counter terrorism measures or laws.

We will continue to look at how definitions of terrorism differ and how legal systems in a country affected by terror changes. What impact could terrorism bring because a person labeled as a terrorist does not get the same treatment as any other ordinary suspect. These countries continue to face the challenge of defining terrorism and the possible implications when such definitions are employed. It is worth noting that after the adoption of resolution 1373 in the United Nations Security Council, nations that previously gave terror suspects the same treatment as an ordinary prisoner had been compelled to redefine terrorism to comply with this new meaning contained in the resolution 1373. The goal of the resolution was to push countries to define contingency plans within their counterterrorism programs.

Countries such as India, the USA and United Kingdom which have seen an increase in the fight in their counterterrorism efforts had a lot of rough time complying with the UN resolution. They were faced with the dilemma of:

- Preservation of human rights
- Effectiveness
- National security concerns
- Adherence to the rule of law
- Public confidence in institutional legitimacy.

In understanding the definition of global terrorism, the use of countries like India and the UK which have their own different experiences with terror groups is good in trying to point to the real meaning of global terrorism. They may be having different structural and societal arrangements in dealing with both internal and external aggression, but they offer valuable lessons as far as terrorism is concerned. These two countries share the heritage of governance or law and are burdened by the consistent threats to their rationale security apparatus. They also enjoy the best governance structures that separate the political process from the power that plays a part in the complexity of the definitions of global terrorism. The societal structures in both India and the UK offer researchers the opportunity to get a clear insight on how dynamic the legal definitions of terrorism have been through the years. These two countries have different historical encounters with terror, but they also tend to form a common base for good comparative analysis of the domestic changes that take due to terrorist activities. The definition of global terrorism is further hampered by the fact the world body the United Nations offers an incomplete definition of terrorism. The definition of terrorism offered by the UN does not augur well with its own counterterrorism evaluations among the member states. Sometimes we may be forced to look at how individual countries deal with domestic terrorism and how their definitions they are applied in those countries and help carry out the legal definition domestically but in line with the global perception of global terrorism. It is through the examinations of such policies that we get to fathom the real reason behind the many definitions of global terrorism. Looking into the legal definitions and obligations within the UN resolution 1373, lessons can be drawn from individual countries, definitions and help researchers get a broader view on the definition of terrorism based on national laws and policies.

Defining Terrorism is an international problem

The struggle by researchers and scholars to define and redefine terrorism goes back to the question of philosophy, law, history, morality, and religion. But a majority of scholars will tell you that the definition of terrorism is intertwined and as such has escaped many scholars who are trying to reach a consensus. It is even becoming more difficult to define terrorism on a moral ground because of the prevailing circumstances. Look at it this way, the way terrorism is defined in Afghanistan is not the same way America will look at it. Having said that, the laws that define counterterrorism policies actually depend on the definition of what terrorism is all about. For any nation to define its counterterrorism laws, then it has to face the problem of terrorism head on so that they may be able to come up with adequate parameters to formulate such laws. Getting the solution to this answer is what will give a country the characterization of a terrorist and to what extent the basic human rights and protection should be accorded to such a person. To define harsher penalties within the legal confines demand that we know what terrorism is.

The inability of the United Nations to give a comprehensive definition

When the world lacks a global direction into the definition of the word terror or terrorism, the definition of the legal parameters to combat terrorism activities become even more difficult to execute. The inability of universal bodies like the UN to guide in the proper definition of terrorism is obstructing the effort needed to effect counter terrorism measures on a global scale. Any scholars are of the opinion that the lack of a concrete definition of terror slows down the counterterrorism operations and its effectiveness in the effort to maintain law in pursuit of human rights obligations

There is some effort being made by countries which try to fill the gap in the piecemeal definition of the UN Security Council by adopting several treaties, protocols, and some Security Council resolutions to create robust counterterrorism measures. This path breeds disparities in the universally accepted definition of terrorism is an open avenue for some non-comparative states to manipulate existing laws and definitions and as such leads to the abuse of human rights and less transparency in defining who a terrorist is and who is not. Different attempts have been made by the UN to come up with an internationally accepted definition of terrorism on several occasions.

In the 60s the General Assembly tried many times to resolve the issue by creating a universal definition that would be agreeable to all parties. On the same quest, there was a 1987 resolution that realized that for there to be an effective struggle against terrorist activities and groups, there has to be an establishment of a generally accepted definition of international terrorism. These two efforts did not bear much result because different nations saw some level of subjectivity on the two definitions. This led to the rejection of certain elements in the universal definition on. The majority of nations on both sessions advocated for the need to exercise freedom in fighting both anti-colonial and related violence that can be tied to terrorism.

The inability to define global terrorism on an agreed consensus reflects the ideological struggle experienced on the ground and the relentlessness of certain nations (developing) to agree with the views imposed on them by the political influence of powerful nations. Some of the elements of the resolution advocated for the punishment of the killing of civilians caught up in an act of war against terrorism.

The changing meaning of terrorism

Terrorism is a word that was made popular during the French revolution. The usage of the word today is a complete contrast to its usage of that time. Then, the term terrorism used to refer to the creation of order at a time when the world was in turmoil because of the many uprisings of the 18th century. The meaning of the word terrorism was used then as a legitimate instrument in the use of force to establish a revolutionary state, today the term is used to mean an anti-government push driven by non-state or independent entities to change an authority or in support of an existing one.

Terrorism then was used as a measure to intimidate rival factions from attempting to take over a 'legitimate' authority. At the same time, anyone who was caught while in the act of treason (treasonous as it was known then), the person was condemned to the guillotine. This form of punishment is more than similar in many ways to what a modern day terrorist is subjected to. Looking at this old definition of terrorism, researchers are aligned to think of it as an old and effective way of enforcing the ideals and virtues of a democratic system. Several revolutionaries of the time subscribed to the ideology that a revolution must go hand in hand with terror for democracy to win. One of these revolutionary leaders was Maximillian Robespierre.

Despite the variations in meanings, there are some distinct characteristics that they old time terror and the modern one share. In the old terrorism, the activities were organized, deliberate and systematic, the other similarity is the end goal or achievement of such activities; to create a "better more accountable authority" to remove the "inept and corrupt systems" in place. Then came the era of nationalism and patriotism based on one identity and does not show allegiance to the royal family. This saw the emergence of the red army in Germany, and in Italy, came forth the red brigade. With the increasing changes in the social economic environment and the emergence of the industrial revolution words such as Marxism and communism were adhered to due to the perceived alienation of the populace from the center of power because of the rise of capitalism.

It is from this melee that a new form of terrorism emerged and it borrowed from the concept of the revolutionaries of the French revolutionary era. This alienation led to the establishment so anti state ideologies that can be linked to modern day terrorism, where violence is seen by the actors as a necessary form of evil not to draw attention to themselves or a particular case, but to educate, inform and eventually be able to rally the masses to a revolution.

HISTORICAL ROOTS OF TERRORISM

To understand the changing context of terrorism, this section will give an analysis of the concept of terrorism as a physical process that has its roots that can be traced from many years ago together with the many researching arguments that have been put forth to formulate our understanding of terrorism as we know it today. From the beginning of time and especially at the onset of the French revolution, to the revolutionary bombers, the antichrist, the red armies of both in Germany and Italy, the African colonial struggle, to the Palestine wars with Israel and ultimately to the religious fundamentalists of the early 60s to date.

All these events have taken place in the timeline of the human history, especially at a time when humans are able to record and analyze the whole concept of terror. Such heinous activities cannot be looked at without looking at the paramount question; what are the motives and justification of terrorism? The change in meaning over the years has brought to humanity so many problems in trying to understand the concept and reasons behind such activities meted on fellow human beings to push through an agenda or an ideology.

Through this section, the arguments will be based on the different perspectives and interpretations that can help in understanding the whole terrorism concept throughout the different eras and historical timeline across different societies and cultural dimensions.

Perspectives on Terrorism

Terrorism is obviously a hotly debated topic that it boils down to the fact that whatever defines terrorism is determined by how it is defined in both historical and modern trends. Looking back in time, (**Rapport,** pp. 46-61, 2004) gives us four dimensions stop, look at when attempting to see at it as a modern thing. These four dimensions:

- The Anarchist wave

- The Anti-colonial wave
- New Left Wave
- The Religious wave

The Anti-Christ Wave

The anti-Christ wave has been linked to the fact that it draws its motivation from the failures of the reform agenda across Europe in the 19th and early 20th centuries. The argument here was that the anti-Christ made several attempts to bring down the governments of the time. The primary tactic used here was more or of targeting individuals such as the key government officials as a warning to others. This form of terrorism is believed to have started in Russia around 1880's and extended its arms to the Baltic States and of course Asia and later in Western Europe.

The Anti-Colonial, Wave

This wave showed its **T**face in the early 1900s. From the name, it can be said the main motivating factor here was the ideology of self-determination while opposing the oppression courtesy of the colonial master. We can look at the Irish rebellion of 1919 against the English as an example. The grievances of the rebels were targeted to both the representative of England and their collaborators. Such representatives included the soldiers, police, judges, and other government officials. The aim of such a rebellion is to make it difficult for the colonialists to settle among the natives. (**Moten,** pp. 39-40, 2010). Such activities were undertaken by non-state actors to use terrorism to destabilize the colonial regimes. Such groups in their course of action turned into movements such as the Mau Mau of Kenya, the Jewish IrgunZvaiLeumi, the Lehi (LohameiHerutYisrael). The Lehi fighters fought for freedom to get rid of the British rule out of Palestine, (Garrison, p. 267, 2004). In an ironical twist of fate, such movements always believe in their cause of "struggling to keep away a government of terror" (**Moten,** p. 40, 2010); this is the reason why most activities of such movements were through the use of hit and run tactics which are solely directed at the security agencies that includes the police and military installations (think of Boko Haram and Al Shabbat)

The New Left Wave

This wave got their inspiration from being alienated from the existing democratic system of government. This alienation will lead to distrust and ultimately rebellion. The leftists are always antagonizing the west and their imperialism and find a lot of inspiration by looking up for nationalism and radicalism. They are well known for tactics such as ho stage taking, kidnapping, assassinations of people it considered to be their principal targets. The Italian red brigade, the German red army faction, and the Japanese red army took to identifying themselves as the protectors of the third world (**Moten**, p. 40 2010).

The Religious Wave

This is the wave that has stretched from the early 60s to the present day terrorism. They clamor for a self-determined religious state at least according to (**Moten,** p. 40, 2010). This wave has been characterized by the Islamic ideologies, even though the Indian Sikhs wanted the state of Punjab to be independent, and this also stretches to the Christians and Jews alike. The driving ideology here is fundamentalism that is religion based or driven. The wave includes such brutality as violence leading to deaths, the slaughter of those who believe differently (infidels), and the violation of human rights. Those who perpetrate such acts of violence were /. Are seen as carrying out the will of their Lord / God and are revered as martyrs who will be rewarded in the afterlife. (**Schmid,** 2004) Schmid further debates that such acts that are committed to "reframe inhumane activities" in the mind of those committing them see it as a war in retaliation (defense) and they do this to make sure that their race/ dogma is pure and not contaminated by the infidels. These are acts of murder that have been euphemized to mean "sacrifice" (**Schmid**, 2004).

In 1979, the best example is the Iranian revolution in which the primary reason behind it was the so called religious fundamentalism of the new era. The biggest and, the most distinguishing factor of this kind of terrorism is the use of suicide bombers. The Tamil Tigers may be having the record of the most number of suicide bombers used between the late 80s and into the new century, (**Moten**, p. 41, 2010). This wave of terrorism proved to be the most frequently used and has the biggest number of casualties on any single attack. They don't only target individuals but also put key installations and infrastructure as part of their target.

Both the Religious and the new left waves of terror use the most advanced terror tactics that are not limited to plane hijackings, using guns and bombs to hold people hostage, and some have even gone hi-tech by being able to use sophisticated encryption software for espionage. Looking at terrorism in the early stages, can be differentiated and uniquely identified in relation to the environment or people's way of life. It is from this nationalistic outlook that terrorism spins out of control and metamorphosed into the global nightmare seen today. Terrorism, particularly gained more international coverage during the religious wave and because the two foremost religions involved; Islam and Christianity have a global outreach and this definitely explains why terrorism got out of the national scope. And appropriately, the world over, there are three forms of terrorism

- Domestic terrorism
- International terrorism
- Transnational terrorism.

In order to understand terrorism better, tracing its roots is one thing, looking at the social and the behavioral part of it will give the discussion an open view on the link between terrorism and other factors such as political, environmental, and social economic situations (**Moten**, p. 45, 2010). Instead of associating terrorism activities to a given region or religion which gives the perception of us looking at the root causes which are according to many scholars are pretty obvious; political alienation, social economic factors and, inequality. These terror groups that use religion as their face of terror, for finance the Al Qaeda network should be looked as offshoots of both the national and international show of aggression. These groups revel on the perception that they are marginalized and have or are still experiencing some form of injustice by the "powerful" forces. This gives them motivation and acts as the driving force to seek revenge through terrorism activities.

A recent study by **Marari**, (1985) shows how most of the Palestinian suicide attackers have experienced such atrocities first hand by having at least one relative killed by the occupation forces. (**Moten**, p. 46, 2010) The statistics on the economy drives associated fundamental terrorism

The demographic and economic determinants of terrorism constitute another perspective of terrorism. This perspective situates terrorism with a linkage amongst economic factors and demography (fertility rate, high birth rate), especially in the Muslim world. Despite the fact that nature does not give all the same standards of living, in a place with a large number of unemployed youths there is bound to be a regular uprising against any regime that seems to sideline them. Such a group of people is being driven into hopelessness, frustration and abject poverty (**Moten**, p. 47, 2010). Moten further gives an explanation by saying, such a situation is made worse by the presence of an authoritarian regime and has no room for libertinism. Unfortunately, this is the case of many Muslim countries where radical Islam takes the driver's seat in perusing the religious driven terrorist activities against such regimes and their benefactors. But instead of looking into ways to make life more comfortable to the general populace, these authoritarian regimes developed repression tactics such as denying them basic rights such voicing an alternative opinion or the use non-violence approach to express their concerns. In such an environment, terrorism by any means seems to be the only way such radicalized youths and fundamentalists see as the only chance they have in changing their status quo.

Several countries do not agree with the view that some terror organizations such as the established ones like the Al Qaeda to be linked to religion (Islam), the same way some secular institutions can be linked to acts of terror. (**Moten,** p.48, 2010). The western perspective of terrorism creates a big division into the two known ideologies; the secular (West) and the religious (Muslim) worlds. The narrative is that the former advocates for peace as the latter is seen as representing (instigator) of violence. (**Samuel Huntington**, 1996), in his book the "*Clash of Civilization*" gave a hint that there is some level of justification that holds on to this belief. He asserted that Islam is surrounded by the bloody borders with a high propensity to resort to violence (**Huntington**, p. 258. 1996). However, **Cavanaugh,**(p. 9, 2007) states that the continuing divide between the west and the Muslim world is so because it is an ideology being used for political gains.

Some western countries led by the United States have been at the forefront of classifying terrorist groups, individuals and nations as being either in support or participate in terrorist activities. This listing brought together many scholars who are of the view that this is done for political expediency and nothing to do with terror (**Moten**, p. 10, 2010), he further states that such a list has been used to impose sanctions the US famous invasion of Afghanistan to get rid of the "haven of terror" is seen by scholars like (**Johnson**, pp. 74-85, 2004) as motivated by economic motives such as oil and political interest. **Moten** (2010, p. 52) added his view on the Afghanistan invasion by saying that this was not done to rid of Al Qaeda in the region, but to overthrow the Taliban who were not cooperating in the oil business in their favor.

The other alternative perspective is the so called "Muslim Perspective" which is seen as a reaction to the western led war against terror (**Moten,** 2010). The Muslim perspective offers the view that is challenging the western view of terrorism as that which involves the killing of any western civilian and but the same definition of terror does not apply to the western capitals killing innocent civilians in the Muslim world all in the name of pacification and democracy (**Moten,** p. 53, m 2010). This view sees the west as the instigators of terrorism the world over because of their capitalistic and domination tendencies.

Justification of Terrorism

Going by the various perceptions of terrorism in the world today, a terrorist in one capital is hailed as a hero, another stands the test of time (**Primoratz**, 2004). This dilemma is what will bring us to the morality question in regards to terrorism throughout all the human history with terror. Many scholars are of the view that terrorism is generally considered to be repugnant regardless of the primary actor (whether by the government or non-state agents), the victims, or the mode of execution (**Coady**, 1985), (**Primoratz**, 1990), and (**Jollimore,** 2007). the ethical and intellectual point of view.

The generally accepted view that terrorism is a bad thing is the same analogy used in the just war theory that underlines the importance of not targeting civilian installations or targets (**Primoratz**, p. 25, 2004). Whenever there is a violation of that then, this is seen violence meted on noncombatants. To get the difference between intentional and collateral effects of war, (**Schmid,** p. 204, 2004) tried to differentiate by making a reference to war being likened to "justified" terrorism. Some are still of the view that terrorism under some dire situations may be justifiable.

For instance, according to (**Kraemer**, 2004), there should be a priority to justify the motive and not the end game of the incursion when analyzing terrorist activities. In this case, terror is seen as the only weapon available for the powerless to use and therefore terrorism from smaller factions or insurgent groups may be termed unnecessary but justice in pressing for their "just" cause or action. It is worth noting that such a perception is held by both the terrorists and the general population at least according to (**Krueger**, 2007) who conducted a study on these views in the following countries, Pakistan, Morocco, Jordan, and Turkey.

It is, therefore, coming to reason as to why in the Muslim world, the West (the US) is seen as unjust to other parts of the world (Islam nations). That being the case, a terrorist does not need any justification to commit acts of terror against the West, because to them and their followers (population back home) this is the simplest form of vengeance. This perception validates the fact that one needs to understand how the enemy perceives terrorist while trying to justify their activities. And in most cases, the reason behind such acts turn out not to be linked to any form of religious fundamentalism, and therefore any acts of terror use religion as a cover of their vengeance.

(**Mark Juergensmeyer**, 2004) advanced the stage theory which highlights the need of looking at the world through the eyes of a terrorist who is driven by religion fanaticism in an effort in trying to understand their own definition of justification. The terrorist guided by religion sees the world as an axis of the good and the evil forces. It is through such perception that an actor is of the idea that he has been appointed to work towards the good of the society. It is at this point that the "US and THEM mentality kicks in and gives the terrorist the more reason and the needed justification that committing acts of terrorism is a show of power in fighting the evil axis (secularism). Performing such acts is seen as an act of nobility and the advancement of good over evil (**Schmid**, p. 212, 2004).

This further enforces the thought of isolating the target from the civilians as a secondary factor to many terrorists. In the words of Osama Bin Laden, all Americans are a target (**Schmid**, p. 384, 2004). In as much as there are convincing views that a justification of terrorism to address grievances is more or less the same as a conventional war fought on the streets as opposed to the bush warfare.

The Historical Timeline of Terrorism

Terrorism in the Pre-Modern World: 13th Century

Terrorism is as old as the human history, though this is the time in human history that acts of terrorism have been experienced than any other time in the history of man. The first-century Sicarri, a Jewish group is thought to be the first terrorist group that killed both enemies and collaborators as they campaigned to oust the Roman Empire in Judea. They used the word Hashhashin, which is a loose translation of the word assassins. They were seen to be the most secretive Islamic sect that lived in Iran or Syria at the time (around the 13th C). They were also mercenaries for hire who executed political figures at a fee. Then came the zealots who were not outright terrorists who depended much on the spread of fear to create that fearful atmosphere among the people.

The Origins of Modern Terrorism: 1973

Terrorism as we know it today emanated from the French revolution. The man in charge of the revolution at the time was Maxmilien Robespierre. During the revolution, Robespierre, who was appointed as one of the leaders of the new state started a campaign of killing his enemies or those who were opposed to the revolution on? He fashioned a dictatorial regime in order to unite the fallen country, through his killings, he justified his ways as a need that the country needed to move from monarchy to a liberal democracy. His enemies, through fear or suspicion that they were to be killed formed different factions to try and oppose him and he became more brutal and it is through this that he laid the foundation of what we know as terrorism today. This followed in different areas of the world as an example, looking at the 19th Century attempts to end the Tsarist rule in Russia.

Non-State Terrorism: 1950s

The war and the quest for self-determinations led to the use of guerrilla tactics by other actors against the state. This was driven by the need to get rid of the colonial settlers and regimes. And this is what brought forth new ideologies like communism. Factions have been formed all over the world that chose to use terrorist tactics to fight the colonial empires, one notable example is the IRA, which was fashioned by Catholics to form an independent republic and move away from Britain.

The Kurds in the Middle East have on several occasions waged wars to seek autonomy as early as the 20th century. They use terrorist tactics to establish themselves. In Sri Lanka, the Tamil Tigers are a minority who embraced guerilla tactics to fight for their independence.

International Terrorism: 1970s

International terrorism came to the fore in the late 60s. It was notable with the prominent and rampant hijacking of planes. The Palestinians through their Popular front hijacked an Israeli plane, followed by the Pan Am Flight Bombing in Lockerbie Scotland. This is the era that really defined the terrorism as we know it today as a composed of many theatrics and acts seen as symbolic of those who subscribe to their ideologies? The 1972 Olympics in Munich, which were politically motivated acts of modern day terror, it is because of this event that the term counter terrorism was first used as well as the international terrorism. The rise of international terrorism was further fueled by the fall of the Soviet Union in 1989. This filled to the proliferation of cheap weapons from the Russian black market. Even in the United States, groups such as the weathermen came out to protest the war in Vietnam by setting off bombs to highlight their cause.

The Modern Terrorism, Religious Terrorism and Beyond

This form of terrorist activity is by far the most radicalized and seen by many as the most potent because of the use of religion to justify their actions. Both the Christians, Judaists, Hinduisms among others practice their own form of militant extremism. Modern terrorists are known to be people seeking to avenge by hiding their agenda under the decoy of religion.

POLITICS, IDEOLOGIES AND STRATEGIES OF BOTH CONTEMPORARY AND OLDER TERRORIST GROUPS

What is an Ideology?

An ideology is defined as a set of beliefs, principles, objectives, and values that can either be significant or insignificant which are defined by a group as a unique identification for political purposes. The identity has what the group calls its aims or objectives. An ideology may come out with a separatist's agenda, politicized agenda, historical agenda, and mythical agenda as well as based on supernatural beliefs or power. Regardless of where an ideology draws its inspiration, its main function is to provide the groups with a theoretical concept of action.

The individual belief of an adherent does not have to be necessarily the same. A leader of a group may see the need to strictly follow their ideology, but to an ordinary member the only motivation they need is the feeling of belonging somewhere. The feeling of belonging can be tied to a perpetual hate of the enemy. Research studies have shown that both in terrorist and extremist groups, it is quite easy to note the stark differences between the ideological belief of the leaders and their followers who are in the group without any clearly defined objective.

In reality, every group's ideology is distinct to their overall cause, and as such the ideologies may fall into one or all of the following categories

- Separatism
- Religion
- Anarchism
- Communism
- Liberalism
- Conservatism
- Fascism
- Organized crime
- Single Issues

Organized criminal gangs and single issue ideologists may not have an overbearing ideology, but are seen to be part of an ideology because of their agenda are politically driven, which albeit through Orthodox means gives them one way of fulfilling their objectives. The single issue groups may not have the clamor to change the whole system or political establishment; they try to inflict changes by infiltrating the system using gaps in policies that are currently being used.

The organized criminal gangs may get involved in activities that may not qualify to be labeled as terrorist groups, but they are not to use violence as a bargaining chip and as a way of exerting their influence in an area by intimidating politicians and public figures into doing their bidding. This is common with the mafia in countries like Italy and Mexico, the drug peddler's network also falls into this category. They use these tactics to gain immunity from prosecutions and ways to conduct their businesses without through subversion and to some extent gain political mileage.

The categories listed above are not interrelated in any way, and therefore a single group can adopt one or more than one to suit their overall endgame. Looking at it from a practical perspective, it is evident that groups like the Basque group ETA and Herri Batasuna were formed on the basis of being separatists and Marxists while the Hamas can be seen as a religious and a separatist group. The mix of ideologies may sometimes be the easiest path to a group crumbling down because of the individual differences in the group.

How ideologies help in terrorists' target selection

If the driving force is not the quest for power and glory, a terrorist group gets motivated by their ideology. The desire to commit terror activities is well defined in a group's ideological view which is also determined by other external factors which may also be strategic. Such factors include the use violence when other "peaceful" means have not yielded anything. The other reason used to justify terrorism is when the group's non-violent means are quashed by the system due to repression.

Regardless of the motivating factor to engage in terror, there has to be one way or the other on how a group reaches its decision to select a target(s). Ideologies play the central role in the determination of who or what the target is based on how the group sees itself in the world. The terrorists' ideology will determine who the enemies are and it can be noted from an ideology how to determine the innocence or guilt of a target. This kind of thought is what makes it possible for such groups to see people who believe differently as their targets. The idea of legitimate targets does not conform to the society's interpretation of innocence and guilt. Looking at the Animal Liberation Front (ALF) has made several claims that in as much as they break the law, they are acting on a higher moral ground that compels them to enforce their ideologies.

The individual or a group's action is what will be interpreted within the confines of their ideology to be classified as terrorism regardless of whether the concerned individual does not associate or ever thought of as terrorists. To illustrate this further, Patricia Hearst and Emily Harris, of the Symbionese Liberation Army of the 70s made a justification for the killings of a bomb attack placed in the police vehicles, their argument was that the law students are studying to be lawyers who will be keen to serve the system and its sympathizers. Their decision to study law, according to Harris' ideological belief is their mindset and not a decision made based on personal choice.

Due to their ideological beliefs, terrorist groups seek to identify their victims by saying they deserve whatever action planned gains them, this does not in any way dawn upon them they have killed innocent people. The collective guilt of their supposed victims is seen an action that helps the terrorists get rid of self-reproach because at least according to them, a person labeled as an enemy has to be attacked. This sort of activity gives the terrorist the ability to legitimize their actions and become bolder in future attacks.

From (**Drake**, 1998), his definition of ideology gives us an idea of how terror groups choose their targets he says that it is through their beliefs, principles, and values that are defined in their ideologies. Many groups identify with such ideologies that are usually the thinking of the founders of the group

Looking at the illustrations on table 1 (below), we can look at the examples taken from data collected on deadly terror activities between 1965 –2005. The indicative pattern displayed confirms some of the forwarded reasons that can be tied to argot selection as explained in hypotheses by (**Drake & Hoffman**, 1998). Taking the example of the first nationalist separatists, their main targets are the security installation that includes the members or people who are associated with the installations. Sectarian violence perpetrators and the right wing have the civilians as their target aiming to bring down the support base of the nationalist governments. The leftist extremists like the red armies in Italy and Germany are deliberate in their attacks, instead, they choose to target government forces and a section of political leaders who to them seem like a blockade in their quest.

Table 2: Government response by target

Political Leadership	77	11	47	135
Security	785	205	409	1,399
Civilian	1,098	183	573	1,854
Rival Terrorists	178	19	81	278
Total	2,138	418	1,110	3,666

Source: Writing on Terrorism, Austin L Wright

Another table below shows how governments in the western capitals respond to terror activities (what is their target?). Do they also use underhand tactic to match the terrorists? Table 2 (below) shows how governments respond to terror attacks based on the type of target that has been destroyed.

There are several patterns that evolve from this table, there is the modal response where the government does not take any action in retaliation, the second view is that when the target were civilians, the government will respond, but with no show of might (force), they at this point try to be diplomatic by trying to exhaust all the judicial avenues through seeking arrests and convictions, this measure will be so taken to reduce the repeat of such an attack in the near future. The other angle that the table brings out when the security apparatus is targeted, there will be a forceful reaction and there will be an attempt to try and destabilize the terrorists by trying to destroy their bases. The final outlook from the table is the launch of an attack followed by a judicial process, this line of action can also be taken when there is an attack on a political leader(s). It is now coming out clearly that target selection is done by the use of a precise strategy that worked for both governments and terror groups.

Geography

Ideology is not the only driving force of a terror organization. Their location may most likely influence the ideology they represent and what they want to be their sphere of influence. Looking at the geographical positioning of terror groups (**Young & Findley**, 2011) through their study realized that many scholars fail to make a clear distinction between domestic and international terrorism. They argue that this may be influenced by the fact that some domestic outfits such as the Hezbollah may once in a while operate an international cell to gain attention or retaliation.

Geography also plays a big role when the defining sphere of control of a terror group, the area they occupy will determine their long term ambition, while (**Hegghammer**, 2005) was reviewing the Islamic terrorist group, he noticed three categories

- The global jihad groups
- The socio- revolutionary groups
- The nationalist-separatist groups.

All these categorizations can as well be used to fit in any terrorist outfit as those that seek to overthrow the government or those with the intention to liberate a certain region. He developed what he referred to as the Hegghammer's triangle, as shown below which serves the purpose of illustrating how geography can be used to understand terror activities based on their location and possible changes with time and in relation to their capabilities. He used the triangle to show the never changing policy of a terrorist organization irrespective of the increasing or decreasing geographical area of influence.

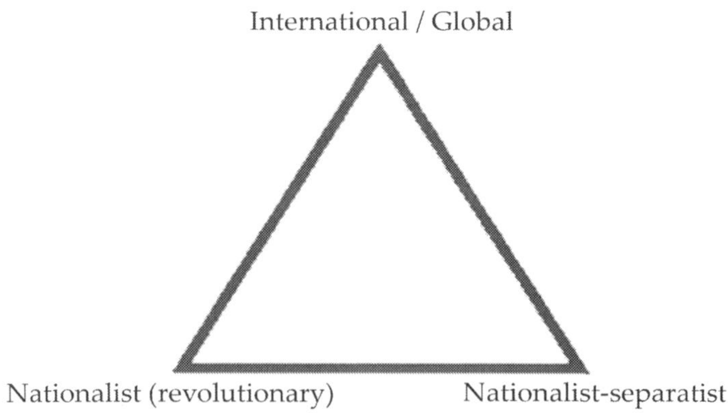

Figure2.1: The Hegghammer Triangle:TerritorialAmbitions of Terrorist Entities

Source: Ideologies and Terrorist Tactics, Andreas Hoelstad Dhaehli

What is a terrorist attack?

(**Drake**, 1998) in his work the Terrorist Target Selection, he came up with the idea that the most viable way to understand who or what terrorists attack and why, one ought to use the actor-based approach: this perspective lets the researcher assume to be in the position of the terrorist and reads their ideology in order to understand how it shapes and changes their thinking framework. In the eye of the actor, all his activities are in line with the group's ideological strategy. This perception will not leave out their target areas, according to (**Nacos, Asal** et al. 2009).

In the strictest sense, ideology cannot be the only defining factor that can be used to explain the aspects of who to attack. Other things that are not widely mentioned include the limited resources, society's immediate reaction, and the prevailing security environment. (**Drake**,1998). Their ambit of operation can well be explained by the illustration on 1. Drake says that an ideology will influence that target by looking at the fundamental limitations on the strategy and tactics to be used. Other factors such the group dynamics (Politics), community reaction and the prevailing security environment determines who will be picked as a target and also helps in the development of its planning strategies and tactics. Being the primary actors in their environment they will have to adapt to the prevailing political leadership, security, the environment and military capabilities.

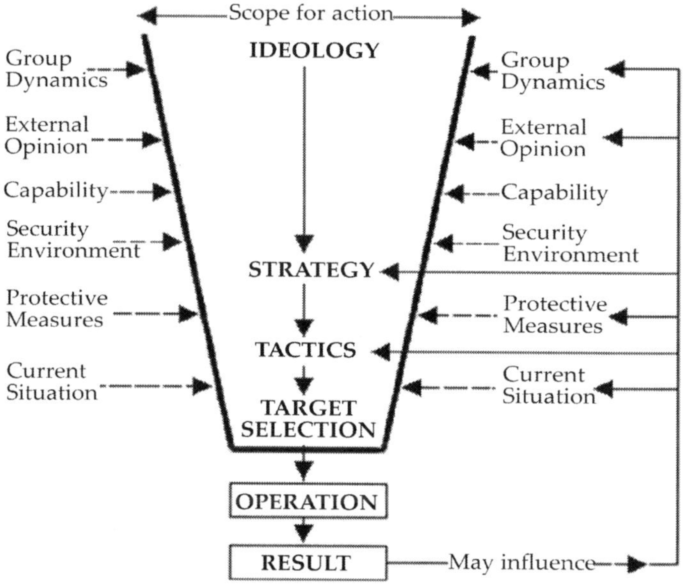

Source: Drake1998a:176

Figure2.2: Drake's Constraints on Terrorist Target Selection

Ideology has had to be connected to the modern day terrorism because of the nature the "new" terrorism has taken; it is considered to be more bloody and full of fanaticism than it was in the early stages of terrorism. Looking back at the religious wave two types of research thought to be less rational seem to be causing more fatalities and their target are the civilians which is a step away from the predecessors whereas the anarchists, new leftists, and the anti-colonialists are quite the opposite. The clear differences in the past and modern day terrorism have earned the criticism of many scholars who tend to think this difference is debated because it may be exaggerated (Field, 2009). The debate still goes on with the mention of the religious blood thirstiness bring an added dimension to create a horrific image persona. (**Stein**, 2002) made an observation on how the then USSR, China, and Iran at the onset of the cold war labeled the worst leadership as imperialists and barbarians.

Hypotheses

Islamists targets more civilians

The cliché that the effects of modern terrorists are sterner than it was in the beginning of terrorism may be difficult to substantiate and it has been met with a lot of skepticism from many scholars. (Tucker, 2001), there is very little that can be said to be new in the so called new terrorism, whatever is seen as new today may not be more dangerous than it was at that time. Their choice of target in both occasions is a reflection of their ideals as explained in their overall strategy and ideology. (Duyvesteyn, 2004). Meanwhile, (Hellestveit, 2005) tried to show us how the Islamists define war and civilians in their doctrines. Terrorizing an enemy of God is seen as a heroic act and a religious duty. The moderate Muslim clerics will categorically say that the killing of civilians in some circumstances is not right. With this kind of reasoning, chances are that there will be a likelihood of more civilian casualties in any conflict that has been instigated by the Muslim terrorists. In support of this claim, (Spencer &Asal, et al. 2009) made it clear that Islam has a high affinity for violence compared to other religious extremists.

Analysis of the larger scale indicates that religious terrorist groups are more likely to have more casualties by attacking soft targets. Another approach to look at it involves the focusing on ideology and the psychological understanding of the process that involves identifying the collective enemy, they develop the us versus them mentality which can be aggravated by tensions lead to the creation of enemies and to some extent the targets may be anyone that are not members of their organization (Asal et al. 2009).

(Drake, 1998) made a claim that an ideology can be used by a group to dehumanize people to objects and symbols. The assumption here is that dehumanizing is an essential tool that a terror group uses to create an image that makes it possible to convince its members that unarmed targets are just the same as any other symbol representative of evil, oppression, and injustice. This changes the perception of the targets as humans, but evil forces that need to be destroyed. Agreeing from the modern terrorism perspective, there is an expectation that religious factions are known to target soft targets.

Islamists target children and elderly

This is another target based approach focuses on how societies are built up. The democratic rules in some areas are seen to be weak representation of the people's will, rivals and critics. This leads to the long practiced traditions that the press ensures that such institutions do not withhold information from the public. When opponents of the regime enjoy the freedom of the press and human rights, liberties in an authoritarian regime, using terrorists against civilians may not bear any fruit. But according to (Wiktorowicz, Kaltner, Asal et al. 2009), terror organizations tend to look at democracy based on morality and not freedoms accorded to them. A good number of terror attacks that have been instigated by the Islamic fundamentalists are directed at non-religious groups. There are other groups too that are linked to suicide bombings such as the PKK (Kurdistan Workers' Party), ASBP (Arab Socialist Baath Party) and the SSNP (Syrian Socialist Nationalist Party). Not to be left behind are the Palestinian terrorist groups that have also been known to use such tactics.

Where Do Terrorists Attack?

Terrorists also look for the most cost effective targets that will affect their target and give them a good coverage and use that opportunity to sell their agenda. It is no longer a question of who or what is to be attacked, but the location of the target. (Meltzer, 2002) is of the opinion that Osama Bin Laden gives an example by looking into the September 11 attacks. He and his organization represent the international aspect of terrorism and to such group's location of the attack is of paramount importance; the same applies to the nationalist separatists.

Studies conducted on the operations of the Palestinian and Chechen terror organizations against the Russians and the Israelis respectively, show that the two groups would always target the occupied territories and to some extent get inside major towns. Their demands were or are still the demanding an end to the military occupation of the areas they have laid a claim to. On both the studies there is some logic involved in the selection of targets, especially in relation to location (McCartney et al. 2008:72) and (Reislien & Reislien, 2010).

In contrast the United States and the western military operations in the Middle East, Russia and Israel are neighbors to these separatist groups. And because of this proximity, the terrorists will have to work a two-way approach to wage a war against their neighbors; one war in the occupied territories, the second war right at the center of the country's capital or center of authority. This situation will turn out be an urban guerilla warfare that will only target the military and other related representatives of the government. On some occasions when the separatist movements get into towns and capitals there is bound to be a target aimed at the non- combatants (civilians) (McCartney et al. 2008) and (Reislien & Reislien,2010). In this scenario, (McCartney, et al. 2008) realized that civilian targets are more likely to be victims in Russia than it may be the case in Chechnya. By causing the civilian casualties in both Russia and Chechnya raises their cause by sending two different messages targeting different audiences. On the Chechen side, civilians will get to see firsthand the soldiers responsible for their plight while the Russian citizens will be faced with the question of prolonged occupation tussle of the region

Terrorist attacks on enemy lines kill more civilians than targets in disputed territories.

(**Resslien & Reislien,** 2010) realized that territory will determine the nature of the attack and the number of casualties. Along the territories, the killings here are done in an assassination manner because the method of operation is target shooting albeit with low casualties and fatalities. On the Israeli example, the attacks on their side are made to be spectacular, which involve the use of explosives with the intent to maximize fatalities and casualties.

Terrorist attacks behind enemy lines are more lethal than attacks in disputed territories.

The technique that is used to give two different messages to different audiences has been associated with the nationalist-separatist movements. This is also linked to the military capability and accessibility of the desired target. There is no safety nct or the population that the movements can use as a shield, this type of attack increases the chances of being caught and does may not have the needed threshold for quality as a prime target. In such attacks planted bombs, and suicide missions seem to be the most logical thing to do in a separatist group. They are abrupt and random, unlike firearms which may result in casualties or fatalities on the movement.

When looking at these approaches as an actor in the terrorist's mind, it is easy to note that who to attack forms the largest part while the wherein decided by other things as location/territory. Many separatists are seen to be thinking the same way when it comes to ideologies. From this perspective, it can be said that an ideology may be irrelevant when it comes who the target is or how to accomplish an attack because all this comes after the location of the attack has been defined. Going back to the so called modern terrorism, terror groups that are based on religion are seen to be more dangerous than the other forms of terrorist groups.

Radical Islam and western totalitarianism in the modern setting

Research studies show that there are four areas that we can look at that gives a close connection between the extremists of yesteryears and the ones we have today. The first thing to look at is the language used by the terror groups or the extremists fascist leaders. The use of words like the vanguard and revolutionary is more or less the same as what we see today and can be said to match words like the capitalist, colonialists, establishment and the reactionary. These words are usually hurled at enemies or people who profess a different kind of ideology from the one being preached. To cite a typical example, every time a Muslim cleric addresses the west, they label them as war criminals and imperialist and their media as a tool for the colonialist to use in oppressing the idle east. The same can be said of the western media reference to the Islamists as terrorists and religious fundamentalists.

In the present day Iran, its efforts to liberate itself from the western influence has been dubbed the 'revolution' and the use of terms like the 'revolutionary guard' instill some form of fear to those who do not want to "toe" the line. Today's religion-based groups use the scripts from the holy books to support their cause for war. Use of the word *Jihad* which has been translated differently by Muslim scholars adds to the confusion and that is when self-definition takes place and every Islamic group want to use the word how they see it fit. The basic understanding of the word *Jihad* may include attacking an aggressor but not in a way that establishes the killings of others in the name of war but just like it was in the old times the fight against enemies is still decided on the basis of whoever is not professing the same ideology is an enemy. The worst part of this form of terrorism is the inclusion in its latest brazen attacks, killing of the innocent (non-combatants) by use of the most barbaric methods of a suicide bomber detonating in a busy place to maximize casualties and fatalities. This clearly points back to the days when communism and fascism were the main political ideologies that killed those who were opposed to the regime indiscriminately. Modern day extremists in similar fashion as the people behind authoritarian rules and ideologies want to force a certain way of order by upsetting the existing one through mass violence that cuts across the population.

Wanton deadly violence is another way that today's terrorists use to carry out radicalism the same way the Marxists and the fascist did in their era by rejecting the simple principle of differentiating combatants and the noncombatants. It is from this view that totalitarian ideologues and societies seek to move away from the call for a complete revolution. Such governments are corrupt are seen as evil alongside their citizens. Totalitarian regimes still see the need to wage war against their citizens as a necessity to them it is seen as morally justifiable.

History: tracing radical Islamism's western roots

By examining the history of terrorism in the decade that followed the First World War, any Muslim scholar at that time will tell you that that was the most painful chapter for Muslims. Followed by the disgrace fall of the Ottoman Empire and then followed the domination of the Middle East by both Britain and France. These two events happened in quick succession and were generally perceived as humiliating and slowed done the progress of Islamic civilization. When the Turkish reformer, Kemal Ataturk abolished the caliphate in 1942 after the fall of the Ottoman Empire it was perhaps the most humiliating thing that happened to the Muslim world at that time.

Events that happened in Germany during the period after the First World War were almost similar to what happened in the Middle East. With Germany's defeat, the humiliation subjected them to the treaties of the harsh Versailles treaty. It is at this time that Hitler blamed all the woes Germany was undergoing to the foreigners and initiated a euphoric restoration of the previous Germany by empowering one race (Aryan) as a superior race that is capable of ruling Germany and the entire world; coincidentally, the Muslim brotherhood was founded just about the same time (era), in 1928. Its founder was Hassan al-Banna, an Egyptian school teacher .Like Hitler blamed the woes that faced Muslim civilization at this time to the increasing foreign influences. He also fantasized of the way Islam could recover its past glory in such a way that the Islamic ideology of the pure pan Islamic movement will be able to rise up and take their rightful place as the "owners" of the middle east and ultimately be able to control the world.

Efrain Karsh, an Islamic scholar who in his book "Islamic imperialist" made a point on how Banna openly admired both Mussolini and Hitler. He went further and created a paramilitary unit and designed its operations in the same way Hitler made his vision through the dreaded SS. He toyed with the idea of terror and the urge to conquer through the cult of death. Banna came up with a phrase to his cause "death is an art, that can be exquisite when practiced by a skillful artist," Banna was both of the idea of using violence ingrained in the traditional Islam and use it to reject the liberal democracy through the use of more radicalism and political ideology fashioned around radical Islam. He even anticipated the opposition from many of Muslim clerics and scholars to regain Islamic control.

The connection of his vision with fascism and the hatred for Jews and Zionists made it easy for the Muslim brotherhood to join forces with the Nazi Germany with the help of the Grand Mufti of Jerusalem at that time Haj Amin al-Husseini, who was seen as a Nazi collaborator in Berlin. The collaboration between Hitler and Banna opened up an avenue in the Middle East for delusional conspiracy theories that was formed around the control of the world's capital and economy by the Jews. Then, there was the infamous Czarist forgery, "The Protocols of the Elders of Zion" which allegedly supported the Jewish plot to take over the world.

By the end of the Second World War, Muslim brotherhood was already big in n umber. They had more than half a million members in Egypt. And subsequently through the years the brotherhood was grooming new generation of disciples and leaders that has led to the creation of the extremist group we know of today. Following the killing of the Egyptian President in 1949, Banna was assassinated by the government. His successor Sayyid Qutb, went ahead and merged Banna's vision with that of Marxism and fascist principles and condemned both capitalism and democracies. He even compared his version of faith alongside secular ideologies. Qutb openly adopted the Marx's stages of history. It is through this that hc believed that in the same way industrialization replaced the agrarian revolution, capitalism will be defeated and by socialism by adding that Islam would be the fourth and the last stage after Marxism. He wanted his new ideology to be implemented from the top leadership downwards. He fashioned the idea of a revolutionary guard and continue to build on Banna's doctrines and was of the idea of using the Vanguard in favor of elimination al that resistant their movement. In 1966, he and fellow Muslim brothcrhood members were hanged on charges of planning to assassinate the Egyptian president, Gamal Abdel Nasser.

The notable member that was arrested at that time was a one-year old child named Ayman al-Zawahiri, who at one point was Osama bin Laden's deputy and chief strategist and also played the role of the chief theorist. He met Osama bin Laden in the mid-80s before joining him in Sudan in the early 90s. He made a claim that Bin Laden was the next Che Guevara. Sometime in 2002 a document that Mao outlined their revolution strategies through indoctrination, violent insurgency and the accession to power (government). In the 70s , the Muslim brotherhood members who lived in Saudi Arabia recruited Osama Bin Laden, who later on moved to Afghanistan, then Pakistan where a fellow member was giving them support in terms of infrastructure when they were fighting the Soviets. This brief interaction is what formed the basis of Al Qaeda network as we know it today.

At present, the Muslim brotherhood public renounced violence which looking through its past was formed as an ideology that found its ways through violence that resulted in what we know today as violent extremism. That took different strides and identities such as the Sunni extremism that followed bin Ladenism, the Shiite radicals of Iran led by Khomeini.

2 SURVEY OF TERRORISM TODAY

INTRODUCTION

Terrorism is a violent premeditated act that involves the use of threat. It is usually committed by a person or a group of people that subscribes to one or more ideologies. The intimidation tactics used are usually targeted at large audiences that go beyond the intended primary target (Enders & Sandler, 2012). Looking at the definition that (Hoffman, 2006; RAND, 2012) uses in their research findings, the definition here is somewhat similar. Violence is the distinctive feature of terror activities, the level of attack range from gruesome to extreme depending on the group that is involved in the attack, the end game is to create anxiety and a horrific scene. To consider one a terror attack, there is always the tie to some political motives which the perpetrators always communicate after such an attack. The definition that is used here has limited the description of terror to domestic tourism and may be extended to define international terrorism, what is completely left out of the description is state sponsored terrorism, this happens when the government unleashes terror to its citizens. There are some instances where a government or one of its agencies is used to commit or aid terrorist groups through funding, logistics, safe passage, and intelligence in the course of their preparations. The end game of any terror activity is to generate fear among the innocent civilians (noncombatants) who may in turn pile up pressure for the government to concede to the demands of the group.

Terrorism for the last two decades has offered many researchers a lot of data to make their analysis on the effects of terror on the following fields.

- Economics
- Political science
- Sociology

These are the only three that seem to be the most closely attached to the study of terrorism.in the field of political science, there have been several efforts made to trace the history of terrorism and its changing concepts throughout the history of mankind. The initial studies of terrorism was based on a single concept that was aimed at trying to understand its definition, causes, tactics, and the ideologies used by individual terrorist organizations(Crenshaw, 1981; Wilkinson, 1986).

In the analysis of terrorism, scholars try to look at rationality based on the predictable nature and not the wishes of the main actors of terrorism. The thought here is, if the government policies make it hard for terrorists to manage an attack and the expected behavior of restraint from the rationality of the terrorists, then it can be said that terrorist are rational beings. One researcher (Abrahms, 2008) who was asked whether terrorists are rational since in the end, they do not achieve their objectives, answered back by saying that terrorists do not achieve their goal by attacking civilians. Contrasting this view is another scholar (Jones & Libicki, 2008) who mentioned that those who renounced terrorism to join the political forces may have achieved their goal. Still on rationality (Abrahms, 2008) had an interesting analysis though he gives a much-chosen evidence. To break down the analytical study of terrorism one has to understand the data collection of unfolding events. (Landes (1978) made a breakthrough when he used the plane hijacking to gauge the effects that the US counterterrorism policies. He applied several methods in order to reveal how the counterterrorism measures deter terrorists from hijacking. The deterrents are things like being arrested, prison time, and the possibility of being convicted. His review indeed showed that the metal detectors reduced the rate of hijackings.

The 9/11 attacks led to the increase in the interest of literature pertaining to terrorism. Data that was available at this time was both conceptual and analytical. After the heinous attacks on 11 September 2001 (9/11), there was an explosion of terrorism literature, both conceptual and analytical. This section will talk about terrorism on an analytical basis, we will go through the policy trends and forecasts, we will take a look at the impact terrorism has on the economy and the social costs on campaigns from both sides of the divide. This cost is what will give us what potential gains an economy can gain from its counterterrorism initiatives. The government needs such figures to be sure that there is some level of effectiveness in their counterterrorism measures so that a decision can be made on whether to continue or discontinue the budget. The other dimension is the study is meant to help us understand the reason why terrorism is an option to the respective groups and if there is anything that can be done so that policy makers can learn about what appropriate measures to take.

We will also present some of the major advancements in the way terrorism analysis is done today, for example by learning new interpretation methods on both domestic and international terrorism. The game theory analysis and its role played by foreign in aid in combating terrorism. There are so many research literature that has extensively explored these areas, we will talki about them here too because terrorism does not seem to end anytime soon and so the major topics will also continue to be with us for a long time. It is also a good idea to look at what the future holds for the study and research of terrorism.

Has terrorism changed since its re-emergence in the 60s?

Many studies in this field tend to start from the late 60s. Starting to look at terrorism from this time creates a specific cycle that can still be attached to the changing modes of operations and ideologies that are shaped by the dynamic environment. To better analyses terrorism trend it is a good practice to stay away from complex undertakings like plane hijackings, the more routine trends like day to day hoaxes, bombings, and threats give the best data (**Sandler & Enders**, 2004). Bombings may seem isolated but in actual sense, it is a composite of many other bombing-related events like explosions, letter bombs, and car explosions. Law enforcements should be able to know the cycle of bombings it will help them in anticipating the next wave of violence and probably find them prepared especially when there is a defined pattern.

International terrorists came to the fore between the years of 1968 and 1980 where there was an increase in terror activities on a global level. Then came the 1980s when there was a surge in state sponsored terrorism (Hoffman, 2006). The mid 90s international terrorism went down; many research studies attribute this to the decline of state-sponsored terror activities and also the rise of capitalism that was commensurate with the fall of the leftists (left wing). Then there was the rising proportion of civilian causalities that corresponded to the growing emergence of separatist groups and terror groups with religious ideologies who changed the terrorism scene by seeking more carnage and used deadly methods to execute their terror. (Enders & Sandler,2000; Rapport, 2004). The period between 1998 and 2005 saw the rise in the number of casualties in every attack. The choice of target(s) also shows a dynamic change with time as new tactics and ideologies are introduced. International terrorists show some rationality in response to the security measures taken or put in place by security agencies. It became increasingly difficult to attack areas or personnel that are accorded state securities and international terrorism resorted to hitting of softer targets. As people continued to increase their security measures on business and homes, terrorists resorted to hitting private events. It reached the point where attacks on businesses were surpassed by these private parties' attacks in the 80s (Brandt & Sandler, 2010, 2012).

In the late 90s terrorist attacks on private establishments gained more prominence over public officials. There was also a surge in domestic terrorism globally, and the worrying trend is that more terrorist's organization fashioned their attacks to unharmed civilians as we entered the early 90s. (Brandt & Sandler, 2010-2012). This attack on civilians may have caught a trend because of two reasons:

- People offer an easy and softer target
- Religious fundamentalist wanted a big number of casualties
- Policy makers and researchers can use such trends to make

informed decisions when looking for ways to formulate appropriate counter policies and allocate the proper use of resources.

Economic consequences of terrorism

Terrorism has a direct impact on the economy of any market. Take for example the September 11 attacks on the world trade center, costs were estimated to in the upwards of $80 billion. At that time the American Gross Domestic Product (GDP) was at $10 trillion (Kunreuther, Michel-Kerjan & Porter, 2003).

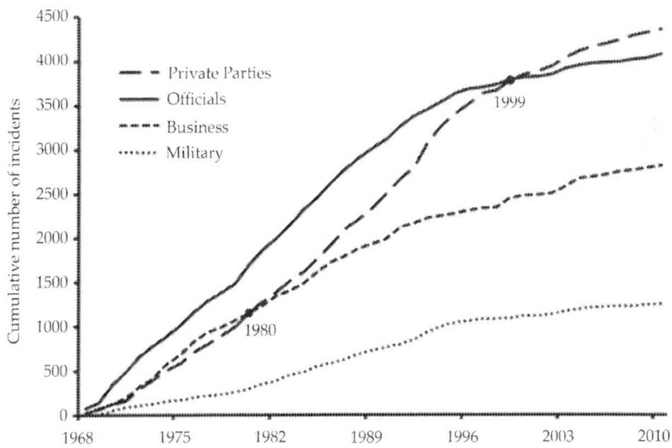

Figure 3: Cumulative number of transnational terrorist incidents by target type, 1968–2010

This is an example of a direct cost of terrorism that shows the immediate loss that an attack can bring bearing in mind that it includes both the structures, injuries ected country. The indirect losses that are attributed to terrorism are the lack of high insurance premiums to cater for such losses, increased security budget, lost business opportunities and increased budget on counterterrorism measures.

When insurance companies pay compensation to those considered to be located in high-risk areas, the high amounts involved can directly be attributed to the high cost of terrorism. The clear line that separates direct and indirect costs from direct and indirect costs of terrorism is not easy to draw. It is important to note that even small-scale attacks have a little negative impact on the country's GDP. The example of a small scale attack like the Madrid commuter was estimated to cost the span's economy about 0.03 % of the GDP (Busea et al., 2007).

The loss of economic value due to terrorism can be viewed in terms of reduced GDP stunted its growth. All the factors that affect the larger economy, such as government expenditures, investment and consumption are also affected by terrorist attacks. An economy that has to endure a considerable number of terror activities will lose investments because of the perceived business risk as far as investors are concerned (Blomberg, Hess & Orphanides, 2004). In addition to that, investors who find themselves in such a position will be forced to send or transfer their resources to other countries that may be having the same rate of returns but with low-risk terror potential. Such situation has placed governments on the need to have in place government initiatives to aid in combating terrorism-related activities as this reduces the cost of security on taxpayers and other stakeholders. Terrorism also has different effects depending on the location or the business sector that has been affected. Some locations are known to be carrying more risks than others when analyzed over a time period. (Enders, Sandler & Parise, 1992) used the Greek example to show that attacks by terrorists affected the tourist industry and led to a loss of about 23% of the expects annual revenue from terrorism in the year 1988, another example would be Austria that suffered close to 40% of its annual tourism revenue for 1988 (Drakos & Kutan, 2003).

When it comes to the economic doldrums that can be attributed to the consequences of terrorism, a lot of research information can be found in great volumes. An important fact is that stable economies are able to withstand the aftershocks of terror attacks, even if they were to experience such attacks on a regular basis. The reason behind this could because of the movement of business from high-risk areas to less prone areas, but within the same country, meaning no loss of business (Sandler & Enders, 2004). This is also directly related to the fact that casualties in developing countries are very few and with even fewer deaths and modest property damage. These advanced economies are able to offset these negative effects of terrorism because of an anticipated fiscal plan that covers for contingency planning. (Enders & Sandler, 2012: 296–298). The smaller economies where terrorism is rampant like |Colombia, Spain, Israel, and Mexico, first will have to come to terms with huge losses that adversely affects the GDP, and it becomes worse when the attacks become so rampant. (Abadie & Gardeazabal, 2003). The developing countries are bound to suffer very significant losses (Enders & Sandler, 2012; Gaibulloev & Sandler, 2011). This is a common feature in failing or failed states, when such happens, foreign investors will not bring their foreign direct investment (FDI) who play a major role in the development of such economies. These countries take the time to recoup and stabilize their markets. In as much as terrorist-hit areas may have a sustained development despite the economic loss, this loss can be seen to be smaller in relation to the entire GDP. The cost of terrorism is contiguous to the place of the attack. Its effects are more localized and only felt in other regions when investments move to safer locations. Terrorists continue to hit different economies, but somehow the stock markets have a way of turning out to be resilient with the exception of major incidences that affect several economies. The stock value of company's remains affected for a number of days when it becomes the target of terrorists (Chen & Siems, 2004).

How effective are counter terrorism policies?

Since (Landes (1978) had done a study on this, several researchers have dug deeper into this area trying to evaluate specific counterterrorism policies. Technology may hinder a targeted terrorist attack but they may still present additional challenges such as terrorists moving to other locations with fewer technological barriers. The transference of an attack as one of the unintended results that come are good policies of mitigating terrorism activities for they ended up changing the terrorist's behavior and change of mode and venue of attack. A typical example is the metal detector that plays an important role in preventing plane hijackings, but a terrorist may see an opportunity for hostage taking. That is why it is easy to see that hijackings went down as the incidences of hostage taking went up (Enders & Sandler, 1993). There is a direct attribution to the increased number of casualties after the introduction of metal detectors in the 70s (Enders & Sandler, 2012). To understand the effectiveness of a counterterrorism measure, a researcher must look into the impact of the intervention mechanism used and the alternative possible attacks that can be anticipated. In some areas where metal detectors were installed in embassy facilities, attacks in such areas are no longer possible and levels of incidences have significantly gone down (Enders & Sandler, 2012).

In order to get the nature of effectiveness of an intervention technique, one has to know the economic value and the benefit that comes from it. Getting the true value of the benefit is a challenge as it involves knowing the number of attacks that happened when there was no intervention in place.

When evaluating the effect of a counterterrorism measure, transference is one thing that a researcher must take into consideration, because terrorists also weigh in on the prescribed measures and evaluate the overbearing risks and use rational thinking to change and their target and location of the attack. (Enders & Sandler, 2012).

One may feel disappointed by counterterrorism measures affected by the lack of the effectiveness of the United Nations resolutions. When treaties are signed, there is hope and great promise. However, studies indicate that previous UN resolutions did not produce any desirable effect on counterterrorism measures (Wilkinson, 1986). This finding may be able to make sense going by the fact that most UN resolutions do not have any tangible enforcement mechanisms and if that is not the case, only a few countries seem to gain from such agreements.

Other studies have also shown that counterterrorism effectiveness in repeat or retaliatory raids led the terrorists to bring forward future attacks as a way of protesting these attacks. An example would be the 1986 US bombing of Libya after the La Belle discotheque was bombed in Berlin (Enders & Sandler (1993). As a follow-up, instead the terrorist attack scaled upwards due to spending resources on the terrorists' side. The overall effect of such intervention did not in any way reduce the level of terrorist attacks.

Another tactic is rewarding terrorists planning an attack to avert their mission. (Dugan & Chenoweth's (2012), empirical analysis shows that such actions led to more terrorist activities that seem to coincide with previous results (Bloom, 2005; Rosendorff & Sandler, 2004; Siqueira & Sandler, 2007).

In theory, it can be said the governments are doing a good job handling domestic terrorism than international terrorism. This is probably possible because the government controls all the external activities of the terrorists within their borders (Enders & Sandler, 2012; Sandler, 2005). When a country is involved in the eradication of a terrorist group that targets on its interests, no other country benefits from such actions because their interests were not affected. For common benefits to be achieved, nations find themselves funding bigger budgets by changing the focus of terrorists to other countries, some countries may enjoy the efforts of common global terrorism approach by spending less to enjoy the services offered by other countries. (Arce & Sandler, 2005; Sandler & Siqueira, 2006).Therefore, this can lead to a negative effect of being involved in counterterrorism on the international level. Countries that have a significant amount of asset overseas may not see a problem in such spending. For example, if a country decided to take its fight on terrorism to say, the Middle East, instead of putting counterterrorism measures in place it decides to eliminate the threat altogether to respond to the killings of their citizens. This will, of course, lead to a backlash from the international community who may see such aggressive acts as excessive. This will eventually bring positive effects on the country with the new focus and therefore under spending factor is restricted.

Root causes of terrorism

Terrorism has shown its dynamism over time and as such it has any causes and therefore terrorism cannot have one root cause. When causes of terrorism are to be discussed, the likelihood of reaching a consensus is remote. This is due to the fact that many studies have been attributed to this subject without any conclusive results. Some of the most reasons that are likely to apply to the many waves of terrorism are:

- Economic discrimination
- Religious persecution
- Nationalist/separatist motives
- Religious fundamentalism,
- Political ideologies

The above are just the common ones which may also be used in the categorization of terrorism. Therefore other common grounds like marginalization can be counted out (Wilkinson, 1986). Several studies have been fronted to suggest that poverty can also lead to radical terrorism, one such study by (Krueger & Maleckova, 2003) was quickly disputed by (Piazza, 2006) as he saw little or no relationship between poverty and terrorism. Looking at several countries where terrorism is rampant (Enders & Hoover, 2012) in his controversial study saw no relationship that could be tied to income and terrorism. In countries considered to be poor, the general population is looking for ways to survive and looking at rich countries where not enough grievances that can fuel radical terrorism. This contradiction among scholars led to a study by (Gassebner & Luechinger, 2011) whose intention is to highlight the differences in the factors that fuel terrorism. To get desired results, they analyzed the strong factors that are thought to be causes of terrorism and looked at data from victims, the location of the attack, and the country of origin of the terrorists. Looking at the recent trends in terrorism attacks, it is easy to note that they key factors that lead to terrorism may differ from country to country. The country that has fallen victim to a terror attack, it is possible to use variables such as the GDP per capita, wars, religion, and possible ethnic tension to determine the root cause of terrorism. The negative factors that can be linked to terror attacks include economic freedom and human rights. For a country that hosts the perpetrators, researchers through their study realized that human rights, economic freedoms, law, and order have a negative influence on terrorism. Factors such as population, spending on the military, involvement on external aggressions, investments in foreign capitals, and the political affiliations with the United states (in line with the voting pattern at the UN) are all positive influences on terrorism.

Looking at the country of origin, things that limit terror activities are economic freedom, physical and human rights, and capacity to communicate freely using technology. On the same note things they promote the growth and spread of terrorism include civil strife and totalitarian regimes. Of course, different studies will have unique causes of terrorism, a cross-sectional analysis on this topic is bound to give an intermediate overview that may still not give you the desired results for particular countries. Using an intermediate view on causative agents seems more logical when looking at international terrorism because at this level most terrorist organizations are probably united by some common grievances.

The dilemma faced by liberal democracies

Liberal democracies have their legitimacy galvanized by the popular support and in return the favor by giving citizens adequate security and improve their living standards. While looking at this (Wilkinson, 1986) noted the dilemma such countries face. He raised the issue of the possibility that a terror group can exploit the lack of or the lackluster response to threats affecting the general populace by the government. There is a dangling situation where if the government refuses to act on terror threats which may be seen as inability to act and may probably be taken out through voting, the other scenario is when the government responds too harshly which may come out as an overreaction that compromises the tenets of democracy and pushes the government to the edge of unpopularity. It is at this point that terrorist ideologies may resonate with the plight of the populace and may possibly motivate them to start looking for credible targets so that the system can no longer stand. When the democracies respond to such attacks, they may without knowing facilitate terrorism by adding more constraints in the name of fighting terror. These constraints lead to things like the curtailing the freedom of speech, association, press, the right to privacy, and the absence of a stable security environment (Hoffman, 2006; Wilkinson, 1986)

Many empirical researchers like (Eubank & Weinberg, 1994), have always raised the concern whether democracies can harbor more terrorists than an authoritative regime, several studies point to the fact that democracies are the primary hosts to terror groups (Eubank & Weinberg (1994). Some other studies still on the same issue show that more democratic freedoms lower the number of attacks on the international level. (Eyerman, 1998). Subsequent studies try to see the link between democracy and terrorism, which in turn proved that democratic values have a positive effect on the number of international terrorism without having any effect on domestic tourism. Further probing into international terrorism showed that democracies that are heavily involved in solving diplomatic ties through their foreign policies increase the chances of being hit by international terrorists. In addition, any visible alliances with the United States result in such democracies experience more international terrorist attacks. This still remains the most interesting area for many researchers. We can also look at the argument fronted by (Chenoweth, 2010) that when terror organizations compete for supremacy to gain more followers in a given region it drives up terror activities in democracies. She was able to prove that competition among the top political players also has a direct impact on the increased levels of terrorism and terror organizations in that country.

Major new developments in the study of terrorism

There are several areas that harbor a lot of interests now and will still hold the same for a long time to come. Several data and result findings have been brought forward to interpret terrorism, both in its domestic and international dimensions. This data is available for researchers to be able to test the different hypotheses. (Enders, Sandler & Gaibulloev, 2011) made it possible to create a clear demarcation between these two forms of terrorism. (Piazza 2011) noted that economic distribution is a clear and an outright determinant of domestic tourism, nonetheless, this differentiation was not a definitive determination of international terrorism. This is so because many attacks on foreign capitals or installation are sometimes motivated by policy decisions and other specific grievances that may be tied to that single terrorist group or several others.

The use of each country's terrorism count data made the discovery that foreign policy is a significant player that terrorist organizations use to plan their international attacks; foreign policies do not relate in any way to domestic terrorism (Savun & Phillips, 2009).

After the 9/11 attacks, the game theory has taken a central role in the study of terrorism. Game theory is the study of the logic (rationale) that is involved in the study and identification of targets by a terrorist. This has been said to be the best tool that researchers can be used to capture all the important interactions such as the complex relationships: two nations being attacked by the same terror organization, government interactions with domestic terrorist groups, rival terror groups, the government, the media, relation between a government and factions within a separatist group, and the terrorist.

Good results on the study of terrorism depend on findings that are either provocative or out of the norm. The trend in game theory analysis mostly involves the use of counterterrorism measures because of the limited data that is available on the measures taken by governments to curb terrorism. It is not easy if not impossible to obtain data on a government's spending on defense or money set aside to mitigate terrorist activities.

Therefore, the evidences given by different research findings usually rely on such scanty data. For instance, (Benmelech, Berrebi & Klor 2012) presented an observation and had their support for (Bueno de Mesquita's, 2005) on the quality of work on terrorism hypothesis. Using the data provided by (Jones & Libicki, 2008), it is possible to say that on terrorist groups, (Bapat, 2011) gave a related analysis in support of the so-called moral danger where countries use their military to support the host countries.

The game theory offers several points and great insights. The first thing one is likely to note is the strategic behavior that includes the involvement allies (commonly targeted countries) which may want to work together to achieve a common purpose (Bueno de Mesquita, 2007; Sandler & Siqueira, 2006). The second thing will be to see how antagonists may also work together to achieve a common goal, such as trying to match the response of the opponent after a terrorist attack (Arce & Sandler, 2005). The third point is the importance of in countering the antagonists based on the belief that they always have little access to information on resources that are available for the enemy (Kydd & Walter, 2002).

The fourth aspect of the game theory is its long-term perception with the argument that terror groups are more than likely to join forces with rivals to increase their presence in a region, whereas democratic governments cannot go beyond the elections. This may affect the nature of agreements that countries can have between themselves because there may be no guarantee that if there is a change of guard the agreements would still stand (Sandler, 2005). The fifth point highlights the fact that there has been an increased number of actors in the game theory model that has resulted in breaking down the model into several stages of the game, where a stage contains two active agents at any given time.

Previous early studies on terrorism also involve a time series analysis which looked into the effectiveness of counterterrorism measures and the effects of terror on the economy of a country (Gaibulloev & Sandler, 2008, 2011).

Recent developments that have dwelled on the study of how terrorist networks are networked, in the late 60s and 70s shows that different terror organizations cooperated on many levels contrary to popular opinion. Their main areas of operation include training, intelligence, financial support, safe haven, weapon buying, logistics, and personnel exchange (Hoffman, 2006). The most notable were the existing ties between the European left-wing terrorists and the Palestinian groups (Alexander & Pluchinsky, 1992). And recently, the Al-Qaeda network which is thought to be operating in more than 60 countries and has profiles of attacks on the global stage advocated for the merging of groups for the purposes of increasing its effectiveness by using limited resources to fight powerful countries.

The best approach in the study of terror networks is through coming up with counterterrorism policies that will be more effective in damaging the connections or associations between terrorist groups (Farley, 2003). This is based on the graph theory where an assumption has been made that policy makers have intelligence on the makeup of the terror network configuration. Furthermore, the assumption is that the existing configuration does not change because the terrorist anticipates the counterterrorism measure put in place to disrupt it. This is an indication that terror groups must give up their networks so as not to compromise their vulnerability (Enders & Jindapon, 2010). An analysis of the terror networks shows that at least every terrorist organization that carries out complex operations need other networks to facilitate communication and information sharing. With such an arrangement when one organization is infiltrated it can compromise the entire network, to ensure that there is no vulnerability terrorist organizations use small terror cells that are loosely linked to facilitate communication (Enders & Sandler, 2012). These networks are quite essential in the game theory when investigating the way international al terrorist delegate tasks to low-level terrorist groups while in the field (Siqueira & Sandler, 2010).

The most recent research survey, (Young & Findley, 2011) gave out the indication that foreign aid reduced the chances of international terrorism when such funds are targeted to education, civil society, health , and conflict resolutions.

RECENT ATTACKS

Terror attacks by terrorist organization all over the globe have been on the rise and increasingly becoming a permanent feature on the international news channels. Many terror organizations make an effort when conducting their terror activities. When looking at the most recent attacks, in late 2016 and 2017, it is important to also note that some terror activities do not see the light of the day because of numerous foil attempts.

Terrorists attack usually fall into several categories depending on the strength and capabilities that include their connections to other terror affiliate groups. Some of this aggression is normally conducted and controlled by their headquarters through their operatives who are trained in other active cells that are responsible for the funding of every aspect of the operation. The operative is supposed to maintain contact with their cell. In some cases, there are individuals who act alone (lone rangers) and are inspired by the terrorist ideology of destroying the western capitals and any person who does not profess the Muslim faith.

This report, has documented several attacks that took place from 2015 to the latest attack that happened in the last days of June 2017. It is important to note that all these attacks happened under the watch of ISIS which some believe their presence in Europe has increased due to the refugee crisis that started a few years ago. This movement of refugees is largely attributed to wars that are believed to have been caused by some western powers either through the quest for resources or installing a friendly regime.

It is quite important that when putting up measures of counterterrorism, policy makers should understand that such attacks are done by a determined individual or a terrorist organization that consists of a determined individual, lone ranger, or a self-radicalized person who is ready to die for a cause.

The table below is a chronology of terror activities conducted by different terror organizations in western capitals

Here is a timeline of the most recent terror attacks in from 2015 - 2017:

June 3, 2017: Van rabbing and stabbing in London
Seven people were killed and dozens were injured by three assailants who ploughed through pedestrians on London Bridge and stabbed revellers in Borough Market.

May 22, 2017: Outside Ariana Grande concert in Manchester, England
Twenty-two people were killed and dozens more injured by a suicide bomber with apparent connections to an organized terror network.
April 20, 2017: Champs Elysees attack in Paris
An attacker got out of a car and fired an automatic weapon at a parked police van, killing the officer inside, before shooting at others standing on the nearby sidewalk, injuring two before he was shot and killed by police.
The French president said the attack was "terrorism in nature" and promised "utmost vigilance."
The Islamic State claimed responsibility for the attack.
April 7, 2017: Stockholm truck attack
Five people were killed when a truck driven by a man drove into a pedestrian shopping street and department store in Sweden's capital city, wounding over a dozen others.
The 39-year-old man allegedly admitted to being a member of ISIS and told police that he had "achieved what he set out to do."
April 3, 2017: Saint Petersburg bombing
A suicide bombing on the subway in Russia's second largest city killed more than a dozen passengers and injured dozens more.
March 22, 2017: Westminster Bridge attack
Five people, including a London police officer who was stabbed and the perpetrator, were killed in a terror attack. More than 40 people were injured outside the Parliament building.
British Prime Minister Theresa May said the act was "sick and depraved."
ISIS later claimed responsibility.
Feb. 3, 2017: Louvre knife attack
A machete-wielding man yelling "Allahu Akbar" attacked soldiers in a shopping mall near the Louvre in Paris. He was shot and wounded by soldiers.
Dec. 19, 2016: Germany Christmas market
A large truck plowed through a Christmas market in central Berlin, which killed 12 and injured 48 others.
ISIS claimed responsibility for the attack and said the attacker was "a soldier of the Islamic State" through Amaq news agency.
Nov. 28, 2016: Ohio State
Abdul Razak Ali Artan, an Ohio State University student, ran his car into a group of students and slashed people with a butcher knife.
The Islamic State claimed responsibility for the attack and called Artan a "soldier."
Oct. 16, 2016: Hamburg, Germany

There was a "lone wolf" knife attack in Hamburg, Germany, which claimed the life of one teenager.
July 26, 2016: Normandy, France
Two men took five people hostage during a Mass at a church in Normandy and murdered an elderly priest by stabbing him in the chest and slitting his throat. The hostages were freed later, and the two men were arrested.
Then-President Francois Hollande said that the men carried out the attack in the name of ISIS.
July 14, 2016: Nice, France
Seventy-seven people were killed in Nice, France, when a truck drove through a crowd on Bastille Day.
ISIS claimed responsibility for the attack.
June 12, 2016: Orlando nightclub shooting
Omar Mateen attacked an Orlando gay nightclub, killing 50 people. Mateen pledged allegiance to ISIS on a 911 call, after the worst mass shooting in U.S. history, and the worst terrorist attack on U.S. soil since 9/11.
ISIS later claimed responsibility for the attack
March 22, 2016: Belgium attack
There were two suicide bombings on March 22, 2016—one at Brussels Airport and the other in the city's subway system. Combined, the attacks killed 32 people.
The ISIS cell that claimed responsibility for the Brussels attack was also linked to those involved in the Nov. 13, 2015 terror attacks in Paris.
Jan. 11, 2016: Marseille, France
A teenager attacked a Jewish teacher in Marseille with a machete. He told police that he carried out the attack in the name of the Islamic State.
Jan. 7, 2016: Philadelphia, Penn.
A man shot and wounded a Philadelphia police officer. The man claimed the attack was in the name of Islam and the Islamic State.
Dec. 2, 2015: San Bernardino shooting
A married couple shot and killed 14 people in San Bernardino, Calif. The FBI is investigating the shooting as an act of terrorism inspired by ISIS.
Nov. 13, 2015: Paris attacks
A series of coordinated terrorist attacks in Paris killed 130 people and injured hundreds more. The attacks consisted of mass shootings and suicide bombings.
The Islamic State claimed responsibility.
Aug. 21, 2015: Paris
Three Americans were at the center of an attempted mass shooting. They helped to overpower a gunman who was armed with a Kalashnikov, and opened fire on a train from Amsterdam to Paris.

The gunman was on the radar of European counterterrorism agencies and appeared to be sympathetic to ISIS.
Feb. 15, 2015: Denmark
A Denmark national who was inspired by ISIS went on a rampage through the nation's capital, killing two and wounding five police officers.
Jan. 7-9, 2015: Charlie Hebdo
There was an attack on the offices of the satirical magazine Charlie Hebdo, and four attacks around Paris followed, killing 17 people

Source: A timeline of recent terror attacks against the west, Newsweek

ANY HOPE FOR THE FUTURE? IS TERRORISM GETTING WORSE?

After the 11th September 2001 attacks, the reality dawned on the world to both serious terrorist scholars and observers that the time had come where no matter how massive the security apparatus of a country is terrorists can still outsmart the system and pose a great threat to the world. Terrorism challenge can be in the form of state actors, individuals or organized terror network. Today in 2017, we are still in the state of war and the phrase " war on terror" is something that has been on the lips of counterterrorism policy makers and the question many people are asking if we are making any success or are we going to have a future with less or more terror activities.

The two questions act a guide on most terrorism research and studies in both the present and the past. We can look at researches that are designed to act as a review of the history, incidences, effectiveness, and the possible future of terrorism. The emphasis of any research is to place its emphasis on the trends and irregularities that are terrorism related. The final aim is to generate create an understanding of the entire terrorism phenomena. The trend and incidence approach is designed to make us see the importance of appreciating the future of terrorism. In this section, our focus will be limited to the terrorist activities that are directly linked to non-state actors.

We will look at the overview and the historical personification and the incidences of terrorism today, thereafter a discussion on the effectiveness of terror activities and the factors that influence it. Special attention will be paid to incidences that use weapons of mass destruction and the general overview of the features of a terrorist organization.

What are the history and occurrence of terrorism today?

Both the state and the non-state actors use fear as the primary weapon to commit acts of terror, this mode of operation has not changed and maybe because throughout history the use of fear has been used due to its dynamism and regularities. Based on these researchers can ask the question of whether changes in the social order, beliefs or notable events has been the reason why the increase and decrease in the incidences of terror have moved from state actors to non-state actors.

(David Rapport, 2004), in his book, four waves of modern terrorism outlined what he referred to as the four waves were the first, he called the antichrist, which according to him started in Russia sometime in the 1880s and went on the fade at about the early 1920's. The second wave he called it the anticolonial that was started in the 1920's and ended in the 1960s. The third wave he called the new left that happened in the 1960's all through to the 1980's, whereas the final wave was called the religious that emerged in late 70's and is believed to be the face of modern day terrorism, especially in the middle east and some parts of Africa.

The wave of the antichrist was as a result of deep hate and lack of trust of the anarchists who were acting slowly in the reformation of societies and this led to several attempts to of the then revolutionaries to create uprisings with the aim of changing the social order. Their initial attempts to bring change through writing and art did not bear any fruit and that is why they resorted to violence. The antichrist view of the society as being yoked to various ways of conforming instead of being free, their way of showing disdain to such conventions was to instigate violence. Their primary goal was to ensure that the defenders of the government noted the terror being meted on them and therefore had to be forced to undermine the rules of the government. To make sure that they get maximum attention, their attacks were targeted to high ranking officials and to some extent even the heads of governments. Through this, the authorities were forced to act by using excessive force in a bid to quell the uprising and this tactic turned against them when their retaliation was also harming the civilians. The weapon of the time was the dynamite which was used to kill any attacking terrorist.

The first wave of terrorism was highlighted in 1890 and it escalated to the 1940s, which researchers aptly call the "Golden Age of Assassinations." It is quite a remarkable period because on average of 18 months or less a head of state from one of the European capitals would be assassinated (Joel Shurkin, 1988). This very period is what prompted governments to start to use war like tactics to combat terrorism. The involvement of States in counterterrorism was adopted after the assassination of the US President, William McKinley. The attempt to pull other states to join the "war on global terror "at the time failed because no consensus could be reached.

The anti-colonial wave came in after the signing of the Versailles treaty that ended World War 1. Nations were angling for self-determination that were able to break out of the crumbling empires made it possible for new forms of terrorist organizations (fronts). The build-up of the Irish republican Army (IRA) and several other Jewish organizations that worked against the British influence in Palestine. This terror campaign was mainly fought in the disputed territories and where the occupying forces did not want to leave just yet. In Palestine, the members described themselves as freedom fighters who are fighting against terrorism by the occupying government.

From the diasporas different countries opted to support one another in the colonial strife and terrorism gained a lot of support worldwide and assassinations became the order of the day. Another strategy that was being used during the rise of the second wave of terror was to eliminate policemen and occupy the military bases which at that time were seen to be less effective in combating terrorism. This tactic was a sort of provocation because the military had to respond disproportionately, which in the long run ended causing more damage to the civilians more than the terrorist could cause. It was very common for the term "freedom fighters" to be referenced to terrorist groups seeking liberation. Another term, "anticolonial" was coined to referee for those who were in the struggles against occupation (Rapport, 2004).

The emergence of the new left form of terrorism was formed in the background of the Vietnam War. This war exposed the effectiveness of moderate weapons against a more sophisticated western show of force. Many youths did not identify with the system that they had in place and this is what led to the rise of terror organizations such as the Red

Faction in West Germany, the French Action Directed, and the Italian Red Brigades.

Their choice of target selection was somewhat similar to those of the first wave international terrorists. And terrorists revisited the assassinations and attack of the prominent figures and new forms of sabotage like plane hijackings, kidnappings, and hostage taking. While the main aim of the anarchists was to assassinate high-ranking officials to create animosity, the new left wave used the same tactic as punishment.

The third wave of terrorism attracted the attention of the world that it warranted international cooperation to formulate counterterrorism measures. Nations through the United Nations conventions singled out hijackings, hostage taking, and the financing of terrorists and outlawed them. At the same time the term "freedom fighting" was no longer recognized by the UN. But the most interesting development was the use of terrorist tactics by the Palestine Liberation Organization (PLO) to promote its ideologies and policies was recognized as part of the United Nations body (Rapoport, 2004).

The religious wave brand of terrorism has been identified mostly by Islam. The movement began following three important events; the Iranian revolution, the Invasion of Afghanistan by the USSR, and the new Islamic renunciation. This was also the error of rhetoric. The US was referred to as the "Great Satan" by an Iranian leader. The war in Afghanistan was a training ground and a breeding ground for Islamic indoctrination for Muslim volunteers all over the world. This brand of terrorism led to the frequency of suicide bombings leaving more deaths and casualties as they also introduced the use of chemical weapons. The most notable group that initiated the use of chemical weapons in its terror activities was the Aum Shinrikyo sect. They made the attack in Tokyo in 1995. Hezbollah, a Shia Muslim terror organization faction conducted a series of suicide missions on US marines and French soldiers in Lebanon. This led to a large number of casualties and forced these two governments to withdraw their troops from Lebanon. It is through the suicide missions that influenced the Tamil Tigers carrying out the highest number of such missions from 1980 to 2001. In numbers, they carried out more than 40 % more suicide attacks than any other terrorist outfit at the time (Robert A. Pape, 2003). Towards the end of the Soviet occupation in Afghanistan, the Gulf War led to an increased number of US soldiers in Saudi Arabia. Many Islamists and particularly Osama Bin Laden saw the need to change focus and turned to America as the number one enemy of Islam (Richard A. Clarke, 2004). When the Gulf War ended Laden moved from Saudi Arabia to Sudan and the Al Qaeda network, which at that time was decentralized in its bid to defend Islam (Mockaltis, 2007) saw the need to have a distinct feature in Islamic terrorist organization that has the desire to destroy American targets. (The desire to destroy American targets is a well-known pattern in the third wave brand of terror) and because of this the single most event that can be attributed to this vision in the September 11 attack on world trade center in New York (Rapoport, 2004).

This attack prompted more than 100 countries to participate in retaliatory attacks either directly or indirectly in a war directed towards the Taliban. Despite the biggest manhunt and support, very little success has been seen in trying to address terrorism. The most visible result is the emergence of more powerful factions that continue to attack the West.

Rapport's version on the history of international terrorism cannot go on without challenges by several authors and scholars.(Mark Sedgewick, 2007) in his argument has no problems with the four instances or waves of international terrorism that are described by Rapport however, he offers a different opinion on the first wave saying that it may have started in Italy in the 1820s and that more terrorists were there between1920 and 1960 than usually recorded by many scholars which can be attributed to the successful change in the strategies that the terrorists use and not as result of other causes as stated.

But (Thomas Mockaitis, 2007) pointed out that in as much as Rapport revealed the general cycles of terrorism, there are things that stand out in his version of waves, one is that most the terrorists who identified with the left wave, called themselves anarchists and anti-colonial yet such organizations may have existed only after 945 and not as early as 1920. The other disparity is that the terrors committed by the fourth wave are mainly caused by people who profess the Islamic faith and most of the activities of such group are committed followers of Islam. The underlying factor that contributes to terrorism, according to Thomas is instability.

In summary, we can say that all the views that oppose or add to Rapport's propositions should be considered when looking at the history of terrorism. With that in mind presently we have been experiencing the highest form or religious terrorism that we have to accept takes place in every day of our lives in several parts of the world.

Looking at the terrorism situation in Europe, it can be said that terror groups are not so active. For a long time the attacks directed to Europe Capitals end up causing limited damage and it can be said terrorist activities deliberately avoid casualties. But of late, we have to accept the reality on the ground and look at the rising cases of terror attacks that are aimed to cause maximum casualties using different methods that have never been used before like driving vehicles into pedestrians. It is worthy to note that Spain, France, and the UK are countries, mostly affected and targeted by terrorists. Of late, we have seen small countries like Belgium, Turkey and Brussels are the new EU countries on the terror watch list (Europol, 2007).

Therefore, it is more likely that the risk of being a victim of terrorism may not be a serious issue in the developed world as it is in developing countries. There are two things that we need to keep in mind: The use of fear by terrorists in not meant to kill, but to change or influence your way of thinking in a particular direction (usually following the terrorist ideology)

The future of another attack is quite unpredictable in both timing and manner or the magnitude of the attack (Terrorists always try to make sure that the subsequent attacks are deadlier).

Does terrorism work?

Does terrorism really get to achieve the end game or the ideology of the given terror group? The question may not make sense and may appear rhetorical based on the previous research findings. However, we need to ask ourselves if by leaving the emotional and psychological meltdown due to the impact of terror they have been able to achieve anything. It is now the work of the researchers to establish whether, through their heinous acts, they have been able to influence the formation of policies. The question we should be asking is if the terrorists have been able to coerce governments to have their expected pattern of behavior.

Different studies are trying to answer this question and as expected, may varying answers abound. To understand this question we need to understand what the terrorists really want and what strategies they use to get there. (Andrew H. Kydd, Barbara Walker, 2006) made a study on these two questions and according to them terrorism is looked at a sale of a very expensive product that people may not associate with due to its high price, and so to impose their will (price) they will use a different target by inflicting pain on it knowing very well that you will react and because of the value that you have attached to the target, you are likely to listen to their demands (pay the price)

In as much the terror organizations have different ideologies, they are all united by their respective ideologies, but there are five goals that any terrorist group can relate to through their militant activities. They may use different strategies to achieve the five goals.

- Regime change
- Territorial changes
- Policy change
- Social control
- Status quo maintenance.

The five objectives above can be pursued on the following strategies that are commonly used by many terrorist organizations

(1) Attrition

(2) Intimidation

(3) Provocation

(4) Spoiling

(5) Outbidding

Terrorism through suicide bombing is another popular strategy that has been used to pursue a specific goal. Those that act on religious motivation to participate in the suicide mission cannot be seen as a rational act but as an irrational activity. The irony here is that terror groups that use suicide as a weapon of negotiating are known to pursue goals that are rational in nature.

After a thorough investigation on how various weaknesses and strengths are being used to negotiate the conclusion by many researchers is the use or availability of information from both ends of the divide. Terrorists must use the information they have or obtain from future victims in a way that they can change their perception and will. This logic works both ways, counter intelligence strategies, and also employ the same use of information when combating terrorism. The regime type also has an influence on the strategy to be used, and democratic governments are more prone to different strategies compared to other forms of government.

The study of terrorism by suicide as a choice weapon has also undergone some studies, debates, (Pape, 2003) made his study on this and he coined a phrase thus "the coercer is the weakest actor and an indication of the disposition to sacrifice his own life to achieve that. The greater the destructiveness of the terrorist activity, the stronger is the seriousness it deserves. It may also create an anxiety in the participation of a bigger attack (punishment) if the demands are not met. To choose a democracy as a choice of target makes it even harder for the terrorist to achieve their objectives because democracies have the propensity to retaliate violently but cautiously. When governments use such tactics, it encourages more suicide missions. The only way terrorists can achieve anything when dealing with democracies is if they try to engage in pursuance of the goals that are moderate and go about it without forcing the state to hand over their vital interests. Pape gave the conclusion stating that from 1980-2001, half of terrorist attacks that used terrorism as a strategy were successful in pushing governments to change government policies.

(Max Abrams, 2006) conducts an analysis into the effectiveness of the strategies used by the terrorist to pursue their goals; his conclusion was that terror groups managed a paltry 7% success rate. The rate of success, according to Max depends on the choice of target selection. Groups that attacked vital installations like military, security and political targets had high success rate as long as the number of civilians was very low. In his conclusion he finalizes by saying that terrorism is a weak method of coercion regardless of the objective being sought.

Therefore the success rate of counterterrorism measures depends on sufficient information to both the terrorists and the state, the objective being sought, the nature of the regime being coerced, and the target selection. Terror being seen as a weapon of the weak by many scholars, seem to work where the state does not have a high stake on the demands of the terrorists, when there is moderation on the use of violence, and there is no threat to the fundamental rights of a person/ people

Established democratic societies seem to be prone to coercion and are likely to change their policies when faced with such threats.

What if a terrorist group threatens to use a weapon of mass destruction (WMD). Will they be successful in their quest? There is no so much date that gives support to this question, looking at several examples will show you they have not been successful. In the 20th century there was a total of the 18 terror attacks that used WMD and a result, nine people died and a staggering more than 900 casualties. In the period between 1970 and 1999 there was a total of 12 of attacks that used WMD, one person died and more than 700 fatalities. The Aum Shinrikyo's sect was a group of terrorist that were known to use biological weapons on its targets. Most of the terror organizations that use WMD usually lack the knowhow of using biological and chemical weapons (Seth W. Carus, 1997). Chemical weapons may sound scary when used on people but in actual sense they are not as lethal or effective as terrorists would want them to be. Even their usage in wars is quite paltry compared to other more efficient and quick methods that can be used to win a war (**Rapport**, 1999).

So we can make the conclusion that WMD cannot be better than the conventional methods used by terrorists. And judging by the expected state reaction when deadly force is used, terrorist also practice rationality on their choice of weapons.

Terror may after all, is not an effective tool in getting governments to change their policies, but when used well, terrorists can make some headway in changing people's perception which in the long run change the policies of the state.

Is Terrorism Getting Worse?

It is not easy to answer this question unless you take a personal perspective on it. Looking at terrorism from any angle gives the impression that it is not only becoming more deadly and common, it is gaining notoriety by being widespread. The death toll in the recent months and years tells everything about it getting worse. The war on terror got its international façade when George W Bush made s declaration of the war on terror that should not end until all the terrorists have been apprehended or defeated.

Unfortunately the war on terror especially in the Middle East has led to more terrorists sprouting up or the existing one re-inventing themselves and this gives the impression that terrorism is becoming worse day by day. Looking at the previous data, number of fatalities may be going down because of improved counterterrorism measures that have been adopted by many countries, however, this does not mean that the number of attacks has gone down. One thing then has been notable with many terror organizations is that if they are boxed out of their region, they look for alternative target sites and in most cases, it is usually the European capitals.

The mode of operation is increasingly becoming worse. ISIS has of late adopted beheading of foreign nationals as a way of passing a message to the world, with such trends, such tactics spreads fear among the populace and creates a pennant anxiety that an attack is imminent. You may ask why is this becoming the near norm with all the efforts countries are trying to use to tame the terrorists. Some scholars and terrorism experts will most likely agree on one thing, the world being in a perpetual war like status creates a lot of instability especially in the Middle East is the number one reason why there is perpetual terrorism. Civil war is a natural breeding ground for factions who think of retaliation they will be able to get rid of the occupying forces.

Collecting data on terror attacks globally is not an easy task and most importantly, it can be quite subjective (it all depends on the individual's ability to understand what terrorism is all about, what to collect and differentiating terror attacks other brutal attacks). Regardless of the quality of data used for analysis, terrorism the world over is worse today than it was several years back. Even before the advent of ISIS, Europe, the Americas, and the United States faces a serious problem because of the new tactics that involve the so called lone rangers or lone wolves who are considered to be more dangerous than an organized platform that is relatively easier to track. But that is not to say that lone rangers are more dangerous than infiltrators who are more trained and are able to carry out an attack with precision (more like the 2015 Paris attack)

The threats caused by civil war in the Middle East

There is the general perception that terrorist seems to be targeting the west more than any other place. This may be true, but their activities have been restricted to the Middle East (considered to be the breeding ground of terror) because the western powers have made it difficult for them to access these countries. Terror activities seem to torment those who live in the hot zones created by the west than they affect the terrorist primary interest.

Civil wars that seem not to end may be happening far away from the western capitals, but the constant fear or a terror act in these cities is palpable. Civil wars create a lot of situations that cause a lot of tensions in these areas and leave very little room for other ways of expressing grievances and the only way out seems to be joining a faction that one can identify with.

Civil wars generate the unending vicious cycles of need and grievances that touch on personal life of a person. For example, being displaced from home, your parent being killed, losing a brother either to the occupation or rival factions, etc. Such grievances will push any sane person to give up on life or only to fight for his or her survival. When such a person gets an opportunity to vent his or her anger against the west, he is considered a possible threat and the only way to solve this issue is to give him opportunities to think otherwise so that he does not see war as an alternative.

The threat posed by terror will not go away any time soon, as long as more forceful invasions in the name of war against terror still gets the support of developed countries and the United Nations. Experts agree that when a seemingly stable government is toppled whether fairly or unfairly, from a counterterrorism point of view, this is a failure when it comes to containing terrorism and prevention of future threats, look at Libya as an example.

In the west, people are threatened by acts of terror across the world. This has led to a lot of attention being paid to likely threats than it was in the recent years. This mode of fear and thinking has already changed our perception of terrorism, which we can also conclude that the terrorism apart from being a constant threat to humanity have also succeeded persuading our minds to think in a terrified manner regardless of what we are doing

TRENDS IN THE GLOBAL TERRORISM INDEX OVER THE LAST 10 YEARS.

The global Terrorism Index (GTI) database gives a comprehensive summary of all possible terrorism trends and patterns. This section will give an analysis of the last 10 years and beyond.

The GTI database is updated and reviewed by institutions such as the Institute for Economics and Peace, University of Maryland, Global Terrorism Database, and the Global Terrorism Database. Data from this database is collected by the national consortium of terrorism and responses to terrorism. Such data command a lot of credibility and is used by researchers who are cresting reports on terror activity on a global scale.

The research herein is a highlight of the quick changes and the dynamic involved in global terrorism. The study also looks at improvements in combating terror, the intensified terror incidences, and the areas that should be of concern, and look into the complex future of modern terrorism activities. The complexity of the data found in any GTI database will at least show which countries improve in their index scores, which ones faltered, and the overall performance in terms of the comparison done over the previous years without forgetting countries that were moderately affected by record levels of terrorism.

The year 2017 saw a notable deviation of the pattern from the previous five years. The year 2016 saw the amount of fatalism increased by ten percent. The number of states that are reporting deaths may have decreased in some countries. The overall decline of fatalities is mainly attributed to the increased military operation in Nigeria and Iraq, which weakened both ISIL and Boko Haram. The increase of activity by both camps in other countries is the look to the new reported threats in Syria, Libya and Yemen. Boko Haram went into Cameroon, Niger and Chad, this movement led to the increase in the number of deaths they caused by more than 150 %. The military action in Iraq pushed ISIL to 15 new territories and therefore increased their operation base to about 30 countries. This is largely the primary reason why there was a number of terrorism incidents from different countries rose in almost every year for the last decade. 2015 saw the decline of terrorism acts by about 10% and the number of fatalities in the same years also decreased by the same margin. In 2014 there were fewer deaths due to the decline of terrorism attributed to increased participation of the military in countries with insurgency problems. These deaths in both Iraq and Nigeria went down further than it was the previous year. Nonetheless, 2015 recorded the deadliest and the highest number of deaths ever recorded in the year for that period. With the increased weakening of both the Boko Haram and ISIL in their main areas of the sphere and influence (both in Nigeria and Iraq) led toe positive change that coincided with the negative trend that led to the increase of terrorism in other parts of the world. This led to the fundamental shift of strategy by ISIL in regard to international terrorism, this was evident in both Europe and the Middle East. The other negative effect or trend affected the Boko Haram because of their expanded territory into Nigeria's neighbors. This in turn raised the terrorism index of both Cameroon and Niger in the GTI database.

This negative aspect led to the increase in the number of ISIL – faction groups that carried out these attacks. The study of this period noted that the number of states that had more than 25 deaths increased to 35, this increase by seven digits recorded the highest number. Six other countries retreated on their GTI scores in 2016 that led to a large change in rank from the earlier year. This is what led to the overall drop in the GTI to six percent. This drop outweighed the gains that were made by both Nigeria and Iraq. The countries that decorticated are Saudi Arabia, France, Tunisia, Turkey, Burundi, and Kuwait.

In the European capitals ISIL changed its international strategies and initiated the use of the lone ranger attacks that seemingly was inspired by the refugee movements and in turn increased the terrorism levels to one of its highest levels ever. This upsurge was evident in OECD nations that led to the increase of more than 600% in fatalities in 2014. The role of ISIS in this increase is quite significant because more than half that year's death were attributed to them.

The ISIS's attack on Paris, Turkey and Brussels were recorded as the most serious attacks in the history of the respective countries and this further contributed to the worrying trend of the international terrorist groups that are linked to Al Qaeda before and after the September 11 attacks. It is worth noting as the focus and attention of the world has been drawn on ISIL on both Iraq and Syria, 2015 recorded one of the deadliest years of the Taliban in Afghanistan. Both in the battlefield and deaths committed by the Taliban went up 2015. This means that terrorism increased by about 30 %, while fatalities in the battle field shot in the upwards of 35%.

This unpredictable global view on terror was at least not without some encouraging and good news where most countries saw an improvement in terrorism rankings. The number of countries that recorded terrorism activities in 2015 reduced by one compared to 2014. This temporarily paused the annual trend of yearly attack increases. The progress of countering terrorist activities by different groups through the effort of international coalitions led to the reduction in fatalities in the Central African Republic, Sudan, and Somalia. Pakistan was on a decline in the level of terrorism largely attributed to the infighting from the different factions. This also coincided with other military operations by the Pakistani army in the FDA areas (federally administered tribal areas). India showed some improvements which as far as history is concerned always carried the highest number of terrorist activities. On the same note was Thailand, which unusually recorded the lowest number of deaths since the year 2005, bearing in mind the 2016 Bangkok bombing.

The economic impact of terrorism in 2016 was largely similar to 2015. It is quite important to note that the economic impact of terrorism is small when compared to other forms of violence. In situations where there are acute levels of terrorism like in Iraq, the cost of terrorism hits the economy hard because of its destructive aftermath.

Statistical analyses on the factors that fuel terrorist activities indicate two distinct factors which are also dependent on the country where terrorism has taken place. The first category of factors are those that are linked to terrorist activities that are politically motivated and are committed by the state and or when there is a conflict. From 1984 to 2015 all terrorist activities took place in countries with the highest level of state sponsored terrorists. They involve the use of extra judicial killings, detention without trial, and torture. On the same note, more than 90% of all terror related deaths happened in countries that are already in some form of civil strife (internal or international). This gives only 0.5% of terror attacks attributed have occurred in countries that do not have any form of conflict or state sponsored terrorism. This emphasizes the related link between existing conflicts, political violence, and grievances. During an analysis of the relationship of terrorism with factors that are dependent on the level of development. In the OECD countries, militarization, youth unemployment, criminality levels, access to weapons, distrust in the electoral system, and social economic factors play an important role when looking for factors that correlate with terrorism. The same factors in OECD countries are the driving factors towards extremism and radicalization.

In developing nations, levels of corruption, history of conflicts, respect of human rights, and inequalities among people of the same group are basically related to terrorist activities.

A terrorist who acts as a lone ranger is very unpredictable but the report gives some statistical representation that helps the counterterrorism policy makers understand the trends and tactics used by such groups and what countermeasures to use in every case. The 2017 GTI report emphasizes on the belief that terrorism is a brutal form of violence that is committed by a person or a small group of people who commit these crimes in a small number of countries.

The five countries mostly affected by the high number of terrorism as fast as the GTI is concerned are, Nigeria, Pakistan, Afghanistan, and Syria. This five accounted for more than 70 % in deaths globally in 2016. Four terror groups are responsible for these deaths, namely Boko Haram, Taliban, ISIL, and Al Qaeda.

Terrorism seen as a form of violence has the major psychological impact on the societies it victimizes. Though it is also good to note that there are other forms of violence such as major armed conflicts that according to this report, carried more deaths in 2016; as it also led to the destruction of economies.

3 THE LAW ON TERRORISM

INTRODUCTION

A person or groups of people may premeditate and plot to cause harm to a target group of individuals, to institutions and even governments. This can be done by use of violence for varied reasons like politics, where members of a certain group may fight in order to over through the government of the day or in order to be incorporated in the running of the government. The other motivation could be for ethnic cleansing to the extent of causing genocide with the aim of ensuring only a certain tribe or clan is in control of power. Further political intention could be for resolutions of taking control of an area with the objective of controlling the resources available.

The second intention could be for religious reasons. This may happen particularly where religious ideology is used in an aggressive manner whereby people or groups are compelled to follow a certain religious belief by force. If not, they are killed and their property destroyed. A known case is where Muslims radicals want to compel other people to abandon their religious belief and follow theirs, like stopping people from attending churches and synagogues and instead worship in mosques. Due to many circumstances that make a group or a person decide to engage in terrorism, it is the very reason why scholars have not agreed on a standard definition. However, key characteristics inform the act of terrorism like, use of violence to cause fear among the populace, there is the destruction of property, murders are common, terrorists aim to kill as many people as possible and cause as much terror as imaginable. In addition, they want the act to be publicized to as many people as possible and to be felt in far-flung areas. Consequently, terrorists want to be perceived as cruel and ruthless as possible. Terrorist ambition is to cause disquiet, also to induce feelings of sympathy, to intimidate, to cause disquiet to non-locals or to immigrants.

TERRORISM-RELATED LAWS

From various acts of terrorism, human cost by terrorist has actually been experienced virtually everywhere in the world. The atrocities cut across all continents from America, Europe, and Asia to Africa. These clearly show that terrorism has no boundaries; it does not matter whether the country is advanced economically or even technologically. Anyone would be pardoned to think that poverty is the root cause of terrorism but considering such advanced economies have been affected, it, therefore, demonstrates terrorism has its own phenomenon.

Africa is rated as a third world continent that is characterized by poverty, diseases, hunger, wars, political instability, low literacy levels just to name but a few. However, just like in advanced economies, terrorism has equally taken root in Africa. That begs the argument, what is the motivation behind terrorism? In fact, the devastating experiences occasioned by terrorism have been felt across all continents. The key players involved are actually the learned because of some of the sophistication that comes with terrorism. A good example is the planning aspect which cannot be done with the precision required if not for school education.

Looking at the targets picked by terrorists, it can only be argued that the thinking can only be from very smart people in the society. Some of the notable figures mentioned in terrorism are military experts, who actually assists in the assembly of bombs and of late Improvised assembled devices commonly referred to as IEDS, trusted religious leaders like Imams, some law students, commoners in the community. These again demonstrate that terrorism can be perpetrated by anyone in the community.

Following the first and second world wars that happened in the past, countries came together and formed United Nations body that was meant to mediate and resolve conflicts in an amicable manner to protect furtherance of war activities and also to protect human life and their property. In line with that, strong consideration for human life was put into focus; the protection of human rights came into play where it was argued that every human being has a right to life, freedom of association among other liberties. Although the right to life and liberties are critical components of humanity, they have come with their own challenges that require regulating to safeguard life and property.

From the various incidences of terrorism, it can clearly be seen that terrorists have exploited the same liberties and rights to cause atrocities. These have awakened governments and United Nations to domesticate laws that will safeguard life and property from terrorists and their terrorist acts. Although human rights activists and lobby groups are opposed to the enactment of terrorism-related laws by arguing the laws are too strict and tough, but the reality calls for even stiffer penalties to deter people or groups that may plan to terrorize others by causing unnecessary anxiety and fear.

However, before considering the terrorism-related laws, it's important to understand the human rights first. The definition of human rights is envisaged in various fundamentals like universal values and legal guarantees that basically protect individuals and groups against oppression by the governments and its proxies in regards to freedom, entitlements, and human pride. These entitlements are spread far and wide from, cultural, political to social rights as well as the right to progress.

Human rights have posed challenges to governments in the context of handling terrorism-related matters and even counter-terrorism. This is because, with a right to life, it becomes tricky to kill terrorists through bombing or other severe measures while knowing very well they may kill but claim the right to life. Human right protects against torture yet terrorists don't give information unless pushed to the limit. These scenarios time and again put law enforcement agencies into very awkward position and yet they stand accused of failing to do their work diligently. These rights serve as a double edged sword.

Human rights prohibits anyone to be discriminated against, however in order to pre-empt terrorist planning and consequently execution, it's important for the law enforcement agents to profile the prime suspects while monitoring their activities however they often get criticized from sympathizers and lobbyists for doing what ordinarily is their job this serve as another challenge to handling terrorism.

Aside from right to association and fair trial, government security agents must do their work but the said human rights are obstacles in protecting the very human beings that are the target of terrorists. Another human right to consider is right to privacy, yet there could be a suspicion that the occupants might be planning to cause atrocities. These are examples of how terrorism in taking roots by exploiting the fundamentals right that they enjoy.

Aside from the many challenges posed by the human rights, there is a universal concurrence that says the right of one person ends where the rights of the other starts. That means despite the difficulties posed by the fundamentals of the human right, it is still possible to craft laws that may be used to protect humanity and their property from terrorism. In essence, the balance has to be found in order to promote and protect human rights while at the same time countering terrorism and customizing laws time and again for purposes of countering the mutating trends of terrorism.

Due to failure to have an international compromise on the correct meaning of terrorism, governments have been forced to look at the domestic laws and customized them in a way that they may as well be used to charge terrorism-related crimes. Different countries have chosen to evaluate the circumstances in their respective jurisdiction and crafted laws that follow the due process of law-making in the respective country. In most of the case, the governments evaluate at what laws best protect their citizens and their property, and even foreign investors. The laws are made in such a way that, they are not in conflict with the constitution of the respective countries.

Therefore, while considering the terrorism-related laws, in view of the understanding that the rules are crafted by individual governments, then it means terrorism bylaws can only be considered by country and not universally. Going by these arguments, then there is the need to look at the terrorism-related laws as they were crafted by the individual country.

First of all, it is essential to have a look at terrorism related laws in India. The common term used to refer to the laws in that country is the anti-terror law in India. It is important to appreciate why India which is one of the most populace countries in the world had to craft some laws to cover terrorism. Considering the country has a hostile neighbor like Pakistan with whom they had been fighting for a while and who was exercising aggressive activities toward it. To cover itself, India had to ensure that any retaliation had to be done within the internationally accepted approach. Some of the earlier laws enacted were the India Penal Code and The Code of criminal procedure, 1973. Both laws contain rules related to terror cases. They included crimes of instigating a war against the India government, breeding hatred among the populace. In addition to the two legislations, other rules have been enacted to cover additional trends as pertain to terrorism. This is because terrorists keep on changing tack and therefore their ways of conduct keep on mutating by the day.

Due to the complexity of matters related to terrorism and the balance with the human rights requirements. India's circumstances were not an exception. The laws had to consider how investigations be conducted within the regulations governing the act. More so, how should the court process be conducted to ensure a successful conviction? This was important because in any court procedures have to be followed to the letter. In absence of clearly defined ruled, judges might release the culprits with no bonds, simple sentences or other lenient pronouncements. Therefore, laws had to consider all that, but at the same time protecting the right of the accused to a fair trial and also considering that they remain innocent until proven guilty. Basically, the threshold had to be well defined within the law.

The absence of such legislations may breed discontent with members of the public who may feel the courts are too lenient to the terror-related offenders. These may bring in a culture of mob justice which is highly discouraged in the modern world that we live in today. If members of the public take laws into their hands, cases of killings on mere suspicion may be rampant or even killings as a result of mistaken identity. The criminal procedure must be well defined to avoid the perception that the courts are taking their sweet time in concluding the matter. (That simply means the procedure must be well elaborated to be predictable). With the complexity that comes with terrorism, it must be clear on what constitutes the terror act, considering that not all criminal activities may be qualified as terrorism. More so, members of the public have a right to association, which means the government must declare in no uncertain terms which organization groupings are considered as terror organizations so that people can avoid them. Furthermore, non-governmental organizations may request to fundraise for a good cause. In that regard, it must be known what constitutes terror financing to avoid falling victim to a kind gesture.

Since terrorism is considered a crime against humanity, therefore as part of the procedure it must be clear how the arrest and detention will be done and what should be the constitutional safeguards. In the case of bail terms, what should be the circumstances and the bail terms? Further consideration of the evidence, that is, how it shall be preserved to be admissible in courts. What type of evidence is acceptable is it audio or video recording, eye witnesses or reports from both local and international agencies. Can their evidence be admissible in the courts of law or where the jurisdiction of the investigating agencies both local and international does start and ends? Are the evidences gathered by intercepting the communication among the terror group admissible? How will the witnesses be protected during the pre-trial and after the trial?

Furthermore, how will the sentencing be done? Will the convicted terrorists be put in separate detention camps or prison or should they be put together with other offenders. If so will they likely to influence other general offenders? In the case of minor terrorists, how will they be treated? How will they be sentenced? Will they enjoy the right of minors considering they are terrorists? Will the offenders have a right of appeal? Which courts levels are supposed to conclusively determine the ultimate sentence? (With so many such questions it can only show how terrorism matters are complex when it comes to successful prosecution). These questions show how complex terrorism/ terrorists trials and to see to their final prosecution.

Global instruments, particularly in relation to peace and security, rest with the United Nations. This is a global body with membership drawn from across the globe. Its main tasks are to arbitrate and look into matters that disturb peaceful order in the international community. Just like the governments in a different jurisdiction, United Nations had also to come up with the direction on matters terrorism. These mainly touch on matters regarding terrorism funding, organization and invent provoking terrorist acts contrary to the values of the United Nations. In its various resolutions, there was a declaration that each member state should take the necessary steps to protect its citizens from acts of terrorism.

The United Nations urged member states to domesticate laws that should deal with serious crimes among them terrorism. They should ensure that any organization or individuals involved in planning and financing of terrorism-related activities should not be hosted and if anything, other members states should be informed to ensure such groups are alienated from the wide international community thereby denying them a chance to execute their evil activities.

In a bid to give direction to its members the United Nations through its Secretariat drew some treaties and protocols that were basically to bind member states. The said treaties and protocols are simply conventions and agreements that members had to consider in dealing with acts of terrorism. Among the treaties were acts committed on board the aircraft, agreement on what should happen in the case of the seizure of an aircraft and probably such a plane is taken to a different jurisdiction from where the act initially happened. Matters pertaining to allowing the landing, re-fuelling and generally what would happen in the case of such an eventuality? Other agreements were on the prevention and punishment of offenses against protected individuals like the envoys. Additional conventions were on safeguard of nuclear materials. These are generally a key concern because if such materials fell in wrong hands the effects could be disastrous.

More conventions were on the suppression of terrorism financing and cutting off ties with that organizations and persons. This was important because for terrorism to take proper effects it needs finances to deal with the massive logistical challenges. These spread from recruitment to purchases of arms to oiling the pockets of its agents and collaborators. Considering all the aspects, it is therefore impossible to further terrorism-related activities without proper channels and sources of financing.

It is good to note that terrorist hits at the nerve center of what the United Nations stands for particularly the furtherance of democracy, and the rule of law, stability and even the human rights. It is therefore important for the United Nations to keep monitoring the domestic laws of the member's states to ensure they are well founded in both domestic and international laws. .Where it is realized the member states lack the legal capacity to put the legal instruments in place, legal experts may be seconded from the united body to guide in drafting. The whole aim of all these steps is to make sure the legal regimes against terror acts are strengthened.

United Nations plays a key role in ensuring the member's states are obligated to submit offenders for prosecution particularly where the arrest has been made in another jurisdiction. The whole aim is to facilitate quicker repatriation of offenders so that they may face justice. Additional matters of collaboration in the investigation so that the evidence is preserved well to aid in the successful prosecution and final sentencing. All these are critical for purposes of deterring the acts of terror from happening. The mere perception that all international security agents and government are working towards the same course may help to mitigate the many cases associated with terrorism. The United Nations may further arbitrate where there are no agreements among the member states on extraditions proceedings of the offenders.

Through the various agreements drafted by United Nations, a general understanding of how the offender will be treated and what rights he will enjoy with regard to communication with the members of their family. The notification on the operating standards of treating the offenders is generally prescribed for all anti –terrorism conventions.

As indicated earlier, different jurisdictions formulate the laws that are meant to handle terrorism-related matters. Among such laws are the laws of Trinidad and Tobago. Trinidad and Tobago is a major Island located in the northern coast of Venezuela and at the southern side of America. The country has formulated terrorism laws commonly referred as Anti- Terrorism Act. The Act is intended to criminalize terrorism and its financier, prevention, detection, matters of how the prosecution will be conducted, conviction and finally punishment of the offenders. The Anti –Terrorism Act also stipulates how seizures of the terrorist property will be done, and also confiscation of the assets and more so how the forfeiture will be done to the said properties and their proceeds, and should be administer them. The terrorism laws according to the Trinidad and Tobago jurisdiction are well elaborated in terms of what offenses constitute acts of terrorism. These offenses may be related to the safety of sea navigation. Considering it an Island state, it can only be understood why marine protection is a key component of their terror laws. This is because most of the commercial economic activities are directly related to the sea, from the general transportation to the logistics in the shipping industries, fishing activities, marine ecosystem and even tourism. These may be a departure from a country whose jurisdiction borders a dry land or a desert. These seek to further elaborate why terrorism-related laws are customized based on the needs and circumstances of the general geographical location of a country.

The second agreement is on the offenses related to the bombing offenses. Considering Trinidad and Tobago is a member of the international community, it has an obligation to protect individuals who are against terrorism. Trinidad laws on terrorism speaks strongly against the terrorism financing. In fact, the laws are clear on what constitutes terrorism financing. The major consideration is whether the party receiving or giving has the knowledge that the funds are meant to commit a terrorist act or the recipient or giver is a member of an outlawed terrorist organization. The law is very clear; it does not matter whether the offense is committed directly or indirectly by use of agents related to terrorism. All the actions constitute to terrorism financing.

The laws are very clear that upon conviction of such an offense in relation to the financing of the terrorist activity they are liable to conviction. The law even clearly states what period the offender will be in custody: approximately twenty-five years. These stiffer penalties are intended to deter any person who may contemplate about engaging in terror-related activities. The act is well elaborated in regards to the process of investigation of an offense or offenses related to terrorism. Who should do it and in the case of detention of such a suspect, how all that should be carried out. The acts also elaborate on the jurisdiction and trial of the offenders. They will determine if it is outside the country or is in the country. It also stipulates what happens when; the offender is a foreigner and the extraditions proceedings in case the arrest was done at Trinidad and Tobago.

Anti-Terrorism Act of Trinidad and Tobago stipulates how information sharing should be done. This can be within the multi-security agencies or foreign security agents. Ordinarily, they agree on the channels to use so that the investigations are not compromised. More so, how the extradition should be carried out considering that offenders have the right to be heard before any proceedings are initiated. In addition, Trinidad and Tobago may have prior signed mutual assistance agreements with other countries when it comes to terrorism-related offenses by its citizens caught in a foreign land or foreigners apprehended in Trinidad and Tobago.

Trinidad and Tobago laws are very clear on how information will be shared and in the case of disclosure of the source, how it shall be done without exposing the whistle-blowers. Seizure and forfeiture of terrorist property are well defined in the law and how future proceeds from such property will be used. For example, it can be for compensation of the victims or for use in the strengthening of the laws further through the institutional framework as set up in the laws of the land. Matters of custody and records of the offender detained are well elaborated.

Terrorism is very dynamic and keeps on mutating by the day. The perpetrators are very smart people who not only understand but also know how to manipulate information technology. Due to the advancement of information technology and in particular internet, communication among the masses is now very easy and convenient. Additionally, any information required can be found on the internet with ease and in a fraction of the time. Unlike in the past where information communication used to take time before it reached the intended recipients. The common practice was the uses of "snail mails," as the world technology advances; fax machines and telegrams took over. However, all these modes of communication were very cumbersome to both the receiver and the sender.

In the light of advancements in information technology, the same has happened to criminal elements who are equally advance with technology. Many terror organizations can still use the legitimate mode of communication to reach out to new and old members. It is possible to recruit target people by use of the advanced technology using a psychological approach to convince the targets that the matter being perpetrated is a just cause. And going by the current trends in the recruitment of membership within the terror organizations it serves as a clear demonstration that it is working. Actually, it is now easier to reach the target members far and wide from the comfort of a desk without necessarily traveling to those locations. Because of this, funding of terror activities is now easier than before because the world is full of electronics means for transferring money across the globe. And by looking critically, it is difficult to have a full proof that the money being sent or received is intended for good purposes. In some cases, legitimate businesses in operation are used as conduits for transferring money or used as facilitators of funding terror-related activities. Despite all the risks advanced by the development of information technology, it can generally be concluded that the world and economies have managed to prosper and sorted challenges like unemployment just to mention a few.

However, governments need to take proactive measure to neutralize use of the very technology to advance a warfare that is meant to harm the public. This can be done by use of laws that may be crafted with a view of directing the good and bad use of information technology. It is clear that as the information technology advances so are the criminal elements advancing by using it to their great advantage. It has bred a new form of crime against humanity, as cyber terrorism. This type of terrorism starts when a person or group of persons decides and plans something that is meant to harm people. The motive could be political in nature, a plan to cause political instability or advancing information warfare against a group of people or government with an aim to create anxiety and unnecessary confusion.

Other approaches hatched may be a plan to attack computers of target group with the sole purpose of stealing information that can be used to perpetrate a crime. Other motives of hacking the computers of competitors with the aim of bringing a downfall or accessing an authorized sensitive or confidential data can be used on military activities, arms, nuclear and even financial data. In line with the global trends, laws had to be crafted to mitigate such scenarios through proper channel of the investigation, evidence handling and finally prosecution of the offenders.

As earlier stated, different jurisdictions customize the terrorism laws are based on the threats within their jurisdiction and the world. An example of such laws is the cyber-terrorism laws of the United Kingdom. The rules were crafted in a way that accommodated the crimes of terrorism perpetrated by use of the information technology. One such crimes is the information warfare. Here the information technology is the main vehicle that is used to perpetuate the terrorist crime. Under the information warfare, the terrorist spreads information on an expected incidence with the aim of causing panic among the populace. This has the effects of sabotaging the economy because people fear being attacked at their workplace or even avoids taking their kids to school for fear of attack. Unless such situations are neutralized by the members of the surety forces they may have a devastating effect on development. More so, unless punishment for getting involved with such acts is not severe then other players may start the same. That implies stiff penalties must be designed to deter such actions.

Another terrorist act that can be committed by use of information technology is communication. It is much appreciated that people must reach each other for business and prosperity but when the communication is intended to convey a plan for purposes of destruction of lives and property then that may be translated a crime against humanity. Such terrorism acts may be committed by use of a lawful mode of communication to convey information meant to hurt others. It can be through emails, websites and other communication approaches like through the use of social media which may include Facebook and Whats App.

Other ways in which information technology may be used to commit terrorist acts is when the user recruits personnel who will commit the acts in varied jurisdiction and more so get involved in logistical support. This can be through appeals where members of the organization accept to use their vehicles to facilitate the crime of terrorism and such like activities. In such a case, information technology has been wrongly used to solicit for personnel and logistical support that eventually is used to commit terror activities.

Since all manner of information is available on the internet, the same information can be used to gather the required intelligence on target facilities or installations. The motive may be wrong; maybe to bomb such a facility with the aim of sabotaging the economy of a target jurisdiction. It is also very possible that people can be able to get information on how to make bombs and nuclear weapons. That clearly demonstrates the dangers posed by exposure of information to the public and in particular the criminal elements. Due to that, they must be laws that highlight how a certain use of information may constitute a crime and upon investigation, a person may be convicted using terrorism-related laws as pertaining to the wrongful use of information.

Other ways that information technology can be used to perpetrate terrorism-related acts may be through propaganda. Here terrorists amplify their actions and also use the same platform to promise even further harms or massacre. The terrorists may go further and give the target areas that are meant to be attacked next. That way they cause fear and seek recognition and sympathy from members of the public. At some point, they use propaganda to justify an act with the aim of creating anxiety to members of the public or attract of funding.

Some terrorist groups may choose to open their own websites that they can use to communicate to the members and the general public about their atrocities. That calls for a constant appraisal by security agents to put in structures and personnel that can monitor the terrorists' activities and to stop them from inflicting harm on people. (In most cases, such acts are committed by selfish individuals or groups whose only quest is self-gratification. Therefore security agents must monitor such groups in order to establish their real motive and device approaches that can be used to counter such groupings). They must be several steps ahead of the terrorists and are not to be outwitted, outmaneuvered by them.

In most cases, the intensive investigation should be conducted to bring a member of such organizations into account and ensure they are successfully prosecuted so that they can deter further harm. All aspects should be monitored from financing to networks used and also the preferred modes of communication. They should dig on who are the people behind the plan whether local or foreign and their achievements to determine the greater vision of such separatists' groupings within their jurisdiction. When proper collaboration is established with international security agencies such groups can be brought to account and make the world a safer place to live in.

LEGAL ISSUES

The threats to humanity have never been as real as in the recent times, thanks to the terrorism phenomenon that have toned down. Although terrorists' activities have been condemned across the globe, there has not been a united front to tackle this monster called terrorism. A number of issues have risen in the best approaches to use while at the same time preserving the converted human rights as envisaged in the bill of rights by the United Nations. International players are in concurrence that governments must do everything within their means to protect the citizens from the clutch of terrorism, however, most often when actions are taken; there has been a major outcry in handling the terrorists. Like when they are killed on site, human rights activities complain that it is extra-judicial killings and must be condemned. The argument is that the governments must ensure that any counter-terrorism measure does not become an all-around approach to deal with the vice of terrorism.

The emerging legal issues are of concern on how to protect the human rights at the same time deal with the phenomenon of terrorism. The major problem is that even when acts of terrorism are perpetrated among the populace, the international law on human rights never stops to apply. This poses a lot of challenges to law enforcement agencies on whether terrorist should continue enjoying the rights just like any other person. For example, right to remain silent yet the law agencies need to get information from such a person, right to a fair trial yet such an individual intended to cause harm; right to life and the individual wants to kill people, All these are fundamental legal issues that need to be deliberated upon by the international experts drawn to lick this modern-day monster.

One of the greatest challenges is the relationship among democracy, the rule of law and a person's freedom. Without democracy there cannot be a rule of law and without democracy, there cannot be freedom of a person, yet the same person is turning against the other person to harm them and the rule of law must be used to prosecute such a person. Citing such challenges that governments must deal with while handling acts of terrorism may call for a review and a common stand on when the human rights may need to be shelved. What circumstances may warrant such setting aside of the human rights without abuse? It can, therefore, be concluded that human rights observation are in conflicts with global terrorism right to life and as such, it remains an emotive subject to discuss.

COURT CASES

Cases of terrorism are on the rise. This is due to the many groupings that have taken upon themselves to ensure the acts are perpetrated as long as possible. Besides that, there are so many unresolved cases that have justified terrorists' network to continue with their evil activities. Some may be historical others are mere excuses for purposes of continuing with acts of terror. Virtually all continents have in the recent past witnessed cases of terrorism. The only astounding view is that terrorism phenomenon has no boundaries, from advanced economies to developing economies and even the underdeveloped economies.

Notwithstanding all these, some jurisdiction has clear laws on how to preserve evidence and successfully prosecute cases of terrorism. Others have no clear frameworks anchored law. However, that said and done, there are varied court cases which have been concluded and others are on-going. The major challenges in all these are the aspect of the human rights that must be considered in all the proceedings steps. In some cases, terrorism-related cases are thrown out for lack of sufficient evidence that can sustain a fair trial. In others, the bail terms are so lenient to deter any such crimes in the future. Citing the circumstances of unsuccessful prosecution, it may explain why the security agents are increasingly getting frustrated and consequently, the state and its agents are tempted to result in extra-judicial killings to protect the citizens from harmful acts of the released individuals who have no respect for human life.

It is clear that terrorism is a global threat to peace and is a problem that keeps on affecting the entire humankind. Terrorism is a systematic use of fear to achieve an intended goal which can range from sabotage to killings for purposes of control of resources or geographical region. In consideration of all these, states must join hands at international domestic or regional level in order to tackle this phenomenon of terrorism. From the acts of terrorism across the globe, no country can be considered safe in isolation of others. It therefore, calls for concerted efforts to deal with the menace and continue devising new and proactive approaches in the hope that the phenomenon of terrorism can be addressed in a foreseeable future.

Some countries have even identified narcotics and other crimes like human trafficking as some of the sources of funding for the terrorist activities. Governments that have major incidences of such a nature are increasing by getting global support to address the menace of terrorism. In addition, there has been a global ban on trade with animal trophies like elephants tusks and rhino horns all these are collaborative efforts to address the key drivers of terrorism-related activities by the international community. Through the United Nations, there is a concerted effort to organize forums and create a committee that can undertake research to address this global phenomenon of terrorism in a more unified approach.

This is by inviting member states to air their views and opinions with a view of changing tact in handling the matter.

4 TERRORISM FUNDING

CRIMINAL ACTIVITIES AS A SOURCE OF FUND TO TERRORIST

It's delicate to evaluate the relationship between financing terrorism and organized crime hence further analysis is required. The fact is that we are able to identify differences and similarities.

A key consideration is the motivation. In fact, terrorist groups may differ. Crime groups or networks organized because of the crime model. Monetary gain is not the sole target to organized crime groups, the groups are known to have given non-financial goals which include; spreading ideologies, carrying out adverts, destroying company plans, spread of terror activities and intimidation in general. Terrorist groups sometimes compete with governments as far as their legitimacy is concerned, which is certainly not the case for organized crime. Meanwhile, terrorism can be difficult in clear and distinct criminal matters: in some cases, terrorist groups focus on the benefits, as well as their ideological motivations. It is essential to understand that the financial resources available to terrorists and organized criminals are of a different order of magnitude. Financial flows related to terrorism are often very low and remain below the thresholds of financial controls and the financial dimension of organized crime has a different

Quality, obviously, has important implications for implementing anti-money laundering legislation. The aggregate size of money-laundering worldwide is estimated at 2 to 5% of world GDP. However, resources for terrorist attacks are generally low. The costs of 11 September amounted to less than half a million dollars. Other attacks on Bali in Tunis, Istanbul, Madrid, London, Sharm El Sheikh were still far from being "cheaper". As a matter of fact, raising funds to support terrorism cannot be regarded as large scale. One might say that this is a small thing that cannot be measured in terms of world GDP. This does not mean that it is not important and that the fight against it has no impact or importance, underfunded, terrorists are able to create dramatic damage and fight against the financing of terrorism worked. But the important point to consider is that terrorist groups are not really based on highly profitable criminal activities, although they are difficult to assess. Where do we see the common points and the similarities between the financiers of terrorism and organized crime?

Logistics can be an overlapping area. The association between well-planned terrorist consortium and organized crime groups, mainly drug dealers take a wide range of positions starting from facilitation, i.e. protection, transportation and taxes, to direct traffic from their own terrorist organizations. Traffic and terrorists are often similar, such as hardware and secret movements of goods, people, and money logistics needs. Drug traffickers have terrorist military expertise, weapons supplies, and access to clandestine organizations. Terrorists are receiving a flow of income and experiencing illegal transfers and illegal profits from recycling operations. Corrupt officials present in both groups have services like access to unreliable documents for instance fake passports and customs as a mutual benefit. There exists also a possibility of easy movement to the traffickers after working hand in hand with terrorists who as a matter of fact control large territories. Terrorist groups and traffickers are increasingly dependent on mobile devices to achieve their goals. Despite the presence of a strong and reliable central leadership, all activities are performed by small cell members. An additional fact is that, terrorist and traffickers use the same means to realize the goal of hiding profits and fund raising. The process is facilitated by use of systems such as hawala, firms to recycle money, possessing multiple accounts and depends mostly on smuggling. They have also learned to make full use of trusted contact network and lead email. In fact, terrorists have increased their use of e-mail messages.

NARCOTICS INDUSTRY

As for some examples of criminal activities used by terrorists, it would be deepening the terrorist drug traffic. The most important cases are obviously known in Latin America. the Revolutionary Army of Colombia (FARC) should be about US $ 500 Million of US $ 1 billion per year of illicit activities, especially tax or participation in drug trafficking.

The ability to provide infrastructure, enable proximity to culture and enhance production in South Asia and Former Soviet Union by traffickers create a great link between the traffickers of drugs and terrorist.

In southern Asia, Al Qaeda, including Bin Laden reported traffic of hereinto support its operations. We have no clear idea of Al Qaeda's involvement in Afghan drug trafficking. A point which doesn't seem to be controversial is when Al Qaeda carried its operational base in Afghanistan; it got support from Taliban government which took a great part of its revenue and taxes derived from trafficking opium. Bin Laden could weaken the west by baring opposition production in Afghanistan which globally contributes to 70 percent of the worldwide production. Drug trafficking and the traffic running from Afghanistan via central Asia to Europe and Russia also benefited another group by the name movement by Islam in Uzbekistan.

The drug situation in Afghanistan remains very critical and clearly one of the major concerns for NATO troops deployed in the country theme. Smuggling heroin routes in the Balkans also have to do with the interaction between crime and terrorism in this part of Europe, where NATO is also heavily involved. Aside from, specific criminal activities and to participating in drug trafficking, terrorists use a variety of additional methods of winning, moving and retaining money. With regard to regional targets group terrorist groups are known for crimes such as fraud, low crime, smuggling cigarettes and forging. Low level criminal practices cannot be underestimated for they are capable of providing revenue for small cells and facilitating their networking. To store goods, terrorists use products that keep their value over time and are easy to market outside the formal banking system. This is especially true for precious stones or metals that can serve as stable financial resources. Diamonds are easy to transcend due to its high value, low weight and the fact that no odor found. The remote location of mining sites, the absence of effective rule of law and fragmentation of the international diamond industry in Africa is a major contribution of illegal transactions... Let me also mention the emerging risk of terrorism involving maritime piracy. This connection is particularly dangerous for international energy markets because most of the oil and gas transport is by sea. According to the International Maritime Bureau, the effects of the frequency and strength of piracy have increased in recent years. The traditional operating areas of pirates and maritime terrorists are the Arabian Sea, the South China Sea and the waters off the coast of West Africa. The narrow Malacca is a particularly vulnerable area. Major seizures by terrorist groups could have a devastating impact on the world economy.

BUSINESS ABUSE LEGALLY

Small firms such as fisheries and farms are supported by Al Qaeda in the recent past, not leaving large corporation like investment and construction organization behind... The network has also been linked to the Afghan national airline. In the 1990s Al Qaeda appeared to have established a number of businesses in Khartoum, including a holding company, a construction company, an agribusiness, two investment companies, a leather company and a transportation company. Terrorists and their supporters use authorized business to execute criminal plans. These companies can be big restaurants or fast food shops that are usually purchased with funds provided by single person. Commercial corporations avail of a portion of profits to the investors as a reward for the financing up to the time full payments are paid for the investment. In several occasion it can be alleged that, “seed” money to acquire the business is provided by terrorist groups. Laundering income from a list of criminal activities and availing of a way out for stolen goods have cash-strapped business as an ideal. They are also convenient places from which informal money senders can conduct business. In addition, it is well established that legitimate companies have been used for years to finance terrorist cells. Here terrorists seem to live the lives of ordinary people and, for example, be just ordinary retailers. In fact, the cell can be activated for an attack. New quality of terrorism has been encouraged by democracy and rule of law, and this is evidenced by globalizing and diversifying terrorist activities. The challenge is that terrorist organizations have increasingly based their activities on countries that offer conditions conducive to their survival and expansion. In addition, their mobility has increased enormously. The above places a great responsibility for the international community.

COMMUNITY TO STRENGTHEN COUNTER-MEASURES

The leading factors contributing to country hospitality towards terrorism and transnational crimes are: financial institutions which are not transparent, misusing the existing legislation, legislation in place, experiencing unfavorable economic condition, corrupt officials, not respecting the law and not guarding national borders appropriately.

Lack of political will to implement the rule of law is a leading contributor to the above conditions, since it is the immediate output of weak national institutions in place or high recorded levels of c corruption. The origin of both national and transnational criminal is attributed to the failing economy of a given state. These purely internal factors may be exacerbated by the geography of a nation or by the impact of unresolved regional issues, such as longstanding territorial disputes. In summary, a fertile ground for criminal firms and terrorists' growth can be attributed to situations like: a weak state in place, absence of civil society, inadequacy of democratic development and lack of a sound economic institution in place. Regardless of the fact that terrorists activities can flourish in developed societies, a strong rule of law can act as a great deterrent. This conclusion leads back to a crucial assertion: having a sound democratic institution in place is the best response to terrorism.

MYTHS ASSOCIATED WITH RAISING FUNDS TO SUPPORT TERRORISM

"Terrorism," "myths" are difficult to define. Essentially, they can carry the simple meaning sacred stories that are used to explain the origin of the world and various natural phenomena. It can be referred as falsehood in a simple language which obviously offends those who treat them as sacred. Political violence was had terrorism as a special form initially but currently is used as a pejorative term. On September 1977, **Antony Arblaster,** published an article in which 11 books on terrorism are reviewed, putting "myths" and "terrorism" in the same bed. The ten basic myths about discussions involving financing policies of terrorists are:

1. We know what "terrorism" is and its difference with upcoming political violence.
2. A clear distinction between terrorism and organized crime is made. (There is also an inverse myth: a distinction between terrorism and organized crime doesn't)
3. The funding of the armed arm of the political movement is funded in a similar way to all the other movement sectors, making all activities to be involved in providing funds for terrorism. This myth intellectually overlaps with one another.
4. We can regard terrorist organization as Weber pyramids with small groups controlling everything. This is in contradiction with the concept of cell structure that revolutionaries have created in 1860 to prevent the penetration of security forces. Strength relationships existing between political movement and armed weapons create a distortion. It follows that financing follows the same procedures due to the stated rules. Funds are created for specific transactions; for outdoor activities; to support the prisoners; for the reduction of poverty, partner organizations such as sports associations. Every activity is independent, although secret activists can be planted within these organizations. There are also separate sleeping cells once again being activated for specific purposes only.

5. Terrorism is a homogeneous phenomenon. It is not. There are many types of funding groups and mixing also being different.
6. While fighting terrorist groups, a major misunderstanding about the services offered by an armed political wing to a given population exists. Violence and execution of contracts is an essential service in which the state is weak. The extermination brought by the underground banking system is treated to be far away from always being a good idea for it allows provision by the groups themselves. The implementation of Maoian agrarian reform was essential to the success of rural guerrillas and the urban guerrilla problem was to find a substitute that could provide services / economy, etc. Security, executions of contracts, police are all areas where these groups can be moved.
7. An example of complicated multi-million pounds at the stock market tentacles was the Al Qaeda is use of the internet.
8. Something by the name "new terrorism" which was different in that it incorporate previous terrorism knowledge. Therefore, it can be treated exactly the same way that drugs, so can fruitfully be applied hence a "successful" war on terror. Follow the Money!
9. Large amounts of money had been stolen which violated terrorist organization worldwide resulting to seizing of small amount and returning the highest percentage of what was illegally acquired.
10. FATF has reduced the debate that a difference between terrorism money laundering and other stated forms of money laundering. The solution is not yet found because originally it was argued that money laundering is not a serious crime while money laundering as a terrorist product was a serious crime

PARAMILITARISM

The process of simplifying the existing relationship between parties comprising a serious political movement and led by a force of guns to fight against terrorism where less complicated actions are taken is likely to produce the unexpected results. Terrorism mainly refers to the condition where individuals and social groups bring forth violence or even built new states. Or even do away with activities important to the state activities for instance execution and delivery of contracts for a given period of time. Disintegrated countries state which is a result of ideological attacks or the collapse of other states which is similar to tales of Sicilian mafia. It facilitates the growth of organized crime and crime organization in a parallel manner to family and friends as discussed below.

Basing on given parts of international community of NGOs, subways of the civil society or land regardless of the state can be created .It is possible to exclude the majority or even the elite community since all organizations are in need of money and involvement in the process of creating an independent state becomes possible. Many have preceded the outbreak of the disease, such as terrorism. They are mainly interested in preserving separate identities which in turn separate the funding process but at long last interpolate others. The arm of movement that can take the path described by Gambetta licensing company can provide execution and even benefit itself. The process cannot be initiated by local political movement but individuals or even regional organization. It is possible to have different relations growing and changing with time resulting to other economies, states or civil society emerging. It is important to have organization with coercion forces for they yield a variety of existing relationship between organized crime and the movement of the armed arm. Structural adjustments are also influenced by types of financial flows from abroad which mainly support illicit business. The conceptual framework available is examined by this article.

When it comes to terrorism, the problem of definition remains centered, it is also time to return to its "academic view of definition of" terrorism. Terrorism is defined to be primarily a disastrous term. Questions about the legitimacy of a country and its moral challenge are regarded as violent. Regardless of the fact that terrorist are individually accused in court dealing with criminal acts by individuals, the whole process is termed to be political. Much debate is evident on political theory on a just cause and its relationship to the illegal means to achieve it (350 BC Aristotle, Locke, 1689). Opponents are trying to call them "terrorist" organizations to prevent them from taking the status of "national liberation movement".

Movements such as OLP national movement are officially recognized and can comprise of examples such the ANC and SWAPO before Namibia's independence can benefit from observing nature of the United Nations (76th plenary session, 1988). This, in turn, facilitates the financial support of other states. The United Nations continues to consider that this is a political riddle, particularly with regard to the Arab-Israeli conflict. The United States has followed the British legal practice to avoid the problem of terrorism definition and terrorist offenses and, on the contrary, the list of prohibited movements. His list includes Hezbollah, Hamas and the FPLP, which will one day be involved in negotiating a global peace agreement in the Middle East. Despite of having an Executive Order 13224 (2008) to block its assets and properties (Executive Order 13224, 2008), the process in which there was no right to appeal or even a sure mechanism through which "no denomination" is possible in itself unlawful and illegal found by European courts. Surprisingly, the United States simply removed Nelson Mandela and ANC designation as terrorists in June 2008, adopting a special Congressional Law to do so. Evidence of forgetting terrorism against the entry of peaceful political process is evident.

It is acceptable to refer para militarism as a useful concept in studying terrorism. It is simply known as "paramilitary" in the context of the peace process in Northern Ireland (Joint Declaration 2003).

TERRORISM, ORGANIZED CRIME AND BUSINESS

Gambetta and others have supported the crime that has increasingly become an organized a business. The feature of network or unreliable individuals' links and groups is always the predecessor of successful business where centralized hierarchical organization is no longer the dominant. Gambetta argument is that even violence, as a "protection" appellation, is in itself a business. The group selling violence is always superior to the one contracting it, which is an easy way to succeed in business or a short leap for some ESAs activities. Organized crimes also have a problem of compliance with contracts. The crime that is organized is a business. There are few studies on paramilitary / terrorism as the methods of economic and financial phenomenon. Paramilitary surviving organizations make it by participating in activities for violence for a period of time. Many of these organizations with a previous Soul of the Foundation's branch fleet and independent-executives have sources of funding. If the author uses organized crime funding copied methods, then successful surviving terrorists groups will be present.

A study, which targeted 16 countries, was conducted by UNODC among 40 crime groups outlining five "broad types of criminal groups". Expectations of discovering further subtypes after dealing with the original group. The "standard hierarchy ", extortion operations are facilitated by the use of violence which can be medium in size say 50-200 people. There exist interesting second groups the regional hierarchy which is a strong social group with a recognized ethnic identity and are known to carry out a bunch of activities. A division by the name the commentary hierarchy exists and it mainly functions by been paid by regional groups in order for them to use crime groups names.

Cluster hierarchy is the third group and is considered to be rare case. It consists of a number of criminal groups which aid in minimizing conflicts which possibly may occur. Groups are termed to as been disorganized and are not applicable to paramilitary organizations armed component regardless of the existence of common ground Autonomists as in the case of red Bridges in Italy. A possibility of providing the relationship between IRA and the whole republican or even between ETA and Herri Batasuna as they appear as clustered unorganized hierarchical continuum. A clear collection of variables on which the typology is based is not present although there is the use of violence and also the involved activity. Most of these types are based on structure and have attempted to have different types of bases developed. On the contrary, spectrum of business activities which were legitimate and illicit and probably aimed at benefiting from updates and with this typology evolved. It is however providing an interesting conceptual framework sufficient for the confrontation of paramilitary groups and well planned crime.

It is possible to compare the series of hierarchy to the classical communist party which clearly is the Leninist where FARC and Sender

Luminous seem to fit this category. Maybe a number of the Shan Armies, with the clause that vast control areas that rural remote territory, contrary to the bands of the UNODC type. The signs of Cali and Medellin can be compared to how the Colombia FARCS were based. Around 1970s the IRA was closer to the regional hierarchy prior and after the ceasefire. There was possibility of it becoming cluster hierarchy or even the ceasefire progress to the main group

For a second point in Gambetta, it is possible for the paramilitary firms to sell organized crimes with the aim of replacing traditional crime due to the need of weapons. They upset smuggling services in the process enabling them to have a separate business for them to sell spare capacities and is very close to realization. This notion of smuggling deals with small volumes of high valued assets which enable rising of funds to acquire weapons. Obvious goods also present include drugs and valuable commodities like diamonds. The above are sure deals and this is the reason for the shipment of arms in Libya back in the 1970s

Who has on this point Gambetta and the third is adding allegory paramilitary more and more "permission" You companies in their Illegal Control Are Operating the United Nations Award. These paramilitaries over a period of several years survive can also be taken to a "Police" role, especially when they have no effective Regions or Controls. To earn points paramilitary SIA potential Gambetta also the second and third roles in a globalized economy. Engaging in organized crime in financial circulation or illegal goods crime groups can find lease effective lease realization and profitable paramilitary services

Order producers maintaining a contract among their drug traffickers and retailers involves relationships with customers named to ascertain the need for an application agency makes and moving sophisticated enough. ETA which is located in Europe and Latin America geographically is known for claiming purposes rather that its main function of provision. United service tel can be of help to people moving from China all the way to Western Europe and passing through Russia, Moldova and may be through other former communist countries. Pouring to provide the industry with prostitution of may be unacceptable paramilitary policy, but for people who provide a job search can be seen as Fair enough and as part of its economic war campaign. This was community of organized crime in China Keeping this operation generates around the Diaspora of the Chinese. In order to avail escort. There is need to cover the operating veterans organizations from the Eastern communist which may further need application services from payee and people affected. The Kosovo Albanian Rises in this area also need money to pay buy weapons for military combat against Serbia. Made an ECCO this in the name of what is virtually impossibility.

The World Economics Certainly Low Similar Conditions have been described Gambetta When a Great Mafia in Southern Italy. The "war on terrorism" in illegal activities in the areas of attraction that can create a new global economy in the execution of contracts cannot do any legality that. Resulting couple organizations these can be sold that violence your OPERATIONS Extender Areas. On response to the economy it is illegal for the establishment of US and EU policies which aim at destroying the economy. Organized crime Organization of a certain measure also converges with cell copy Organization paramilitary structures. It is composed of the More Multiple Networks of People who can get a specific Transaction operation and the remaining time can be completely different in Organizations engaging and working and even completely different legal, especially when these people are attorneys or accountants. People in illegal activities have committed themselves collectively can engage in legal activity at the same time. This is also true in the IRA. There were five cells present in 1968, active man or service unit (ASUS) in relation to the Northern Ireland context. What is operational, but autonomous, requires logistical and other forms of support, which could consist of forming a Fund from another collection, as well as the activities entirely under the provincial and independent council of the Army Center, the body should have " Runs "the recent IRA volume of 26 Million Bank £ Northern Ireland Bath illustrates how we need to know to what extent these operations were VIEW by the United Nations central structure or the IRA have continued to become organized crime as described Reuter In "disorganized". The Other Questioned Behaviors Characteristics Means Common Organized Crime and paramilitary created in the same way in return for afternoon. Neither "paramilitary" nor "organized crime" are mono-dimensional phenomena.

In the case of organized crime, the main aim is to seek profits through crimes such as violence or even persuading political goals violently by use of paramilitary criminals which are illegal activities. They can also play a political role which involves pursuing political power and protecting its illicit profits gaining advantages in favor of political gains. Engaging in economics wars is also present I this case. A mix of illegal and legal is often the mode of operation and they have a less organized hierarchy which makes law penetration in their agency difficult.

The causes of problems and mythology

Remembering the nature and sources of paramilitary or terrorism has proven to be problematic. The information on non- accusable reference on the past is available to the author. Propaganda tool must be the last resort when corroboration cannot be obtained. I had to have the press justify my IRI' s finances which proved to be dubious. At one point all the newspapers had stories which focused on the success of security against IRI finance network. In order to pressure US politicians visit, the association between IRA and the US was exaggerated. This increased the sale of Sunday times newspapers for stories to do with the IRA were always interesting to the readers due to security reasons it had devoted more space to the Northern Ireland as opposed to its competitors due to the losses attributed to it. It is always important to take in to account the problem of verifiability which is a tradition of the insight team of 1970s when considering pseudo-data which constituted my IRA-PLC prospectus

It also applies the case of Al Qaeda data. The largest source of the information is from Sudan where most of the information available was anxious in that Ben laden and his collaborators in Manhattan. He had been given super grass and trial in the early month of 2001. The data is contaminated for it includes those who had to flee Al Qaeda after hijacking some of its funds. Information can also be outsourced from Intelligence services but the problem of overestimating the nature of the threat is present. This is the aim of gaining more resources to fight the threat. Political interests also steps in to minimize the crime to a level that the public can cope up with. Although in contrast the governments of the new law as evidenced by television documentary play on the fears of the people with an hidden agenda of advancing their political interests much has to be done for these napoleon which now refers to as paramilitary funding. Due to the work needed for organized crimes, the UNODC project is a useful first step. Regardless of it been a true typology, it develops ideas to do with paramilitary organization and organized crimes.

The structure of paramilitaries: over ground political movement, armed wing, NGOs and businesses

A brief review at IRA PLC

The review of data is worth especially in business. The previous articles spending figures do not show structural aspects. As a hypothesis, the IRA is limited to the size of 100 paramilitary operators located in Northern Ireland. The safety rackets, money been collected from taxi drivers, companies constructed cubs/school, fraud and pirated CD sales is not their responsibility. groups involved in carrying out similar activities may have some costs and subsidies made in the category "semi-retired staff in Ireland "As shown below, the data approaches represents the image of organized crime group UNODC 2, 3 or 4.the models to be followed is a major concern and it will be possible to know more about the deals to complete the peace process and the asst recovery bureau

The main aim IRA was created was to raise money to remain in business rather than just carrying out business. Despite of the catchy title of "IRA-PLC" talking about the republican PLCs is more correct. The prior definition gives IRA the responsibilities to control Republican movement branches which in real sense cannot be asserted. Sinn Fein, the Women's Movement, Social Clubs, Gaelic Sports Associations, the Ex-servicemen's Catholic Association, prisoners support organizations and various illegal and illegal activities are all organizations within a larger movement. Questions like Who controls who goes hand in hand with who finances who and how not just for research but often used for political controversy and are controversial issues occasionally presented before the court rooms.

The adventures of money quoted in my prospect, has equal chances of been or not been under the control and also to pay a percentage to the Army Council and has no possibility of taking place in areas treated as the republican movement "Control". the relief activates have possibly been thrown out by the final stage and some companies in particular pubs, clubs where leisure activities take place come out from the cold and others lack franchise of illicit companies which are known to produce the obvious case. The question on who to provide coercive apparatus to aid imposing contracts on the insidious market arises.

Existence of networks of different individuals who specialize in different roles has been witnessed since 1979.the structure of IRA seem to converge with the changing structure organized crimes in relation to this extend. A central planner is responsible to coordinate network specialists for single purposes or even for long term business. The same case where organized crimes have executors and smuggling or transport specialists, the IRA has adapted the case. As it happened in the shipments of weapons in Libya, the IRA had bought specialists and organized criminal specialists to facilitate the same. This was an indication of presence of central recycling operation through financial specialist who was employed in Caribbean of the United States which was an indication of spectacular or different operations.

There is a possibility that IRA had moved licensing and execution of contracts to those who carried out illegal businesses in Northern and Southern Ireland no situation of change in organization has been witnessed but the organization of terrorist's episodes may be attributed to the impact of fundraising activities. IRA has records of maintaining political priorities, despite of having disagreeing projects in the area of fundraising. Large areas posed by the catholic community in the Northern ,South Ireland and the united states have mechanisms of high integrity maintained and this opens room for further studies another important question arises ,should paramilitaries give business at a rate which is faster than creating in order to have legitimacy and integrity maintained? Is the same true for organized crime?

In discussing the Islamic civil society and the discussion of Hamas, Taliban, Hezbollah and Islamic corps of Somalia, we should apply the same analysis. This can promote the thesis in that for example in the cases of Hamas without differentiating between political and military social protection. Apart from been general the thesis consist of individual incidents where the associations of armed activities and the terrorists can be described creating the importance of not considering activities related to Hamas armed .it is important to consider all the funds of these organization has been linked to terrorists doing away with Levitt consideration of legitimate businesses. The ruling away of poverty is a

Hamas terrorist guide which results to the recruitment of more terrorists. Suicide bombers are associated with football teams which ranges them as terrorists.

This is not a proportional argument. If more than 99 percent of their staff is not members of the armed forces, less than 1 percent of "rest" or "underground" is not a model of close organization. For example, it is argued that there is an increased activity of charitable terrorist organizations in the United Kingdom there by criminal organizations in general. Of course, this will raise the question, which part of the organization could make it accessible? A safe relationship exist between crowd and teamsters located in New York .the people concerned observed that the union was not closed by the government due to the presence of corrupt reports presented by the McLennan although AFL-CIO was expelled from the association. On the side of funding, in order to have a proof of occasional use to finance terrorism pushed to have responsible person in place rather than closing the organization as a major way of reducing poverty.

The observing writer in his record said that Hezbollah will remain to have a perfect separation from other activities and armed clandestine armies. The newspaper cited a "US Army study", arguing that Hezbollah is completely decentralized. Knowing if this is a useful funding term case is important although the image present in training is not clear to the fields described in Iran, Lebanon and Syria. There is enough evidence available to ascertain the possibility of discussing western civil society in the Islamic denominations.

Group types

Here is a brief summary of the types of issues in a departmental of Legal Sciences at Aberystwyth University. It concludes that, difficulties are present in familiar with funding because groups use a list of fundraising activities from time to time bearing the change of ideologies of state supporters.,. A success against terrorism is aware of inherent changes that can be incorporated, rather than leading to "total victory" in World War II style.

Large state groups can acquire sponsorship and develop national governments in exile under the presence of all the traps. It is allowed that the small nationalist can copy the others and have a "revolutionary tax" that is easy to describe as raw extortion.

During the 1960s, paramilitaries are mainly funded by bank robberies. The Soviet Union is responsible for financing the groups either directly or indirectly. Or ISP services and some divisions have undoubtedly provided a secret training in East Germany. There exist a period where a shelter is planned for the Soviet Union, Algeria. North Korea and Cuba have often been blamed of occupying

A clear relationship between type of purpose and the activity of fundraising existed until illegal low risks activities were discovered in 1970s. Structures started changing during this period; the implementation measures were on their way to been professional. Any association that did not observe a cellular structure was directed to make it under penalty of being destroyed. The surviving groups are those listed above. Short-term survival may be as a result the existing rural retreat or strong support from a closed ethnicity, Diaspora abroad or, in minimal occasions the international community avails support. In the long period of time, they have faced economic and political opportunities that determine whether a given group has survived or disappeared.

The Al-Qaeda problem. New terrorism?

The operation of al-Qaeda's headquarters is a paramilitary activity, although it raised funds for long-term campaigns such as Chechnya and Iraq. It has operations outside Afghanistan and this has been for a long period of time. Comparing IRA and ETA can be facilitated by having six activities on average per day, a steady period which mainly occurs in Iraq. The nature of the event to be participated on or the nature of cash flow is a major determinant of how the Al Qaeda is funded. Most of the funds are received during the month of Ramadan and this is according to an 11 report which is always compiled in September due to the abundant donations from present and willing donors. This gives a good idea to the Al Qaeda in relation to what is going to happen throughout a given year. The most stable cash flows and several ongoing fundraising operations are with IRA and ETA

Al Qaeda seems to be in support of separate organization in 24 individual states and a possibility of it acting like a franchise is evident.

In the current time, it is not supported by any state although it has worked with Sudan in the past and it is unlikely that they have benefited from Afghanistan. Osama Bin Laden claimed of having witnessed huge financial losses after working with Sudan but had huge benefits after working with Afghanistan. The operations in Iraq were announced to have a cost$ 200,000 per week in December 2004.

It is not a new thing to talk about multinational operations. Irregular foreigners were recruited by George Habash and Wadie Haddad during the time of hijacking planes with the help of activists from Europe and South America and a matter of fact they were in control of OPEC. In South America the attempt to Create second multi-state operation by the name revolutionary board was witnessed .its operations were transferred to Europe as direct action. A certain talk of very organized "International" in the right organization Europe and North America in the past .Mocking this phenomenon is prudent for Al Qaeda shared funds and ideas of Zionism.

Funding al-Qaeda: the associated myths

On a given period of time, Osama was introduced as a superman: tracer teacher, the terrorist billionaire not forgetting the classic known public enemy. He was known to be fond of the US enforcement strategy in Sudan. It was difficult to understand financing the Al Qaeda and their firms. This is because it' is entirely legitimate organizations that they perform, as well as being used as conduits for their business .Hawala system and the Islamic banking system was what He used.

Extortion of individuals took place on an unimaginable scale in the West for a total of more than $ 1 million per person. Individuals with a lot of wealth in Islamic denominations must now choose between the risks: US detection or al-Qaeda killing. Likewise, donations from governments and directed towards foundations that distribute money for Islamic causes should be monitored more closely by donors, performance of the same should also be monitored.

The image of the Al Qaeda could have collapsed at the point where Sudanese Authority dismissed all the 35 companies associated with it. However, Al Qaeda is rich enough to have the organizations established again if companies are created against Sudan. Things like money, information dissemination, strict orders and having potential soldiers ready to carry out in globalized political systems. These require new businesses and the creation of new business opportunities. Reporters argue that, Bin Laden did not need such complicated communication systems in Afghanistan but maintains that all the outside networks should have remained intact. They argued in a basic document to the September 11 report is only but a myth, bin Laden's Al Qaeda funded through family wealth shares. Another myth is that the organization is funded through returns of the sold Sudanese business. According to recent information, the Saudi government in 1994 used force on bin Laden family directing them to sell part of Osama family farm and put it in the form of frozen bill. He also states that from the year 1970 all the way to 1993/1994 the received amount by the family per year was one million dollars. A recent intelligence report now states that the state of the Sudanese took all the assets left. No previous evidence, that $ 150 million were lost in agricultural projects and construction in Sudan.

All companies have disappeared with the departure of Bin Laden in Sudan. This is because there is a possibility of having other companies in the Muslim locations, no explanation as to why the "spectacular" were so meticulously planned.

5 CHRONOLOGICAL SURVEY OF MAJOR TERRORIST ATTACKS, EVIDENCE AND OTHER RELEVANT EVENTS

During the last decade of the Cold War, the concept of "state-sponsored terrorism" was given full conviction. Bulgaria, East Germany, Libya, North Korea and Syria were designated as Soviet sponsors to control the anti-American terrorism. However, proper evidence was never presented to support the inclusion of these nations, as a sponsor, much less under Soviet direction. That Soviet KGB often encouraged anti-American violence. There were many terrorist groups and incidents that had no direct involvement in the US-US conflict. And the Soviet Union. Most of the terrorists were in the non-governmental organizations that established their ideological, ethnic, nationalist or religious ideas. Without pretending to know why the five nations are enumerated (and not just as plausible to others as Cuba and Iran), it can be assumed that US politicians have found it useful to label the Soviets as a type of terrorism and to associate regional threats particularly problematic (Israel, Western Europc, and South Korea) with the terrorist network of putative Soviet (Sterling 1981). (Turk, 2004) With reference to September 11, 2001 events, when the World Trade Center in New York and other parts of the United States were attacked by suicide pilots, killing more than 3,000 people, people have precipitated a collection of events whose end cannot be predicted easily. These include the wars in Iraq and Afghanistan, and a proliferation of anti-terrorist laws and practices carried out in United States, including other parts of the world. (Chaskalson, 2008)

1950- This was the era of the recorded Cold War and the emergence of McCarthyism in the US. It was the year that Alger Hiss was convicted of perjury in the United States relating to espionage for the Soviet Union, when Klaus Fuchs was condemned in England of espionage for the Soviet Union and endowing it with information of the Manhattan Project for the development of the atomic bomb, the year in which war exploded in Korea. The tension was high and there were fears that we were on the brink of a new world war. In that environment of Western leaders, questioning Cold War concerns with the earlier principle, they were not relentless to the pretense of the apartheid government in South Africa under the conditions requiring anticommunist legislation. (Chaskalson, 2008) Replace terrorism with communism and that has the framework for much of the legislation adopted by several countries since September 11. (Chaskalson, 2008)

After World War II - Geneva Convention

The weighty reasons that led to the negotiation of the Geneva Conventions after the end of World War II are well known. The atrocities committed against the civilian population during the war are undoubtedly one of the most, if not the most important. Such atrocities are often evoked and the most emotive accounts were writings, memoirs and novels to describe the horror. Rarely, however, has the story of the victims been described, or fictionally represented by the butchers' perspective. I was too stunned to read a novel that has been very successful in the francophone world, apparently less in English speaking countries. The book I mean is *Les Bienveillantes* Jonathan Littell, later translated into English as the benevolent. Besides the bright title, refers to the transformation of the terrible fury, goddesses retaliation and punishment hearted *Eumenydes cycle of tragedies* Esquilo Orestíada, the book is a work of art - particularly for how realistically depicted the carnage and massacres perpetrated by the SS in occupied Einstazgruppen this and all the other atrocities that have been committed by the Nazis in concentration camps and extermination. Fear, anguish, humiliation, degradation, fear, and even the grotesque are skillfully represented by the author, which makes us to experience, through the medium of literature, the Civil Down feelings. The particular body, suitable for disonorsa discomfort that you get in reading horror. Even the unspoken, what the reader imagines, is a powerful depiction of horror and human depravity. (White, 2011) 9-11

The search for understanding and blame for the attacks related to terrorists recorded in September 11, 2001 also began before the shots would stop. Competitors, politicians and analysts have also launched the accountability network. The Clinton and Bush are expressing to let bin Laden slip through his fingers. The intelligence central body and the sole body to carry out investigation were criticized for interpolation in the face of an imminent threat. Other analysts see outside the United States, painting a picture of Al Qaeda as a formidable opponent against which even the most robust counter-terrorism program would be a failure.

Of the many disturbing features of the attacks, his incredible surprise was more disturbing to many Americans. The attacks shattered the complacency of US and replaced by fears of a new and sinister organization that seemed to endanger our own survival (Byman 2003). As noted by journalist Peter Bergen, (Byman, 2005) *"Suddenly, the happy days billionaires*, legal problems, Puff Daddy and evasions of Gary Condit about Chandra Levy disappeared failure as a delicious Mirage-dot com"

Strategic amazing terrorist attacks

Warning failures including catastrophic, are not new to those who are responsible for national security. Betts has even argued that intelligence failures are natural and inevitable. Pearl Harbor is perhaps the best known of surprises for Americans, but other remarkable surprise attacks include:

- Egyptian crossing of the Suez Canal the start of the Yom Kippur War in 1973,
- The 'German attack on France through the woods of the Ardennes' in 1940, and
- the German invasion of Russia in 1941, each of which victims

caught flat feet (**Byman,** 2005)

Identification of impending danger can be exceptionally difficult. Analysts and politicians have to transform fragmented and weak data into a coherent vision of the future, a task that challenges even the best minds. His imagination has to jump, discerning a future threat where none previously existed.

Biased and prejudiced analysts and policymakers determine how they receive and process information. Such a framework is necessary; information cannot be interpreted in a vacuum analytical. Sometimes, however, the image filtered contradictory information indiscriminately, leading to disaster., for example, Israeli intelligence (and political) grabbed the "concept", the belief that Egypt militarily inferior does not start a war unless it has the ability to attack Israel proper and neutralize said force, despite evidence of Egyptian air Israel prepared to attack Similarly, one reason for the tragic fire incident that led to the deaths of two US helicopters Black hawk on Iraq in 1994. It was expected that the F-15 pilots, wanted to confront the enemy but incorrectly "saw" the black hawks like back Irachini helicopters. So "they created the two Hinds, then demolished" (Byman, 2005)

The opponent Nature

The problem of terrorism warning is exceptionally difficult, compounding the challenges analysts, bureaucracies and individual politicians face in relation to strategic surprise. Underpinning supports,

The basic problem of terrorism for intelligence is both simple and chilling time. A group of isplotters conceived a plot. Only a few conspirators know their intentions, even if you could get help from others. They mention nothing of their plot to anyone who can absolutely trust. Communicate anything about their programs in a way that can be intercepted.... They live and move normally and discreet, and any preparation cannot be made behind closed doors so as part of these movements. The problem is: How can we learn from the story?

Terrorists In addition, as one of the pillars says, "The purpose of intelligence is not only proven in someone who could commit acts of terrorism in the future" The problem is particularly troublesome. Investigations of attacks before Sept. 11 warning noted that the tactic may be lost, even if the strategic warning was sound. In 1985, the "Report of the Secretary of State's Advisory Group for safety abroad" ("Inman Report") has examined the barracks bombing of the US Embassy and the Marine in Lebanon, and concluded: "If you have certain equipment, well - trained and funded and you are trying to hurt, eventually you will succeed. " research Khobar Towers attack in 1996 and the 1998 survey embassy bombings. Strategic warning was sound but lacked tactical alertness. During the first month of the year 1999, the "Report on the review of the Councils bombing Responsibility embassies in Nairobi and Dar es Salaam" (better known as "Commission Crowe"), he argued that "we cannot rely on intelligence to warn of such attacks."

Deception and denial aggravate the problem of surprise. Skilled opponents do everything possible to thwart the gathering of information. Encryption limits for distributing sensitive information, and other means are used to inhibit standard means for collecting information. Opponents also scheme to deceive the other. As it is well known, the British secret service during World War II successfully pushed misinformation German officials on British shores to take his deception on the location of the Allied landing on the French coast, an operation of vital deception for successful landing in Normandy. Ironically, the fear of disappointment can also lead to failures; suspicion of fraud can bring intelligence agencies to discount real information. The fear of disappointment also reinforces the importance of existing analytical distortions. Contrary information may be suspected of being "wrong" while confirming information can be treated erroneously as accurate.

The four points of view mentioned above are analytically distinct, but in practice they interact. It is better to see the components of surprise and warning as a system, system characteristics occur often than any particular component thereof leading to errors and disasters. Out September 11

September 11 is a failure, but the nature of the failure is unclear. Many things have gone wrong in many places and at many levels, so the exact problems are difficult to identify, promote accountability, and obscuring the road ahead. This section discusses whether an alarm sounded and then see the various opportunities that analysts and politicians will lose.

Was he alarmed?

The intelligence community, especially the CIA, has done well to provide strategic warning of a threat of Al Qaeda. The identity of the enemy, the scope of his ambitions, and its lethality are known and communicated in a timely manner. The CIA had begun his warning about Al Qaeda, even before the simultaneous attacks on two US embassies on August 7, 1998 gave the clearest danger to many observers. After the attacks on the embassies, warning against al Qaeda has become a priority, and also weakit pieces of intelligence led to sound the alarm. Journalist Steve Coll said that It was a button, the large network, self - perpetuating, highly sensitive constantly alert.

In 2001, the system was on alert, and any policy maker (or member of the general public) who cared to look could see the concern of the CIA. In February 2001, Director of Central Intelligence (DCI) George Tenet publicly stated that Bin Laden and his organization poses "the most serious and immediate threat" to the United States, an example of strategic warning horn. High-level policymakers of the Clinton and Bush have declared that tenet and other CIA officials warned that Al Qaeda was planning mortal "shows" against the United States; the FBI has also added his voice to the warning. Louis Freeh, then director of the FBI, testified May 10, 2001, a first objective of Al Qaeda "is the design and construction of large, high profile terrorist attacks high victim against US interests and citizens and those of our allies around the world."

This records a strong strategic warning, Nevertheless, it was accompanied by an inability to learn clues about the specific characteristics of the attack on the land of US origin, which resulted to failures whose implications were not desirable i.e. tactic warning If politicians have listened to the intelligence, they would know Al Qaeda was coming, but no one knows when, where and how.

Missed opportunities for intelligence

Although the conspirators made several errors and "the system was blinking red" in the words of the 9/11 Commission report, much of the activity of the conspirators continued undetected missed opportunities are as follows:

Working with internal security forces of Malaysia, the CIA has covered a meeting of key players, many of whom were involved in the conspiracy of September 11, but lost his trail when the meeting ended.

The CIA did not "prevent" two key plotters, Khalid al-Midhar and Nawaf al-Hamza, to travel to the US. Both FBI and CIA did not listen to the reports that they were seen travelling in the US.

Several beautiful wires were not prosecuted. For example, in July an agent notified FBI in Phoenix, Arizona office and said in an electronic communication that "too many people of investigative interest" were seeking flight training in the area and asked for a more comprehensive 'investigation into the matter –it was a warning ignored by FBI headquarters.

Jihadist Zacarias Moussaoui fell into the hands of the FBI in Minnesota on a suspicion that he might be trying to hijack a plane. Moussaoui had links with many of the conspirators including Ramzi Binalshibh, one of the masterminds. This information was not reported at the top of the chain of command at the FBI (although DCI Tenet was informed!) Despite the high level of threat that communicates in general.

That time in the United States, the kidnappers had several contacts with Islamic radicals which the FBI was already monitoring.

The CIA has scrapped a plan to kidnap bin Laden although some experts believe they have a reasonable chance of success. Several military strikes against bin Laden were also suspended due to concerns about the intelligence of uncertain reliability.

Policy errors

In retrospect, the US policy toward Al Qaeda also had several fatal flaws that have allowed the organization to thrive. American politics has left unresolved the question of terrorist sanctuary. In Afghanistan, Al Qaeda has allowed to build an army of radicals who think outside the reach of the United States without forgetting its compatriots. Richard Clarke, the top counterterrorism official in the white house during Clintons time and the Bush administration until 11 September, pointing to his regret that the United States allowed "the existence of a large scale to Qaida bases where people are trained to kill Americans "even more troubling, al Qaeda enjoyed a permissive environment in the West, where he could recruit, raise money, and still maintain their cause. Before September 11, the US had no coherent anti-terrorism policy towards Pakistan and a vague policy toward Saudi Arabia, although both were for efforts against al Qaeda. Pakistan was the main sponsor of the Taliban, and also supports jihadist groups as part of their campaign against India in Kashmir. The Saudi regime has no copies of itself Al Qaeda directly, but often closed his eyes as its citizens were financing and swelled the ranks of the jihadists affiliated groups. The result has been the political deadlock and threatening metastases.

The United States has also relied too much on the tools of law enforcement such trials and arrests of anti-Al Qaeda before September 11. Law enforcement has several weaknesses as a tool to combat terrorism. Even with the success of measures enforcement often they fail to catch the masterminds of terrorism. In addition, studies raise significant resources needs of the intelligence community that could be used to prevent future attacks. Arrests and trials did little against the army under construction at the port in Afghanistan, This was perhaps the greatest challenge in the fight against Al Qaeda.

Why have there been missed opportunities?

The four frames derived from various social science literature offer an insight into why analysts and politicians to miss these potential opportunities to disrupt the plot and to adjust policies to tackle Al Qaeda in the United States.

Cognitive failures

Even the most concerned with Al Qaeda did not realize the magnitude of the threat. Former New Jersey Gov. Thomas Kean, who was the chairperson of 9/11 Commission, shows a "lack of imagination" Politicians often failed to recognize that, unlike terrorist groups in the past, Al Qaeda had both the capacity and intention to cause mass casualties of America. President Bush initially thought the first air strike against world trade center of the North Tower. Center may have been due to a heart attack of a pilot. Even Clarke, who is recorded in the list of perceptive observers of Al Qaeda, has the threat underestimated; unfortunately, an attack in which "hundreds" of Americans die was predicted by him.

However, the "lack of imagination" was a more complex practice. The problem for officials, as Tenet, Berger, and Clarke was not failing to imagine that Al Qaeda could and would kill thousands of people. In fact, they have devoted considerable attention to the possibility that Al Qaeda could acquire and use chemical, biological or nuclear weapons or agents for this purpose. However, his imagination has transformed their day to day actions. Richard Armitage who was the deputy secretary to the state noted that after the attacks, "I do not think it actually made the leap into our minds that we are no longer safe behind these two great oceans." Their minds often gone up, but not your bowels shake.

Analysts looking for Al Qaeda, the problem of signal to noise ratio was immense. In 2001, CIA analysts monitored the possible plots of al Qaeda in Europe, Africa and the Middle East. The US territory was also of concern, but lost in the morass of information data related to attacks abroad. These threats were not always pure noise, but were often signals. Al Qaeda was actually planning attacks in Europe and the Middle East, as subsequent events would show.

The FBI has suffered a sprained assumption that the threat will focus outside the United States. Analysts of the Bureau" preconceptions are not questioned, although in 1998 it was clear that bin Laden was looking for recruits to facilitate the attack of the United States and discourage infrastructure development which was in progress. FBI correctly recognized that Hezbollah, Hamas and other religious-nationalist groups are operating mainly in the United States to raise funds. Carrying out an attack here would be illogical, killing the golden goose. Al Qaeda, however, has had in the past proved willing to jeopardize their logistics and fundraising bases in the search for a successful attack.

The CIA has also had its set of blinders chance at home, partly because of its successful collection of inaccurate information. The CIA has gathered considerable intelligence about the danger of attacks by Al Qaeda abroad, which has led to warnings in Italy, in the Persian Gulf and elsewhere in 2001. More general indications of a major attack were interpreted in the light of the information referred to an outside attack.

Another problem for the alert was changing tactics of the opponent. The innovation of aircrafts as weapons had used little intelligence level enabling the Al Qaeda to use them. Different platforms for attack were in use. (Truck bombs in Africa, a pump boat in Yemen, and so on) has led analysts to predict that the organization innovate again.

The enormous sensitivity to any potential threat led to over warning. Any mention of the activities of Al Qaeda was forwarded to the high-level policy makers, and in fact often the same President. This resulted to "warning fatigue" regarding Al Qaeda, a problem that only grew after September 11.

Cognitive failures were perhaps even worse among politicians than among intelligence analysts. Despite repeated warnings from Tenet and others, it is not clear that terrorism was a global priority list of the United States. Many former and current officials of the United States claim that terrorism is "a priority" long before Sept. 11, but the Clinton and Bush, so were Iraq, China, the Balkans, missile defense reform military, and other foreign policy issues. Policy makers "knew" Al-Qaeda was a growing danger, but they were not able to change and reflect this approach.

As a result of this lack of priorities, each agency focused on the issues most important to them. The CIA was responsible for the war in Iraq and support combat in the Balkans, China and monitor other potential rivals, which provides economic analysis, and so on. Neglect and mistaken priorities characterize US policy toward Afghanistan for many years. Before the embassy bombings in 1998, Afghanistan has been overlooked. In its regional policy, the State Department focused on issues ranging from a possible nuclear exchange between India and Pakistan for the interruption of democracy in Nepal. When Afghanistan appeared on the radar screen, which was usually about narcotics or violations of human rights, not terrorism Although the United States has focused much more on terrorism as the decade went on, these other problems have not disappeared and greatly complicated efforts to pressure the Taliban against terrorism. As seen by Clarke, the Taliban knew it would not produce bin Laden escape US pressure; the United States still insist on the rights of women, drugs and other issues. Another indicator of cognitive disjunction between knowledge of people and logical actions to be derived from that knowledge is limited attention to defensive measures against terrorism, particularly in the United States. Despite the discovery of several commissions that specific tactical intelligence is likely to be absent when faced with an opponent and expert alert the intelligence community that al Qaeda was planning a few lethal defensive measures of political leaders initiated attacks U.S. They invoke the defense intelligence, but intelligence knew (especially at home) was hard.

Bureaucratic disorders

Part of the reason for the lack of tactical warning was that the intelligence community and other institutions have not responded to this strategically and sufficiently strengthen its capacity to collect, analyze and disseminate information and act on what they knew. In addition, some institutions, including the US Army, do not embrace fight against terrorism as a mission, despite the high level of strategic alert.

CIA continued weakness

On December 4, 1998, George Tenet, said: "We are at war I want no resources or people spared in this effort." However, despite this rhetoric and the great efforts of Tenet politicians to warn of danger, the CIA did not significantly change the resources from other priorities to combat terrorism or change their culture and focus. As an intelligence officer for a long time involved in the evaluation of Al Qaeda, intelligence officials lower level "complained knew a moving train came against the United States, documented this fact, then watched helplessly, or were banned to speak, as their principal leaders delay action, the intelligence services downplayed, ignored repeated warnings.

Resource allocation is an important area in which the action does not match the level of threat. How much can lose Tenet? Lack of budget authority DCI contributes to this problem. From the ICD controls only perhaps 15% of the budget pre-September 11, intelligence, much of the intelligence community felt no obligation to comply with the directives of the DCI if they went against their own bureaucratic imperatives Therefore, even if the ICD "declared war" on Al Qaeda, no agency has radically changed its priorities.

If the DCI had controlled most of the budget of the intelligence community and the people, it is plausible that the amount of money that could have been devoted to the fight against terrorism. History as evidence of Tenet at the CIA, however, suggests that changes would be limited. Before the attacks, when pressed by politicians to transfer more money to the efforts of Al Qaeda, the CIA said none of its other programs may be terminated or reduced to free up resources. However, under the principle of the CIA it has expanded efforts to combat terrorism, US intelligence budget for other programs decreased. This indicates that other agencies also may have increased spending on the fight against terrorism. In theory, most of the money went to support military programs through technical means, dwarfing the amount spent on human intelligence; it may have been transmitted to strengthen human intelligence programs of the CIA.

Operational deficiencies exacerbate budget problems. The CIA also did not penetrate the upper echelons of Al Qaeda. As discussed below, this failure is due in part to the nature of the opponent, and it is clear that at the end of 1990 the penetration was a priority for CIA for an incorrect claim the contrary. However, some critics argue that 'agency does not have the correct orientation for jihadists approach - an error of institutional response, not only gathering information in general. In part, this was because the Agency has continued to operate with the staff of government structures erected on the grounds of United States, including its "unofficial cover" (NOC) officials tended to be false businessmen. None of them has been able to operate in a mosque without giving it away. A former CIA official said: "The CIA probably not a single fund for Arabic speaking of truly qualified official in Middle East can play a believable Muslim fundamentalist who would be willing to spend years of their life with food shit and no women. Analysis in Afghanistan "mountains of Al Qaeda "was often weak. Despite awareness of the danger of the CIA, he lacked the detailed knowledge of the enemy. Clarke, for example, criticized the CIA for failing to recognize the importance of Khalid Sheikh Mohammed, September 11 mind saying that could have been ripped in Qatar had been known. This problem was not simply because of difficulty in obtaining information about al Qaeda. Rather, the emphasis was CIA operations against Al Qaeda and efforts to build a complete picture of the organization have not received enough support. In fact, a thorough assessment of the intelligence of Al Qaeda has been processed until after September 11. This lack of an assessment seems to go against the traditional emphasis on detail of the CIA, one of its fundamental missions. However, the more detailed the CIA analysis, long term has been conducted by the divisions of area Intelligence Directorate, while the main theme of the center of CIA counter - terrorism (CTC) has been in operation (is refers to DCI through the Deputy operations) Manager, which made it less likely to focus on the analysis. Most "analysis" of CTC focused on issues related to financing transactions rather than on broader strategic assessments and estimates.

Risk aversion is another problem for the CIA. Acting as 9/11 Commission, CIA was "an organization capable of attracting people extremely motivated but institutionally risk aversion. James Pavitt Director of Operations, for example, wondered if the effort to work with the Northern Alliance against the Taliban was worth the high possibility that as an officer he could die in a helicopter accident in rickety road- an example of what other critics have called risk aversion generally a physical hazard.

This risk, however, is reasonable from an institutional point of view. As Coll observed, the CIA has been "conditioned by the decline of history 'allies' enthusiasts at the National Security Council." The institution had learned that these allies often intended for covert operations in place to make difficult political decisions, and when things went wrong the CIA- hung to dry.

Cultural and procedural, the CIA has focused on the external threat. The CIA, of course, is prohibited to operate on American soil, as a result of several scandals revealed in1 970, the agency is exceptionally sensitive to the burden that can spy on Americans. As a result, resources, ability to collect, analyze and focus on the external threat. Not surprisingly, even when identifying the "sign" of an attack on US soil his activities have focused on "sound collection" (or, more precisely, other signals) related to the activities of Al Qaeda abroad.

The problems mentioned above reflect how the broader institutional mission successfully interfered against terrorism. The reluctance of the CIA to divert resources from other concerns, collecting platforms change to emphasize NOC, focus on hazards in the home rather than abroad, and participation in covert political risk reflects the history and the identity of the institution rather than the threat of al Qaeda.

Was FBI switch asleep?

The list of deficiencies in the FBI revealed after September 11 is long. The FBI has not only failed to catch the conspirators, but generally do not appreciate the danger that the country faces a stark contrast to the CIA. Before Sept. 11, the FBI was not structured or oriented to terrorism or, more generally, for intelligence work correctly. This error occurred in part because of the culture of the FBI, but also because the organization has not learned and respond appropriately as information about Al Qaeda has grown.

Before September 11, the Office often failed to gather relevant data to the fight against terrorism information. For example, when Abdul Hakim Murad was interviewed regarding his involvement in a plot to bomb a total of 12 aircraft over the Pacific in 1995, the FBI did not paid attention to their possible plans to crash a plane into CIA headquarters-an omen the plan Sept. 11. Neither the FBI rather than opportunities for collection in a context; for example, could not connect suspicious activity flight training in Arizona or the arrest of an Islamic extremist (Moussaoui) in Minnesota by the national threat level, he intensified. Overall, the FBI did not train its vast collection of operational information or provide collectors with sufficient resources, particularly with regard to monitoring and translation.

Often what information the FBI has collected has not been disclosed, even internally. Ante-deluvian approach to computer system and record means that information was not properly approved from the field to headquarters, or other FBI agents and analysts who may be working on similar problems. The FBI did not see himself as part of national security and did not share the information with the national security community.

As a result, the FBI did not inform lawmakers of the jihadist threat in the house. Two former officials from the White House working in the fight against terrorism at the National Security Council wrote to learn the information from the FBI transcripts of the trial of suspected members of Al Qaeda, and said, "No wonder policy makers, agencies and external analysts FBI never heard this information, most of FBI did not even know. "

Neither the FBI conducted a strategic analysis. It portrays the FBI as exhausting and retrograde, comfortable in their ignorance of Al Qaeda (p. 192). The office created for strategic analysis atrophied. The FBI had only two analysts look at the information about the threat of Bin Laden, and has not prepared a document, such as the National Intelligence Estimate to assess the threat from Al Qaeda to the United States or the radical Islamic presence in this country the culture of the Bureau and the organization encourages these problems. Before Sept. 11, FBI was primarily law enforcement and was probably the best in the world. But police focus on finding a case instead of understanding of a wider network.

Law enforcement emphasizes the collection of specific evidence, not the collection and exchange of information, may be relevant. Given this organizational philosophy, it's no wonder that terrorism was seen as a criminal matter and treated accordingly. In addition, the leaders stressed FBI to find the perpetrators of the latest attack, instead of stopping the next.

The organizational structure of the FBI has reflected this culture and worse. The field office decentralized office structure allowed to set their own priorities, some of which focused on terrorism or Al Qaeda. 56 FBI offices in the United States were independent fiefdoms, where local priorities take precedence,

The FBI has also faced political control and restrictions in many grat functions in relation to the fight against terrorism. For instance, in the year 1996, civil liberties joined the right wing to block legislation likely to allow wire-tapping multiple points, which are useful for tracking terrorists who change phones or use multiple phones. In addition to limiting the tools that the FBI could use this strange alliance that the FBI investigates exceptionally sensitive to religious terrorism based in the United States. Congressional investigations into the deaths at Ruby Ridge and Waco further increased the sensitivity of the FBI. Overall, the FBI prefers to err on the side of respect for civil liberties, setting a high bar for surveillance.

FBI procedures that separate the intelligence of the application of jurisprudence called "wall", reflected Mesa problems on this issue. The rules were confusing and often have been interpreted narrower, which have hampered efforts to track the activities of Al Qaeda in the United States. However, given the culture of law enforcement FBI, the inherent problems of the wall were not as worrisome as they would for an intelligence organization. In addition, because the office did not appreciate the growing danger, little need to change course felt. Thus, despite complaining among the ranks, FBI executives do not press hard to reduce the wall.

Problems arose from the direction of the wall. Former FBI Director Louis Freeh said disdained technology and therefore do not invest in systems to improve data storage, retrieval and sharing. Much of the attention Freeh fight against terrorism was connected to investigate attacks that had happened abroad, such as the bombing of Khobar Towers.

Freeh also worsened the problem of local fiefdoms, cutting staff in the seat and put the 'initiative in the field of operations.

MILITARY FAILURE

CIA, FBI, and other members of the intelligence community are not the only institutions in the firing line. The army been unable to embrace missions is a great source of criticism. Policy antiterrorist creators turned to the military for help against Al Qaeda, but left empty handed. In addition, they did not prepare a plan for direct invasion and opposed military special forces to snatch al Qaeda in countries like Afghanistan, Sudan and Qatar. The military also rejected the use of President Clinton suggested RAID special operations force a way to intimidate Al Qaeda. More generally, military applications for military options NSC resisted. Clark says, "The White House wanted action. The high-level military has done and what has made it almost impossible for the President to overcome their objections" (p. 145). Clinton noted it, "It was clear to me that the high-level military did not want to do this.

A special military concern seems to have been the inappropriate use of limited force against Al Qaeda. General Henry Shelton, then the chief of the Joint Staff of the United States, believed that the deployment of special operations forces or other "boots available on the ground" missions will likely fail, because intelligence was poor and had no secure base. In his view, any military mission must involve thousands of soldiers otherwise run the risk of becoming an operational humiliating disaster rescue mission as "a desert" unfortunate hostages in 1980.

Shelton has a point of view. The army has a role to play in the fight against terrorism, but the direct invasion block, the role of which is very different from the normal function of the military, which is literally a stand between the American people and their enemy. Limited uses of military force do a poor deterrent, rarely inflict significant damage that reduces the ability of terrorists, allies' anger, and can mobilize supporters of terrorists.

The military, like the CIA, tried to minimize the risks in the fight against terrorism. The use of Special Forces or launching cruise missiles has a high risk of failure, given the hostile operating environment and lack of accurate intelligence. But these risks would be more acceptable if the military leaders had considered the main problem for everyone. They did not. In addition, the army has not taken steps to improve their capacity significantly, both for collecting their own intelligence to improve the likelihood of success of a mission of special operations force or by organizing bases in parking areas. Even while warning of threat has grown, the military did not fit.

There is little to report on the responses of others related to national security in terms of Al Qaeda agencies. Only those in the corridors of power in Washington heard the drumbeat of ongoing strategic warning that Al Qaeda was on the way. Neither the report of threats on a daily or even a public witness made a strong impression, national security agencies, state and local authorities may as well disappear, as the Immigration and Naturalization and immigration service's don't treat terrorism as a major concern. Referring from the 9/11 Commission report. "In short, the National Agency mobilized in response to the threat does not make sense, and they had a plan to set the borders. There were no tough transportation systems, no fortified Electronic surveillance directed against an internal local threat. The public was not warned"

Institutional Management Limited

It is possible to put in place problems faced by the FBI, CIA and other institution in one part, at the feet of political leaders. And 'duty of those elected to impose their will on the chosen elements of the government, and have the authority to do sov.a poor job done by the policy makers is evident , this is supported by the fact that they were interested on their own self-interest. The several bureaucrats who were present were also not aggressive enough to fight terrorism. The investigation of President Clinton and FBI for several scandals has given effective immunity for overseeing the White House. Neither the president has imposed his will on the military level, perhaps because of widespread distrust of their credentials in the field of military security and the public.

Despite their efforts, often frantic on issues of fighting terrorism, the Clinton administration has suffered from a lack of will to fight terrorism in the context of the overall foreign policy of Terrorism Made in USA "is primarily a foreign policy issue as a national security issue "(p. 9). key decision makers, including the president, vice president, the national security adviser and the attorney general, paid little attention in relation to the war against terrorism in conjunction with the integration of countries for example Afghanistan, Pakistan or Saudi Arabia, or broader concerns which include such fundraising terrorism, popular hostility towards United States located in the Middle East, putting into consideration other long-term issues against terrorism. Group activities supporting terrorism Clarke were often independent of regular political meetings and in relation to the foreign agency relations. The result was repeated surges into action, but only sustained limited institutional change.

Resources is another problem. Neither the administration has provided a huge boost of resources to key agencies to combat terrorism; nor do they ensure that current budgets of these agencies have been properly dedicated to the fight against terrorism. FBI's budget has grown considerably in the 1990s, and so did the CIA resources for the fight against terrorism. The FBI, however, has spent most of their money on concerns related to Al Qaeda. The CIA also tried to use cost increases to preserve many of its other programs rather than divert resources to deal with Al Qaeda.

The White House did not provide clear authorities, particularly in connection with the killing of Bin Laden. To direct the CIA to kill him through covert operations require a significant change in the rules for covert CIA operations, which normally prohibited murder. Not surprisingly for a bureaucracy burned on charges of "criminal" behavior in the past, the CIA tried to have his glass authorities. The White House, however, preferred to give general guidance, keeping denial, and the Justice Department wanted to avoid giving the authorities unlimited CIA to kill. Each institution has followed its own political and bureaucratic imperatives, and the result was the worst of all worlds, a disjunction between policy makers and senior professionals in the field. Clinton's top aides recall that the desire of the President to kill Bin Laden and his associates "It was very clear to us from the beginning." In the absence of clear authority, however, the CIA told its Afghan client, "You are to capture him [Bin Laden] alive"

Political boundaries

Policy problems often stemmed from legitimate political boundaries or commitments they have made it difficult for senior executives to focus on Al Qaeda. Moreover, even the politicians concerned with Al Qaeda faced ignorance, indifference, or conflicting preferences of other political actors. Many of the "obvious" answers for the growth of Al Qaeda has become politically possible only after the killing of the attacks generate political will.

Policy makers often had different priorities in the fight against terrorism. President Clinton, for example, met with Prime Minister Sharif of Pakistan several times in the years before Sept. 11; Pakistan's nuclear program topic was the topmost part, as well as the a war between India and Pakistan on Kargil. The Saudi Arabia also proved difficult for policymakers to deal with. When anti-terrorist specialists criticized the kingdom, its advocates in the State Department and the Pentagon responded the other, the most vital interests were at stake. As a result, the financial support of radical and so, massive Arabia has not received enough attention.

The problems are related, but a clear solution (even in retrospect) was coy. The leaders of the policies of the Bush administration have seen the problem of Al Qaeda in relation to the problem in Afghanistan, which was in turn linked to Pakistan. Developing a policy towards which requires the development of a policy at all a logical step, but it has slowed efforts to tackle Al Qaeda even if the threat of reports has been increasing pressure from both countries, moreover the United States had few levers. The sanctions already in place because of Pakistan's nuclear programs has made trade incentives or threats were not available, because there were no real economic ties. Military-to-military relations had deteriorated too. Saudi Arabia, of course, was a key US ally depended for many of its vital interests, especially with regard to Iraq. The peace process started at the Middle East, and also a move to stabilize oil prices was put into consideration. Standard forms of military or economic pressure that was not available, and almost certainly would have failed

Drastic as to the defense of national territory, or go to war against the Taliban was also a politically difficult change. The 9/11 Commission indicates, "It's s harder to mount a major effort, but a problem still seems minor. Once the danger has fully materialized, evident to all, mobilizing action is easier but then it might be too late. "It is noteworthy that no political leaders of both parties were demanding a drastic change from the defense of the national territory, the US policy toward Afghanistan or Pakistan, or other tectonic shifts that seems obvious only in retrospect.

Policy makers acutely felt as far as possible, and then returned to the repressive measures that were viable and demonstrate responsiveness to the various attacks. They knew covert action was at best very little chance of success, even under favorable conditions. Clinton Sandy who advised the nation on security matters, the state secretary Madeleine Albright have argued that Congress, the citizens of America and US allies oppose the use of ground forces in Afghanistan against Al Qaeda before the attacks carried out in September. Why was apparently the military option off the table? Enforcement remains one of the most important means of combating terrorism, along with the use of the CIA and intelligence services allied to destroy activities abroad. Congress considers the 9/11 investigation that this trust was truly a defect rather than a strategic decision, with many police officers will see their functions, in addition to other measures, including military action.

Policy makers also had to balance the risk, especially when the military is used. There have been several cases in which the CIA may have had information about the location of Bin Laden (or, more significantly, its future position), which made it vulnerable to attack cruise missile. This information, however, usually comes from a source whose accuracy is questionable at best. Failure could be disastrous. The 1998 missile attacks on Afghanistan had idolized bin Laden. In addition, if the strike killed one of the women and children at the target site it would further damage the reputation of the United States. Other officials feared that the United States had been described as a "mad bomber" for his attacks on Iraq and Serbia and that the attacks could destabilize Pakistan. A strike was called off in part because it could kill members of the royal family in the UAE that may have been hunting bin Laden. It is really difficult to judge the course here. CIA then found that bin Laden was present only in one of the three alleged sightings. Risk errant strikes could have elevated the status of bin Laden, reportedly committed a key ally in the Gulf, and made America stupid and brutal look at the attack on noncombatants.

The nature of the adversary

Too often, the assessments fail to focus on the mistakes of the victim, rather than on the ability of the rival. Most terrorist groups fall into the category of intelligence "hard targets." Its members are difficult to identify, their actions are difficult to predict and difficult to infiltrate their organizations. Only 50% of terrorist groups survive in one year, and only 5% survive a decade; those who usually carry on are experts in minimizing their exposure to the forces of government enforcement and intelligence agencies. Typically, terrorist groups are composed of small cells, where the ties of kinship and neighborhood often cementing a strong ideological commitment. Often, they mixed in the beautiful local communities, or bullied often unwilling to cooperate with the security services. Much of the intelligence analysis of the standard in the market, such as image analysis, is of little help in the fight against terrorism.

Even in the rarefied world of terrorism, Al Qaeda is a very difficult goal to fight. Al Qaeda is also known for great standards terrorist firms and their association in relation to other radical groups are even bigger. The hard-core terrorists who have sworn allegiance to bin Laden probably numbers in the hundreds and the organization has helped train and support tens of thousands of insurgents who have passed through his camps in Afghanistan. Al Qaeda is also linked to radical groups as far away as South Africa, the Philippines, Mauritania, Uzbekistan, and dozens of other countries. Globalization has increased the power of association, thus helping his players together and preaches his message from the remote borders of Afghanistan and the increased survival of United States resentment or collapse of a terrorist group that depends on its ability to maintain operational safety. Inner core of Al Qaeda is extremely sensitive to this problem. For example, the manual *jihad* Al Qaeda has spread attention to the mix and ensures that the overall organization is not interrupted. Bin Laden has invested only trust; the Arabs as bodyguards and avoided using mobile phones. The Sept. 11 conspirators also tried, unsuccessfully, at times, to maintain operational secrecy.

Al Qaeda has demonstrated the ability to review their methods and structure in response to setbacks or failures. Its agents regularly review the lessons learned in order to improve the chances of success for future attacks. This gives the organization the ability to recover quickly from a disaster or success measures.

Before Sept. 11, Al Qaeda had also forged an unusual relationship with a state. The organization had an exceptionally close relationship with the Taliban, united by shared ideology, friendships, and the provision of manpower and financial support to Al Qaeda regime. US failed to persuade and force the Taliban to renounce Al Qaeda. For those responsible for intelligence and US policy, the opposing nature has tremendous consequences of failures caused to stop attacks. The safe haven in Afghanistan has made it much more difficult collection and obliges member states to remove a power system in order to disrupt the activities of Al Qaeda there. Al Qaeda has also been difficult to stop because of its large transnational nature, which have made it possible to lose a cell or qualified operators are still operating elsewhere. Finally, the professionalism of the organization has made collecting and difficult to break because, unlike many terrorist groups, it has relatively few errors.

Upcoming non-response

When we examine the failures of the fight against terrorism before September 11, it is clear that no single measure by itself would make America safe. Although this trial breaks the weaknesses that have contributed to the success of Al Qaeda attacks of September 11 in several categories, these problems are highly interdependent. A simple change to one degree or another would have profound repercussions, but they were needed the most extensive changes to address the broader danger of Al Qaeda.

On September 11, the authorities have tried to solve many of these problems. Terrorism, of course, has become a priority for the Bush administration, with the full support of Congress and the American people. At the institutional level, the military, the CIA, the FBI, and the various agencies involved in national security made numerous changes designed to better help them fight al Qaeda. Foreign policy belonging to United States has on the other hand changed dramatically, were the United States has to overthrow the Taliban and Al Qaeda to make a priority in many of their relations which can be termed to be bilateral.

Despite these measures have resulted in significant progress, new problems have emerged. Support for *Jihadism* has increased, although Al Qaeda as it seems decent organization under siege. Anti-Americanism in particular is widespread. Stop "next 9/11" will require not only avoiding the mistakes that allowed the first attack, but also adapt to the changing strategic context. However, we must recognize that when it comes to terrorist organizations in general, and when faced with such a smart organization like Al Qaeda, including some attacks inevitably successful.

In fact, more than three years after the attacks, warning that another catastrophic attack is imminent remain constant. Therefore, politicians should focus not only on preventing the next attack, but the need to ensure the correct answer should remain an attack. This effort includes consequence management, ensuring that hospitals, firefighters and other emergency personnel have proper procedures, training and resources. Equally important, however, it is managing expectations. Terrorists "win" through the spread psychological damage, not through physical carnage inflicted. Leaders, however, the wet feed this panic will do much more to defeat the terrorists who would do as particularly covert action or a military attack. (**Byman,** 2005)

6 TERRORISM. IDEAS OF THE LEFT AND RIGHT

INTRODUCTION

Ideological terrorism is a form of terrorism in which a group terrorizes with the aim of imposing its ideals on others. These ideals range from political, religious to single issue ideals. Examples of single issue ideals include issues on anarchism, abortion, animal rights, and ecology among others. The ideals that govern the terrorist group fuel their activities and determine the target group.

Ideological terrorism first emerged as a form of anticolonial terrorism. This was evident in Africa as the locals ganged against the colonial masters who has settled in their land and mistreated the locals. The ideology behind anticolonial terrorism was freedom.

Frantz Fannon in his book *'the Wretched of the Earth'* (2006) noted that the colonialist had dehumanized their colonics destroying their culture and replacing it with western ideals. This kind of terrorism was a revolutionary one. Terrorists use violence to get their target audience to submit to their ideologies.

While far right extremism targets the minority and weak groups, far left extremism targets the majority. The right wing extremists are concerned with the influence or interference of minority groups in their cultural identity. On the other hand, far left extremists are concerned that the majority and the powerful are reaping huge benefits and costing the average citizen.

Far rightists will attack the elite, big corporations, popular beliefs while the far leftists will attack the minorities and unpopular beliefs that are beginning to gain traction such as abortion, homosexuality and minority groups in the country.

Both right wing terrorism and left wing terrorism are domestic terrorisms. Both far right extremism and far left extremism pose great danger to countries. Any act of violence from extremists can cause injury, death and destruction of property.

The big distinction between right wing extremists and left wing extremists is their ideologies. Left wing extremists are anti-communist, anti-anarchism and anti -socialism. They support ideologies of neo-fascism, neo Nazism, ultra nationalism, populism, and anti-immigration. Right hand extremism exhibits characteristics such as xenophobia, homophobia, anti-Semitism, ethnocentrism and anti-ziganism.

Both extremists are fighting for the common good of the average citizen. The main difference is that the rightist think that the minority are the hindrance to achievement of the common good while the leftists think that the powerful and the elite are the hindrance to achievements of an ideal society.

Left wing extremism is more of a class struggle. It aims to overthrow capitalism and conservatism and replace it with socialism, anarchism and Marxism. Marxists believe that to be able to achieve an ideal socialist state, it would call for leadership by a group of professional revolutionaries that comes from the working class who have a clear understanding of the socialist consciousness. The goal of adopting socialism would be to develop to full-fledged communist society. A communist society that would be classless and means of productions would be equally owned by members of the society.

DISSATISFACTION FROM THE LEFT: IDEOLOGY AND BELIEFS

Left wing terrorism is an ideology based movement that is against capitalism, feudalism, marginalization, exploitation, inequality and state failure to offer good governance.

The ideal of left wing extremism is to overthrow capitalist and conservative cultures and replace them with socialist and anarchist cultures. This ideology is by a great extent influenced by socialist, Maoist, communist and liberal practice ideals.

Origin of left wing extremism

Narodnaya is one of the earliest left wing terrorist group. In the late 19th century, the group killed Alexander 11 of Russia and propagated the concept of "propaganda by the deed." The concept meant that to spread ideals and principles it was better done with deeds than words (**Assaf**, 2012). Anarchists and socialist's movements were using violent deeds such as regicides and bombings to assert their principles and ideologies.

In the early 20th century, anarchist terrorism became prevalent during the cold war. It continued to develop in the mid20th century in Western Europe. Some of the left wing terrorist groups included Red Army Faction in Germany, Red Brigades in Italy, communist combat Cells in Belgian, Shining Path in Peru and 19th of April Movement among others.

Characteristics of left wing terrorism

Left wing terrorism is mainly driven by ideologies of Marxism, anarchism and socialism. Often, this kind of terrorism is internal. Most of the times, leftist groups in a country are composed by members of the country who attack its own people both citizens and governments as they fight ideologies that are against communism.

In the modern era, leftist terrorism has taken interest on single issues such as ecotourism, anti-globalization, and animal rights among others. They come across as activists for minority issues and will often protest. In extreme cases they use violent methods such as murder, bombing, kidnapping, burning down facilities among others.

Left Wing terrorism around the world.

Third World Countries

In the middle of 20th century, many third world countries were struggling to get independence from their colonies. While their tactics were considered as terrorist, this was a case of a weaker country using the means necessary to fight stronger, richer and more powerful foreigners.

This revolution saw an increased solidarity among members of the third world and nationalists as they struggled for independence. While the colonizers deemed this violent revolution as terrorism, Victimas, 25(1997) saw the actual *terrorizersas* the governments of the colonizing countries. Therefore, the terrorism in the third world countries was not on individuals but rather on states and governments.

In line with this argument, the third world has called for a differentiation between their methods to free from foreign control as acts of terrorism. They argue that their quest for self- determination using violence was a last resort to fight foreign occupancy. The countries continue to fight colonialist ideologies through elimination of foreign interventions. Third world countries repeal the use of principle of sovereignty in place of terrorism. For them to reconcile, both blocs have to be willing to compromise and allow for ambiguity that allows for appropriate interpretations in different international environments.

Western bloc

Countries such as Germany, Italy, US, Japan, Belgium and France have fallen victims of left wing terrorism, either internally or externally. Some popular left wing terrorist groups in the western block included Ceccules Communists Combats(CCC) who attacked Belgium and France, Second of June movement in Germany, Weatherman in the US and Red Brigades in Italy among others.

These terrorist groups used methods such as bombing and kidnapping citizens and diplomats. The events in the late 18th century and the better part of the 29th century led to a strong emphasis to define terrorism and come up with ways of fighting it. The United Nations and members of the Western bloc were interested in promoting international cooperation to fight against any form of terrorism. This required enactment of legal instruments and procedures to prosecute and extradite terrorists. In Canada, the Front de Liberacion du Quebec left wing extremist group promoted the independence of Quebec and a socialist insurrection. In its quench for independence, the group was responsible for 160 bombings and kidnapping and later murdering the Quebec politician in 1970.

In the US, modern left wing extremists emerged from the remnant of the Weather Underground group and students for a democratic society group. These groups advocated for communism at a time when the US was fast adopting capitalism. In addition to the terrorist activities of the two groups, the Symbionese Liberation Army kidnapped heiress Patty Hearst. The leftist terrorists were responsible for at least 75% of terrorist attacks in the US in 1980. Many of the leftist terrorist groups dismantled after the cold war as communist ideologies lost support in the US and other parts of the world. However, the 2017 congressional baseball shooting is said to have been fueled by Marxism apologists.

Asia

The Japanese Red Army and the Liberation Tigers of Tamil Eelam(LTTE) were the main left wing terrorist groups in Asia. Stefan, notes that the LTTE later transformed to a nationalist movement.

In India, the Armed Naxalite leftist group is considered among the largest internal security threats in India. This group propagates Maoism and mostly operates in the central and eastern rural areas India. The group has over the years engaged in numerous attacks and human right violation activities.

Communist Party of Nepal also propagates Maoism and has conducted hundreds of attacks on citizens and government. The United People's Front of Nepal (UPF) in 1994 resorted to an insurgency when they were excluded from the elections. They wanted to overthrow Nepal's monarchy, takeover the private industry and collective agriculture The Maoist extremists attacked private schools and in 2005 demanded closure of al private schools. This led to bombing of two private schools in western Nepal on 15 April, 2005

In 1969, a group of students who were impatient with the communist party formed the Japanese Red Army (JRA). The group later joined hands with the Popular Front for the Liberation of Palestine and created a base in Lebanon. They have been responsible for numerous terrorist attacks including attack on the Tel Aviv airport, hijacking planes, hijacking a French ambassador and bombing a night club in Italy. The group is no longer considered a terrorist threat by the US government as its activity declined in the mid1990s and the later its leaders announced its dissolution.

Eastern Bloc

In the late 19th century and early 18th century, the Soviet Union used terrorism as a tool to get and maintain power. However, in the late 20th century, Moscow condemned terrorism. For the most part, the western bloc is the one that was struggling with rising cases of terrorism and the eastern bloc was rather unaffected. The low prevalence of terrorism and the double edged relationship of the eastern block and terrorism saw a complacency in the bloc's effort to fight terrorism. In fact, on several occasions, the Soviet bloc extremists had on several occasions hijacked planes headed to the west.

Modern left wing terrorism

Left wing terrorism in the 20th century was large as the Islam terrorism is in the world today. However, with the collapse of the Soviet Union that was a major proponet of the Marxist ideologies, Marxism lost traction in many parts of the world. However, the left extremism has taken a different angle this time not taking up socialist and Marxist ideologies rather as advocates of single issues.

Some of the common single issues extremism include ecotourism, animal rights, and environmental conservation. In the US Examples of modern left extremist groups include the Animal Liberation Front, Earth Liberation Front, Earth First, Eco tourism, Black Liberation Army, The May 19th communist organization, 8United Freedom Front among others.

According to 2008 FBI report, Eco tourists and extreme human rights activists were among top sources of domestic terrorism threats in the US. These left wing extremists were responsible for over 2000 crimes and caused damages accruing to $110million since the late 20th century.

In Europe modern era leftism has been evidenced by instances such as French's anti-capitalism riots when some French students in 2006 rioted against poverty and unemployment in France. In 2008 some Greek anarchists burnt down a library at the University of Athens. In 2010, the anarchists burnt down a bank in Athens killing 3 employees.

Incidences of left terrorism have significantly decreased in the world in the 21at century with an insurgence of Islam terrorism taking the center stage.

RIGHT WING DISSATISFACTION: MARX-ISM AND MINORITIES

Right wing terrorism is fueled by idcologies such as anti-capitalism, neo-fascism, neo Nazism and anti-abortion. Right wing extremists aim to overthrow the government and government systems and put in place nationalists or fascists regimes. At the core of the ideologies of right extremism is a belief that governments need to rid themselves of foreign influence in order to rightfully serve its citizens. Therefore, there is often an antiforeigner and racist dimension in this ideology. It is driven by ethnocentrism and anti-immigration.

Falk (2001) suggests that one of the main causes of right wing terrorism is the state of unemployment in a country. He noticed that in many countries that had experienced right wing terrorism, as unemployment rate increased so did the incidences of right wing terrorism. The pattern was true in Germany, US and UK among other countries.

Causes of right wing extremism

As **Ferrante** (2003) points out, work and employment serves crucial purpose in a society. It not only offers an opportunity to earn an income but it also key to self- identity and personal fulfillment among citizens. Therefore, when there is a high rate of unemployment, in people suffer and becomes intolerable, hence, it fuels right wing extremism.

Another cause of right wing terrorism is populism. Populism ideology advocates the rights and well-being of the common citizen and is against the elite in the society. Populism creates a social climate that divides the society therefore extremists will look at it a s a situation of 'us versus them'. The "us versus them" mentality easily fuels conflict and acts of terrorism follow.

Right Wing Terrorism in the world.

Africa

In Africa, South Africa has been the epitome of right wing terrorism. Incidences range from apartheid to recent cases of xenophobia.

America

Michael () notes that there has been a long history of right wing terrorism in America. In the late 20th century, the number of right wing terrorism incidences was more than that of Marxists driven terrorism. Right wing terrorism is also referred to as white terrorism or domestic terrorism. Other than fighting socialism, the right wing extremists also fought the black communities, abortion and homosexuality.

In the 1980s, The Order, a white nationalist revolutionary group killed a radio talk show host by the name Alan Berg, robbed banks and bombed cars among other acts of terror in the USA.

Eric Rudolph was a staunch right wing ideologies apologist. In the late 1990s, he was responsible for a number of terrorist incidences including bombing of the Centennial Olympic park that resulted to two deaths and over 10 injures. One reason for the attacks was to have games cancelled as he claimed that they caused global socialism. In 1997, he took responsibility for bombing an abortion clinic in Atlanta. In 1998 he bombed two more abortion clinics one in Birmingham and the other in Alabama. He also confessed to bombing a lesbian bar in Atlanta.

In the bigger America, countries such as Brazil, Colombia and Canada have experience one form or another or right wing extremism violence. In Canada, right wing extremism was behind the Ecole Polytechnique Massacre and shooting at the Quebec City Mosque.

About 70% of political murders that happen in Colombia every year are conducted by paramilitary right wing extremist groups. The paramilitary groups are supported and financed by the elite in Colombia including far right politicians, drug traffickers, far-right corporations, landowners and members of security forces. Victims of paramilitary violent attacks include peasants, human rights workers, teachers, unionists and left wing political supporters.

Europe

France, Poland, Italy, Ireland, UK, Sweden, Norway, France and Germany some of the countries in Europe have fallen victim to right wing terrorism.

1980, a right wing terrorist attack was carried out in Munich, Germany that resulted to over 200 injuries and 14 deaths. The German National Socialist Underground right wing extremist group conducted bank robberies and were responsible for the cologne bombing.

In 1970 and 1980, Italy saw an era that was referred to as the "Years of lead" as it endured numerous incidences of terrorist attacks both from left wing extremists and right wing extremists.

One of the most notable right wing terrorist incidents was the bombing of Piazza Fontana in Milan that was conducted by a right wing extremist group, Ordine Nuovo's group which was agitating for neo-fascism. The incident led to 16 deaths and caused over 90 injuries.

Ordine Nuovo continued being active throughout 1970s and 1980s. It conducted several terrorists attacks including the Bologna bombing in 1980 in which a neo-fascists apologist, Nucei Armati bombed the Bolgana railroad terminus killing 85 people and injuring 200 more. In 1972, the group attacked antifascist activists killing eight of them in the Piazza Della Loggia bombing. Hilter was a far right extremist who blamed foreigners for all of Germany's problems and an ardent anti-Semitism apologist.

In 2011, Norway saw one of its worst terrorist attacks when Anders Behring Breivik, a Norwegian neo-Nazi and a fascist proponent carried out a series of attack. He first bombed government buildings in Oslo where he killed 8 people and injured 30 others, he later went to Utoya disguised as a policeman and shot at political youth rally attendants causing over 60 injuries and 68 deaths.

In Poland, right wing extremists attack the ethnic and religious minority groups such as the Jews, Muslims and Romanian people. There have been incidences of hate crime such as physical violence and arson targeting the minority groups.

UK suffered numerous neo-Nazi attacks in the late 1990s. David Copeland, a Neo-Nazi sympathizers conducted a series of 13 bomb attacks across the country. His aim was to eliminate minority groups such as blacks living in London, gay communities and Bangladeshi. The explosions took place in Brixton, Soho, Brick lane killing 3 people and injuring over 100 others.

Modern era right wing terrorism

Modern era right wing terrorism incidences are rampant across the world and particularly in the US. Right wing terrorist attacks have claimed more lives than jihadist attacks in the US. Since 2001, there have been over 21 incidences of right wing extremism with some being fatal. The government accountability office noted that up to 73% of violent acts of extremism that caused death were instigated by right wing terrorists.

The most recent incidences in 2017 are the Portland train attack that killed 2 people. In this year also, Timothy Caughman was stabbed in New York. The Charleston church shooting of 215 was one of the most fatal incidences that left 9 people dead and caused injuries to many more.

Right wing extremists in their acts of terror have attacked police officers, civilians, government officers, government properties and private properties, public places and religious facilities. Their tactics of terror include kidnapping, murder, bombing, robberies, shooting, assassinations and ambush among others.

Donald Trump, has come up as a far right politics sympathizer. He has depicted ethnocentrism and anti-immigration tendencies. This is evidenced by the executive order 13769 that he issued as a travel ban to curb migration to the US from Muslim majority countries. He also enacted an immigration policy that proposed construction of a wall on the border of US and Mexico to prevent illegal immigrations by Mexicans into the US. According to Trump, the rampant immigration to the US threated economic success of the country and threatens the vales and identity of US.

Elsewhere in Europe, the incidences of right wing extremism rose significantly in Germany in 2015 and 2016. Mainly, the attacks were xenophobic. The Old School Society, a Munich based right wing extremist group in Germany openly displayed their ideologies on racism, anti-seticism and anti-Islam. The group that had initially began with 4 members gained popularity and its membership rose to 30 people. The group was responsible for the Munich shooting. It planned several other incidences but members and leaders were arrested before they could execute.

The German government reported a sharp rise in incidences of right wing terror attacks most of them that are xenophobic in 2015 and 2016. The incidences rose from 316 violent xenophobic incidences in 2014 to over 600 similar offences in 2015.

7 COUNTER TERRORISM

INTRODUCTION

Terrorism is a subject that evokes strong feelings among different people. It therefore becomes challenging to address the matter objectively and rationally. The subjectivity of the subject and ideologies around terrorism had posed a great challenge in resolving the issue completely. Efforts that have been made to find a balance and discuss the matter legally often end up eliciting bias among people who have different views.

Baxter (2005) argued that the legal concept of terrorism is ambiguous and imprecise, the concept is deeply inflicted on us with a ambiguity and with a biased legal point of view.

Whichever approach is used to discuss terrorism, and for whatever reasons the topic is brought up, the subject will almost always bring up strong passion and strong reactions from different parties.

A legal reasoning approach on terrorism is likely to be politically biased to the legal systems of the country that came up with it. While international Humanitarian law (IHL) could be an ideal structure for addressing and combating extremist violence, it is perceived as a technical branch of law. This branch of international law is understood by a few individuals' majority of them are based in Geneva. It therefore lacks an international appreciation and therefore does not make it effectively applicable in handling terrorism issues across the globe.

The indistinct nature of international law was evidenced in the attempt to resolve 9/11. The meeting of various stakeholders in an attempt to address the issues resulted into a clash of ideologies and legal cultures (White, 2011). The international and humanitarian law applicability remains unclear and inaccessible for the majority of the world.

Humanitarian law allows for detention of people who are deemed as a threat to state security. This instrument in the international laws can be applied in various situations including when there is a terrorist threat as a tool of curtailing planned violent activities. However, there is no direct link between terrorism and IHL. Up to now, there is a challenge in characterizing terrorism and setting laws that lead to identification and handling of terrorist activities (White, 2011).

TECHNIQUES OF COMBATING TERRORISM

Democratic regime

American leadership has proposed that terrorism results from authoritarian regimes and therefore promoting democracy and economic prosperity can eliminate terrorism. George Bush and his administration was one of the major proponents of this position. He suggested that an international call for democracy would be the magic stick in winning the war on terrorism across the globe. In his second inaugural speech in 2005, President Bush said "the best antidote to radicalism and terror is the tolerance to become free societies". He used this logic explicitly to justify regime changes in Afghanistan and Iraq to democratic practices (Chenoweth, 2013).

In 2011, the US government issued a national management strategy to combat terrorism. The strategy stated that "promoting representative and accountable government is a basic principle of foreign policy and directly contributes to our goals of combating terrorism"

During the Global Forum against terrorism held in 2012, Hillary Clinton, the then secretary of state stated that "experience tells us that democracies are better equipped than autocracies to stand up against terrorism. They offer constructive outlets for political grievances, create opportunities for mobility and prosperity that provide alternatives to extremist violence, and they tend to have more effective institutions."

The call for democracy however led to an uprising in North Africa and Middle East as extremists fought against the gaining popularity of democracy. Juan Zarate, a former counter terrorism expert in the Bush government argued that "If the protests lead to a peaceful and pluralistic transition, which does massive damage to the account of al-Qaeda".

Although there is skepticism in adopting democracy to combat terrorism, many stakeholders are optimistic that global democracy could end terrorism in the world (Chenoweth, 2013).

Force Defense

Questions have come up on whether the use of force by the US of military force against Taliban and Al Qaeda in Afghanistan was acceptable under the United Nations Charter. This question was recently discussed in a conference with majority delegates were German international lawyers. The conference concluded that it was illegal for the US to use military force on Taliban and Al Qaeda. The judgment came as a surprise for Americans.

The conference presented the following concerns and proposal to demonstrate the allegation of illegality of the use of force by the US:

(1) Violates Article 2 (4) of the Charter prohibition against the use of force except when authorized by the Security Council under Chapter VII. It is not like this. While Article 2 of the Charter (4) prohibits the unilateral use of force, the prohibition must be read in conjunction with Article 51, which recognizes "the inherent right of collective self-defense, individually or, if an armed attack occurs against a Member of the United Nations."

This provision was included in the Charter, as publishers were concerned that the system of the forces of collective security in standby mode provided for in Article 43, which will be distributed by the Security Council, could not be reached to exist and whereas, therefore, states had to continue to rely on its "inherent right" to self-defense. This concern has been established.

Article 43 languished waiting and no force was never created, much less deployed against any of about two hundred armed attacks that have taken place since 1945, leaving the state security in his hands and willing allies. This interpretation is consistent with the practice card. A unanimous resolution adopted the day after the attack on the United States, putting the Security Council on record as "[r] which recognizes the inherent right of individual or collective self-defense in accordance with the Charter,"

(2) Self-defense is unacceptable after an attack has ended; i.e. after September 11 2001.

(3) Self-defense can only be exercised against an attack by a State. Al Qaeda is not the government of a state.

(4) The legitimate defense can be exercised against a real attacker and right. The Taliban are not the attacker.

(5) Self-defense may be exercised only "until the Security Council has taken measures necessary to maintain international peace and security." Since the Council adopted the measures in resolution 1373 of 28 September 2001, the right to self-defense has been replaced.

(6) Self - defense can only come from a test that is directed against the real attacker. The United States has not provided this data. (**Charney**, 2001).

Using force to combat is an irreversible approach. Often use of military force leads to numerous deaths, injuries and property destruction. The United Nations Charters provides exceptions for when to use force for self- defense against terrorism. Before going into war, a country must therefore have substantial evidence of a roaming terrorist threat (**Charney**, 2001).

A REVIEW OF THE UN GLOBAL STRATEGY AGAINST TERRORISM

The UN Global Strategy against terrorism was created to control the use of force in international relations. This was in line with the objectives of many members states of the UN (**Charney**, 2009). The charter provides exceptions for which use of force is allowed.

The Security Council

The Security Council plays a major role in giving permission for use of force in the fight against terrorism. The Security Council and the government seeking to go to war negotiate extensively as the council looks at the evidence available to necessitate a war. The Security Council does not only stamp approval of the demands, but it also stipulates regulations and conditions for going to war.

The Security Council and the entire UN has a responsibility to combat international terrorism. The situation is, no country across the globe is safe from terrorist attack whether internal or external. Many terrorists are non-state actors and therefore they are able to plan and execute terrorism attacks that cause extensive damage without leaving a trace of their identity (**Charne**y, 2001).

Some countries have expressed their resetion on the integrity of the UN as a body. Claims have been made that the body works in favor of military and economically strong countries. However, modern terrorism has become an international security threat. It will be difficult for individual states to win it on their own. The Security Council comes in handy in building systems and regulations to control the use of force as self- defense against terrorism.

The UN committee Ad Hoc

The global community faced difficult times in the 1970s in regards to terrorism. Incidences and frequency of terrorist attacks had significantly increased. In September 1972, the Black September terrorist group slaughtered Israeli athletes at an Olympic in Munich. Earlier on, in May 1972, the UN secretary general was killed in a terrorist attack at the Lod Airport in Israel. The attack had been perpetrated by the Japanese Red Army terrorist group. These and other terrorist attacks that were happening in the globe caused a sense of urgency in the UN to combat the growing terrorism.

On September 8, Kurt Wadheim, an official of the UN urged the assembly to give a special focus on the growing international terrorism. An item dumped "Measures to prevent terrorism and other forms of violence which endanger or take away innocent lives or jeopardize the freedoms fundamentals" was added to the agenda.

The UN became proactive in combating terrorism and suggested the development of a "Draft convention on the prevention and punishment of certain acts of international terrorism.' Led by the US, the west came up with a draft of the proposal. However, the Third World Bloc was not in agreement with the US resolution strategy. They saw it as a westernized strategy to legitimize a new form of colonialism.

Third world countries called for exceptions of specific situations from being referred to as terrorism. In particular, they called for an exception of use of struggle for national liberation as terrorism.

The third world block was a majority in the UN general assembly and it succeeded in having the proposal redrafted affirming that governments had the right to self- determination even by using force to achieve sovereignty. The third world also managed to insert a clause in the draft that condemned racism, colonization and alien regimes.

The next stage was a call for a detailed analysis on the causes of terrorism. The draft linked terrorism to apartheid. Its wording was rejected by the western bloc which argued that it was not right to use apartheid as a justification of terrorism.

The draft went through numerous changes. At this point, instead of banning all acts of terrorism, the proposal provided exceptions for situations that could justify the acts of terrorism. On December 1972, the western block rejected the proposal. It voted against the General Assembly Resolution 3034 (XXVII) on the grounds of lack of consensus on the clause "Measures to prevent international terrorism."

However, the third world bloc that formed majority general assembly adopted the general assembly resolution 3034. The Soviet Union was in favor of the stand taken by the western bloc but seeing that they would not match the numbers of the third world bloc they joined it. This was also a strategy by Moscow to gain favor and influence the third world bloc in particular the Middle East.

Eventually, the assembly adopted Resolution 3034 and established an ad hoc committee of six that served as the legal counsel of the general assembly in regards to international terrorism. The committee met every two years.

Due to the reservations that the US had on Resolution 3034 it pulled out indefinitely. However, over time the third world had been able to shift the focus of the debate to discussing specific measures to address the root cause of terrorism. That and the increased modern era terrorism across the globe have caused the US government to seek a more collaborative approach to combating terrorism.

For the better part of the late 20th century, the outright divide in perception of terrorism between third world countries and the West has significantly derailed any concrete effort by the UN to deal with terrorism as a unit. International terrorism meetings were basically a platform to agree and disagree and in most cases, if no consensus was reached. Ad Hoc committee did not on many occasions manage to give suggestions to the general assembly but they insisted that the issue should remain in the UN agenda.

By the late 1970s, the committee had practically become obsolete. The UK, US and many countries in the west wanted to dissolve the committee or reelect members of the committee. They considered the committee useless and a threat to the western interests. However, Germany thought that committee was crucial for the stage of development that the third world was at. There was likelihood that if the west opposed the renewal of the committee it would lead to more obstructive policies by the third world countries that would worsen the terrorism situation. In meantime, Germans persuaded the rest of the western bloc to keep the committee.

In 1979, the committee reached a resolution that was a compromise for both the west and third world. The resolution suggested that the committee not only studies the causes of terrorism but also establishes measures to oppose it. This resolve formed the basis for gradual developments by the UN in condemning and dealing with terrorism.

The ad hoc committee despite the challenges it faced formed the basis for starting and continuing a conversation about the problem of terrorism. However, the western bloc felt that the third bloc used the committee as a platform to attract attention on matter of national liberation and to turn the world against the west.

Despite the relative impact of the ad hoc, other international issues were gaining more interest. Issues of the foreign policy and the development of the cold war to a new phase as characterized by intense tension redirect attention from the fight against terrorism.

NATO's role in the international fight against terrorism

NATO is an acronym for North Atlantic Treaty Organization. NATO was formed in 1949 as a security alliance for countries in North America and Europe. The organization has 29 member countries. The main goal of NATO is to safeguard the security of its members through countries through the necessary military and political means. The organization is also guided by its democratic values.

Leaders of the member countries came to a consensus that for efforts to combat international terrorism to succeed there needed to be a multifaceted approach to it. They also agreed that they were stronger together than they were individually. By pooling the member countries strengths and resources together they would be in a better position to combat terrorism.

The alliance has since 2001 exhibited a strong determination in dealing with terrorism. During the Prague Summit, head of states of member countries committed to improving the strength of their military. In June 2014, during the Istanbul Summit, NATO came up with an agreed to forming an elaborate defense plan against terrorism. The strategy was formed on the basis of international laws and the regulations provided by the UN charter.

NATO understands that terrorism is fueled by different reasons including political, economical, military and diplomatic reasons. To all the causes, NATO believes that the ultimate solution to beating terrorism is democracy. It is therefore in the frontline in promoting democratic reforms both among its member countries and in new areas including the Mediterranean, Iraq, Afghanistan and Western Balkans.

NATO is also committed to build better and deeper relationships within its members and with the relevant international bodies to enhance collaboration and stability. NATO also serves a key role in promoting exchange of economic and financial information in regards to terrorism to enhance policing making in matters of combating terrorism.

During the Prague Summit, NATO adopted an action plan to fight terrorism. The action plan stipulated that members would freely exchange information and opinions in regards to economic aspects of international terrorism. The action plan also prohibited members from any involvements in financing terrorist groups and activities. NATO pays a keen attention to the financial ability of terrorist groups.

NATO is therefore concerned with the following financial aspects in fighting terrorism

- Investigating terrorist funding sources including charities and improper use of finances within NATO member states
- The relationship between organized crime and terrorism financing
- Investigating payment systems, money and resource transfer and financial activities of terrorist within NATO countries.
- Determining the terrorists' networks by following their financial transactions.
- Rating the impact of terrorists on the economy of the member countries.

The Washington treaty highlights that an attack on one-member country is an attack on all members. The treaty also requires that member countries consult each other on common interest matters of security. The determination of the Soviet threat, NATO's mission to Afghanistan and Kosovo peacekeeping mission are some of NATO security initiatives. Other matters of security interest include cyber -attacks and piracy in relation to terrorism.

Besides its core role of territorial defense of member states, NATO plays a key role as the leader of the UN mandated internal security assistance force (ISAF). NATO also offers extensive military training and security support to partners across the globe including the United Nations, European Union and African Union.

WEAPONS OF MASS DESTRUCTION AND MASS CASUALTIES

Weapons of mass destruction are weapons that can kill or cause harm to many people at a go. The common ones are chemical weapons, biological weapons and nuclcar weapons. Examples of nuclear weapons include atomic weapons and radiation weapons while examples of biological weapons are natural toxins and pathogens. On the other hand, examples of chemical weapons are poisonous gas.

In the last decade there has been a proliferation of weapons of mass destruction. Different countries are manufacturing and acquiring these weapons as part of their military resources. The challenge however is that with the proliferation the chances of these weapons landing in the hands of terrorists or malicious dealers are very high.

Considering the amount of damage weapons of mass destruction have the potential to cause, it is essential that safety standards in transporting and mitigation of proliferation is put in place. Various treaties have been put in place to control and mitigate procurement and manufacture of these weapons.

In 1995, Aum Shinrikyo, a Japanese extremist group released Saringas in Tokyo killing people. There have been fears that soon terrorists will be executing attacks using more advanced mass destruction weapons such as biological attacks and chemical attacks. It is believed that in the 1993 World Center attack the perpetrators used cyanide (**Bet**t, 1998).

Legacy of the cold war

During the cold war there was a nuclear arms race that was a competition to establish nuclear supremacy between the US and Soviet Union. During this period, US, Soviet Union and other countries specifically Britain, China and France developed stockpiles of nuclear weapons.

By the end of the cold war, there was an abolition of nuclear arsenals to reduce tension in the general publics on the use of nuclear weapons. While the two super powers did not detonate any nuclear weapons, the war for supremacy focused on building their nuclear capacity deterrent measure. However, there still exists a public and state fear that terrorists could create and use nuclear weapons in their attacks.

Chemical weapons of terrorism

Unlike nuclear weapons, chemical weapons are more readily available and easier to make. However, chemical weapons are not likely to cause as much damage as nuclear weapon. During the 18980-1988 war, Iraq used chemical weapons to attack Iran. International efforts continue to eradicate chemical weapons from landing in the hands of terrorists.

Biological weapons of mass destruction

Biological weapons are easily accessible and can also cause large scale damage. Nuclear weapons have a greater ability to destruct than biological weapons and chemical weapons but they are more difficult to obtain.

In 1993, a research by the Technology Assessment bureau found that 100kg of aerosol spread anthrax spores had the ability to kill between 1-3million people in a night (**Betts**, 1998). Anthrax spores are bacillus that when exposed to the human body multiplies fast producing toxins that cause rapid bleeding.

Biological agents range from bacteria, viruses to toxins. Examples of biological agents that can be used as biological weapons include Anthrax, Botulinum toxin, plague, brucellosis, staphylococcus enterotoxin B virus, viral encephalitis, Q, tularemia fever, small pox and viral hemorrhagic fever. These agents can be dispersed in aerosol and can stay in the environment for long. These biological agents can be easily transported in industrial sprayers. When exposed to humans they can cause fatal disease; some communicable while others are non- communicable.

Consider the case of exposure to anthrax spores

Anthrax is Bacillus Spores. The Bacillus spores can remain in adverse environment for decades. In the case of a terrorist attack, the spores could have been released in the environment through aerosol administration. Once inhaled, the spores settle in the lower respiratory system. They then germinate producing mediastina bleeding hemorrhagic necrotizing vegetative bacilli. Symptoms of anthrax include fever, fatigue and malaise. Symptoms can then progress to a non-productive cough, chest pain and vomiting. Normally, the symptoms may appear to improve within 2-3 days and then the victims progresses to severe respiratory system distress leading to meningitis and then death within the next 24-16 hours (**Franz et al.**, 1997).

Medical responses to an anthrax attack range include pre exposure and post exposure treatment. Pre-exposure and active immunization with antibiotics helps to prevent the disease. However, in the case of a terrorist attack, individual are most likely aware of the upcoming exposure and are therefore not immunized. In the case of post exposures, considerations are made on whether or not the symptoms are already present or not.

Other factors to consider are whether the patient has recently been treated with antiviral and/or antibiotic drugs. Often, if the symptoms of anthrax by inhalation are active, treatment is likely to be ineffective. In such a case, medical professionals are only left with the option to diagnose and offer medical support to the patient awaiting death.

Penicillin can be used for anthrax treatment if infection by inhalation occurs. The challenge is that for the treatment to be effective, a patient needs to be administered with over 2 million units intravenously every two hours. Years of research have found that streptomycin is more effective in treatment of anthrax by inhalation.

In case of such an occurrence, apart from the adverse effects on the patients, the medical facilities would normally not be prepared to handle such situations especially when there is an avalanche of patients. Large amount of medical supplies and drugs would be required which would normally not be readily available. Medical practitioners would also be exposed to bacteria and special quarantine facilities would be required.

In case one is expecting exposure to anthrax, pre-exposure treatment using aluminum hydroxide can be administered in doses on 0,2,4 weeks and again at 6,12 and 18 months. This pre exposure treatment would be accompanied by annual amplifiers (**Franz et al**., 1997).

What is to be expected in case of a biological weapon terrorist attack? Normally, protection devices would not be readily available in the public domain. Humans would be the top victims. A challenging aspect of biological agent attacks is that they cause unspecific symptoms making it difficult to make a diagnosis on the victims. While epidemiological investigations would lead to accurate diagnosis, in such a situation there isn't enough time to do the investigation. The focus is on the first few hours and days after an infestation would be focusing on managing symptoms and reducing death rate.

Increasing threat of mass destruction terrorist attacks

While the US government has taken deliberate and stringent measure to protect its citizens and government from terrorist attacks, America remains a target for numerous terrorist attacks. Attacks range from diplomatic, military attacks on citizens and government officials. Many planned attacks have been caught before they were executed but there have been several others that were executed. Terrorist attacks in the US have ranged from attacks using small simple weapon use to major attacks.

Since the cold war, an agreement was reached between the superpowers to destroy nuclear weapons. With some countries having openly tested their nuclear weapons there is a concern for terrorist nuclear attack across the globe. However, much as there is a concern for the possibility of nuclear terrorist attacks, acquisition, transportation and operation of nuclear weapon is much complicated which discourages many terrorists from acquiring it. A rising and justifiable concern is the use biological weapons in terror attack. The biological agents are more readily available, can be easily transported and cause significant destruction. Chemical weapons seem to be less fatal than biological and nuclear weapons.

With that, no country or people would succumb to any of the weapons of mass destruction let alone any acts of violence. It is therefore necessary for the international community and states to put measure to mitigate possibilities for mass destruction attacks and put in place response strategies in case of an attack

Need for mitigation and response planning

It would be easier to appreciate the value of contemporary effective measures that could be taken against the most limited attacks. A series of measures, which are actually much cheaper than trying to provide a defense umbrella to attack missiles are available to mitigate the death and sufferings of those occurring in a chemical or biological attack.

Examples include storage or distribution of masks, distribution of decontamination equipment, implementation of training programs, mass inoculation vaccines (or at least one program backup), the creation of emergency relief programs with Antibiotics and public education efforts to strengthen co-operation on evacuation, shelter and medical care. These attempts should limit death and injury, but he could not even remove them. It is best to act against the limits of defense is not to deal with it.

Planning and mitigation action plans should take into account the problems and organizational limitations that could arise in the event of a terrorism catastrophe. This can be achieved by considering how citizens would respond and how different institutions such as media, government and medical institutions would respond.

A discussion on behavioral preparation should be conducted both in the government and public domain. Engaging the media to lead such discussion and carrying out grass root level sensitization would come in handy in creating a vigilant and highly responsive public. States should make policy changes to enhance preparation and mitigation of mass destruction attacks.

In June 1995, the White House issued the Presidential Decree 39 (PDD-39), "US Policy on Combating Terrorism." The decree outlined the measures to be taken to reduce the country's vulnerability to terrorism and discourage terrorist attacks. It also came up with an action plan to manage use of nuclear weapons, biological weapons and chemical weapons.

Non-Proliferation of weapons of mass destruction

Following the World War 1 and 11, the adverse effects of using WMDs were clear. Since then various treaties and policies have been put in place to curb proliferation of WMDs.

During the cold war, the superpower prevented use of nuclear weapons by mutually agreeing to destroy their nuclear weapon stockpiles. This improved the sense of security in the world.

The nuclear non-proliferation treaty was signed on July 1 in 1968 and effected form March 5, 1970. The international treaty's main objective was to prevent and reduce spread of nuclear weapons and to promote collaborative peaceful use of nuclear energy. After expiry of the treaty period in 1995, treaty members met and agreed to continue with it indefinitely.

The treaty members as of August 2016 were 191 states. North Korea withdrew from the treaty in 2003. Of the UN countries, three countries are not members of the treaty including India, Israel and Pakistan. South Sudan is also not a member. Countries that are believed to possess nuclear weapon include South Korea, UK, US, Russia, China, Israel, India, Pakistan and France. While India, Pakistan and North Korea have openly accepted to possessing nuclear weapons, Israel has remained deliberately ambiguous.

Pakistan and India are neighboring countries believed to be in an arms race. Both countries have developed their own nuclear weapons and ballistic missiles. Before1990. India developed chemical weapons but after entering the Chemical Weapons conventions it stopped manufacturing and destroyed its stockpile. Both Pakistan and India have refused to sign the comprehensive test ban ().

North Korea manufactures and sells nuclear weapon. The country responded that its nuclear reactors has been shut down upon the signing of the NPT treaty in 1994.

Libya is believed to have chemical, nuclear and ballistic weapons programs. At some point the US bombed one of its chemical weapons factories in Rabta. Syria is also believed to have nuclear and chemical weapon programs. Although Iran has signed the nuclear chemical and biological weapons proliferation treaty it is under suspicion for operating a nuclear weapon program.

NATO and its member countries are committed to prevent proliferation of WMD through active political agenda such as arms control, disarmament and non-proliferation. Aside from promoting non-proliferation, NATO and its allies is also engaged in assessing risks and strengthening defense efforts to prevent and respond to any attack using WMD. This preparedness is also geared towards preventing and managing terrorist attacks with WMDs.

Arms control, disbarments and non-proliferation are keys in curbing the manufacture, spread and acquisition of WMDs. Since the end of the cold war, NATO has made deliberate effort to reduce the number of nuclear weapons in Europe. Member countries are committed to destroy chemical agents that can be used as weapon and have supported other countries in doing so. NATO member countries are discouraged from having biological and/or chemical weapon programmed.

Other treaties that control WMDs include

- Geneva protocol
- Anti-ballistic missile treaty
- Biological Weapons Convention
- Chemical weapons convention
- Comprehensive nuclear test treaty

Although different treaties, agreements and policies have been put in place to control weapons, arms and WMDs, some countries have refused to be part of the agreements. Some countries have signed the treaties but have broken the agreement for example Iran. A power imbalance can be associated with engagement of these countries whether the countries feel that the west has power and so they choose to have WMDs and other weapon programs for self-defense.

There has been a concern on the methods of transportation of WMDs and other supplies used in their manufacture could give terrorist access to WMDs. Often, countries that manufacture WMDs falsify end user or destination of the products to prevent raising attention. For instance, if WMDs supplies are being imported to Iran, manufactures may have the supplies be delivered in a neighboring country and they will later find means to get the supplies to the country. Some organizations and countries also commit documentation fraud to cover up.

8 ASPECTS OF NATURAL PSYCHOLOGICAL WARFARE: WHAT MEASURES MUST BE TAKEN TO RESPOND AND CURB?

EMERGING THREATS FROM AMMUNITIONS OF MASS DEMOLITION

In a Japanese faction in 1995AumShinrikyo discharged Saringas in Tokyo - a small group of people were executed. Sooner than later an atomic, organic or synthetic fear monger assault or culprit in a metropolitan range in the United States? A few investigators trust that in 1993; the World Trade Center assault by cyanide, yet not when consumed in the blast (**Betts,** 1998). Future fear based oppressor endeavors might be more powerful to uncover their objective populace to their most loved weapon.

THE HERITAGE OF THE COLD WAR

When, the cold war came to an end the fear of common atomic decimation with the nullification of atomic arms stockpiles of the two superpowers has to a great extent scattered among the overall population (Betts, 1998; Christopher et al, 1997). In spite of the fact that worries stay on the issue of "little arms", the United States has been effectively attempting to alleviate. Atomic weapons, be that as it may, are the only concern. The most preferred WMD are those which are synthetic or natural. This most plausible alternative for the lesser nations or psychological oppressor bunches are plainly burdened contrasted with the customary weapons capacities in the United States are progressively considered. The US technique in the harsh elements War time concentrated on prevention through regular and atomic limit. Substance and organic decimation masses speak to a more impediment challenge. This is the case if WMD are in the hands of fear based operators. (Betts, 1998).

EMERGING HOUSEHOLD RISK

Over the years, in the United States organizations of the main noteworthy bureaucratic gatherings have come up with ways that make it difficult to assault American staff including fear based oppressor structures abroad (Simon, 1997; Tucker, 1998). 177 psychological oppressors propelled attacks on the USA conciliatory, military and different authorities of the American government in 1980.Ten of these demonstrations occurred in 1995. Americans continued to be the objective of fear based oppression, expanded safety efforts abroad were essentially executed by the US government. Tragically, this achievement has most likely been to some degree balanced by the likelihood of disturbed fear monger assaults liable to commandeer some less difficult assaults, for example, representatives from the United States or other regular citizen targets. Shouldn't something be said about the US residential populace? Ok for psychological oppressor assaults, for natives living inside US outskirts? The World Trade Center shelling in 1993, the 1995 Tokyo Sarin gas and the Oklahoma City besieging underlined the requirement for more prominent familiarity with US and US relief exercises. The White House issued the Presidential Decree 39 (PDD-39) in June 1995, "US guidelines and frameworks on Combating Terrorism." The DP-39 accepts systems to decrease the nation's weakness of fear based oppression, dishearten and react to psychological militant operations and to build capacity to avert, also to deal with the outcomes of the utilization of atomic bombs (NBC) organic with substance ammunition, including tools and structures for mass annihilation.

End of what can be called the third world war, necessitated that any subsequent inner fear monger ammunition's potential needs to pass regular explosives for enormous demolition of CBRN specialists (Betts, 1998; Steinbrenner, 1997; Zilinskas, 1997). While atomic and compound bombs of mass decimation stay of extraordinary attention is to be paid to organic operators that might be further appealing to fear based oppressors. How can this take place? Amid the third world war, weapons of mass devastation were at the principle agenda of US outside arrangement.

The hypothesis of atomic prevention recommends the assault to be deterred by super secured proportional annihilation. Due to the disintegration of the old Soviet Union and the lessening of atomic munitions stockpiles by the American government and the old Soviet states, atomic superpower atomic fighting count that struck utilize atomic weapons by maverick governments or psychological militant gatherings. The trouble (and cost) to convey atomic weapons of mass devastation to assault and the probability that the creator approaches some of these weapons, utilize this potential fear based oppressor choice, yet is more improbable than different alternatives.

SYNTHETIC WEAPONS OF PSYCHOLOGICAL OPPRESSION

In the period 1980-1988 Iran was attacked by Iraq which used chemical weapons against the Iranian troops. Concoction of ammunitions are a great deal exceedingly accessible than atomic bombs. The innovation used in creating them is less demanding. Be that as it may, concoction weapons are not fit for dispensing a substantial number of regular citizen losses in a solitary shot by an atomic weapon. This does not imply that endeavors to kill concoction weapons aren't right. It basically guarantees that atomic weapons are presumably liked to chemicals by the individuals who are attempting to deliver substantial misfortunes rapidly. Nonetheless, there is another option that is superior to both.

NATURAL WEAPONS OF MASS DEVASTATION BY FEAR BASED OPPRESSORS

Natural ADM has the upside of joining greatest devastation with simple get to. While atomic weapons have an extraordinary capacity to execute, they are hard to get; While substance weapons are anything but difficult to get, they don't have awesome capacity to slaughter. Technology Assessment Bureau found that 100 kg of vaporized spread Bacillus anthracis spores on an unmistakable and quiet night in Washington, DC, could slaughter 1 to 3 million individuals from a research conducted in 1993 (Betts, 1998). Bacillus anthracis spores are the dormant phase of a bacillus that duplicates quickly in the body, creating poisons and fast seeping inside days of presentation.

Microscopic organisms, infections, or poisons can be utilized as natural operators. Cases of conceivable organic specialists incorporateviral hemorrhagic fevers, viral encephalitis, Anthrax (B anthracis), botulinum poison, brucellosis, staphylococcus enterotoxin B infection, Q, tularemia fever, smallpox andtorment (Yersinia pestis) (Franz et al., 1997). They can be scattered in the mist concentrate sprayer remain in flight for quite a long time by inward breath for some potential casualties. Vaporizers can be conveyed by basic modern sprayers from a plane or pontoon to where wind may blow. Ailments due to such specialists can be incapacitating or fatal to regular people. Some natural operators (for instance, Anthrax) deliver transmittable maladies among people, but others create these specialists.

Example

B anthracis, a Bacillus sporulation causes Bacillus anthracis. It is actually located in the dirt; the body is on the planet. Bacillus anthracis spores can stay essential for a considerable length of time in unfavorable ecological conditions. Airborne organization would in all probability have been utilized as a part of a fear based oppressor assault with this natural operator, which would prompt inward breath of Bacillus anthracis. After inward breath, the spores find their way to the lower respiratory tract, sprout and create mediastina draining hemorrhagic necrotizing vegetative bacilli. Side effects start with fever, discomfort and exhaustion. They may incorporate non-gainful hack and heaving chest torment. It might appear to be enhanced for a few days, or the casualty can be straightforwardly dislodged into serious respiratory trouble, meningitis and demise in 24 to 36 hours (Franz et al., 1997).

The therapeutic reaction relies upon the way that the estimations were started before, a great many exposures, however earlier or after the signs show. Dynamic inoculation with anti-toxins can keep the illness if regulated before introduction - an impossible probability in the regular citizen populace when all is said in done. After presentation, yet before the side effects are available, dynamic or latent vaccination, and in addition a previous treatment with restorative anti-toxins or antiviral medications that can enhance the side effects of the ailment - a therapeutic reaction legitimate if the rundown of psychological militants who is, where ,when what was done and if medicinal supplies are accessible in adequate amounts for an adequate number of medicinal staff to manage an adequately delicate populace (everything appears to be tricky). Once the manifestations of Bacillus anthracis by inward breath happen, treatment is probably going to be incapable. Finding of sickness and bolster treatment is by and large the main legitimate alternative for medicinal services experts (Franz et al., 1997).

On the off chance that you are expecting for subsequent risk antibody, aluminum hydroxide can be given in dosages of 0, 2 and 4 weeks and afterward again at 6, 12, year and a half, trailed by yearly speakers. After introduction, penicillin was basic for Anthrax inward breath treatment. Two million units directed intravenously like clockwork. It was discovered that streptomycin was giving a further favorable position. Clearly, notwithstanding the unfriendly wellbeing impacts of the objective populace, the medicinal services framework could be altogether influenced because of a remarkable number of providers flooding patients. A lot of medications and antibodies would be required, which are not by and large accessible in standard pharmaceuticals. Human services and research facility staff might be presented to natural dangers of expediting settlements (**Franz et al**., 1997).

What would we be able to expect if a fear based oppressor assault happens with an organic operator? Assurance gadgets and immunizations are at present not accessible to the regular citizen populace all in all. On the off chance that we are not aware of an assault, human casualties are probably going to be the first indicators of a natural assault (Franz et al., 1997). Most ailments are due to organic specialists that have unique, effortlessly misconstrued as regular occasions. Epidemiological examinations of such scourge maladies are probably not going to happen rapidly enough to stay away from undesirable outcomes. In spite of the fact that a packed pestilence bend with a crest in a couple of days or hours is a decent marker (in normal episodes, occurrence step by step increments as individuals are bit by bit uncovered, individuals presented to organic assaults countless likely when an assault couldn't be checked and distinguished pathogens **(Franz et al.**, 1997) are reached with the operator around the same period.

REASONS FOR CONTROL AND RESPONSE PLANNING

A plan is necessary so that they will know what to do during an attack by fear based operators. There should be a program that will help during crisis. Over the year an attempt to come up with a program for crisis has been ridiculed and often ignored. However in recent years a program has been constructed and policies have been implemented. There are several attempts that have been taken to control events during emergencies caused by terrorist attacks and they include.

- Creation of training programs and their implementation-training personnel that will help out in times of crisis. Rescue teams and soldiers
- Creation of help (relief) programs like the United Nations programs that cater for different crisis. This programs aim at public education so as to enhance cooperation in tasks such as medical care, rescue teams and shelter
- Masks- the storage and redistribution of masks in crisis.

The above efforts should take into account:

- How the society will respond in case there is an attack- will the people panic or will they do what they are supposed to in time of crisis.
- The cohesion of the various organizations in the country- will the different departments i.e. the defense and crisis management departments work together to get through the terror attack

- The role of the media before, during and after the terrorist attack.
- The medical challenges a country faces may affect how effectively it will take care of the victims of the terrorist attack.

A comprehensive research was carried out on the effects of the weapons of mass destruction such as the biological weapon. The research covered a period of 35 years and above to see the effects on the masses as a whole. From the research it was concluded that we are not fully prepared in terms of our reaction to and control of terrorist attacks.

America is a superpower because it the largest stockpile of WMD thus, lesser nations are inferior to it. The USA is therefore in a position to give guidelines and control measures for the production and storage of ammunitions for mass destruction.

The middle class powers like Canada and Netherlands are used as examples in this case. They are headed by the USA under a union that comes from the desire to hold and manufacture weapons of mass destruction. They have a couple of similarities 1) they are members of North Security Alliance. 2) They produce at the same level of technology. 3) They belong to global unions and regional unions at the same time.

The two countries are independent on other sectors of their economy but are dependent on other nations such as the USA when it comes to security or military powers. The two countries have the same goals and objectives in terms of administration and economic growth. They put a lot of resources in their security sectors but in spite of all these efforts they are still inferior to the G5 nations or NATO powers.

MEDIA PIANO AND POWER HYPOTHESIS

Feeble nations, for example, the Netherlands and Canada do not have much impact on a person on the universal scene, especially in the field of security. Their choices are for the most part restricted to the nature of their commitments to worldwide associations and administrations. For example in the G5 summits only the superpowers are the major decision makers what they say goes so lesser countries have to go along with the decisions made. Each country in the world belongs to a global union and regional union and due to these there has been formulation of theories if international regimes that govern the relations of these countries. That is the reason why lesser countries are inferior to the NATO powers. In this global union the heads are superpowers of the world and in recent years other developed countries .e.g. the Dutch government.

NO PRODUCTION, IS THE NPT IN EMERGENCY?

The framework and foundation among customary ammunition control administrations, the Non-Reform Treaty has an emotional meltdown. The rule on which administration is constructed and its authenticity is progressively being addressed. An opinion piece in as of late compelling daily paper called it the "Settlement of Nuclear production", in an examination in light of the NPT's awful encounters with North Korea and Iran. The NPT is seen to be naturally inadequate by the way that it is really an arrangement of respect. While engineers pledge not to utilize an atomic vitality program to utilize atomic ammunition, the International Atomic Energy Agency (IAEA) has the ability to examine destinations that the agreeing nations have announced contain atomic substances In spite of the proceeding with endeavors to reinforce the consistence framework through the policies and rules, which permits the LAEA to lead challenges assessments on a presumed area, it is fundamental that notices of issues are subjective to the individual nations themselves and not on outside reviews. And, after it's all said and done, the nation's thought to be "agreeable" have the ability to do so. "Canada is focused on more exchanges on rocket protection with the United States," Global Security Newswire, 16 January 2004, www.nti.org; "MPS to vote on the Bloc movement finishing off with accommodation talks. The development (Bloc Quich ~ cois) was vanquished by 150-71. Canada's enthusiasm for NORAD can be viewed as a benefit and a risk, the last being motioned by Canadian Foreign and Security Policy (DFAIT) Minister James Wright when he cautioned that "NORAD could be marginalized if Canada does not take an interest in rocket trouble. " are shy of amassing an atomic gadget that successfully makes the atomic states. Likewise, the NPT was assaulted by two sides. Notwithstanding the issues with the signatories (Iraq in the mid-1990s, North Korea and Iran right now), it was tested by the accepted procurement of atomic status by India and Pakistan and, probably, Israel. At long last, there is the late advancements in the development of the significance of atomic weapons in military situations (other than the customary part as discouragement), and additionally its one-sided assertion on preventive assaults, as a deviation from the NPT. Feedback of the NPT administration depends on four fundamental focuses.

This initially, as expressed above, is the thing that the Wall Street Journal calls his Hon. our framework. This basically infers excessively trust in the nations' readiness to participate. Second, intentionally settled as a "biased" arrangement, the program has been progressively tested. The underlying condition of the providing atomic states (haves) and numerous non-atomic (non-private) expresses, whose preservation was observed to be honest to goodness and reasonable before 40 years when the NPT was arranged, dissolved. Likely there are most likely nine atomic weapons, four of which are nuclearized. Additionally, it is hard to contend that authorities fulfill dreams they have concerned with moving towards atomic demilitarization, as it ought to be. Truth be told, the development of atomic weapons is a long way from the genuine several key issues that are called "and labeled Tanya Ogilvie-White and John Simpson" NPT and its 2003PrepCom meeting, "I don't remark on expansion, "Iran is enrolled for the most stringent control of atomic offices", Financial Times of London (European version printed December 19, 2003), 13. Libya secret recognized that work the atomic program Of 9 December 2003, the choice to intentionally disassemble its offices has "helped" to some degree by the interference of a shipment of uranium advancement parts, with the goal that it was completely covered the Wall Street Journal on 31 December 2003. The following Libya's narrative revelation extend uncovered the presence of a "Wal-Mart" atomic material, which was driven by AQ Khan and Palestiniaianists in Iran, Libya and North Korea, of incredible worry for the IAEA. Saudi Arabia would likewise deliberately consider atomic operation Togo; perceiving how future Bunker destroyers, the thrashing of specialists' weapons and formal articulations of conceivable employments of a safeguard framework) in our arrangement, a few spectators consider additionally decoupling of non-expansion and atomic demobilization. Third, the central administer of the TNP administration - that atomic weapons are characteristically awful - disintegrates. The ramifications of their utility against AC is dangerous as in the last US NSS, are they "ordinary? Pen and shared danger of their utilization in Pakistan's local emergency for the 1998 Kashmir emergency and the talk of North Korea's virgin recommends an absence of hesitance to utilize. At long last, and eventually, more questions are anticipated onto another essential element of the TNP, since it doesn't imagine trades between rich individuals and does not comprehend the information of atomic innovation for serene non- military personnel purposes. Contrasted with the way that common atomic vitality is thought to be significantly more vital than it was for a long time the free legitimate business in double atomic utilize was addressed after obvious instances of misuse by trading and bringing in nations. "On February 11, 2004, President Bush particularly tended to this issue by proposing a modification of the TNP assentation.

He required the crevice to crumple, for example, Iran and North Korea to change atomic substances that can be utilized to manufacture pumps under the control of common atomic projects.

9 ARGUMENT FOR TERRORISM

MORAL YARDSTICK

In the period 1809-1880 Karl Heinzen formulated the first systematic justification of terrorism in two parts. The first essay was entitled "Murder" and was published on January first 1849 (Heinzen, 1978). A year later the essay went to the press after the communist manifesto during an uprising that was all over Europe between 1848 and 1849. Heinzen broached on the subject of murder fervidly saying it was wrong to kill another person, however a, despite stating a one of a kind advantage in issue, so he needs to protect this Privilege ... " he criticizes those who choose to defend the interest of humanity as a whole person should be able to defend him/herself against somebody who is trying to kill them. If one kills without hesitation or a conscience then they lack principles. Heinzen further argued, "Murder is evil and it's not wanted however if our opponents are not of similar thoughts, if one can legitimize a murder

RELIGIOUS TEST

In light of the above discussion it has been noted that Tamil Eelam liberation Tigers, a Marxist-Leninist Democratic Independence Group of Sri Lanka, have been the world pioneer in suicide psychological warfare before the rebellion in Iraq. Pope's data analysis (2005:210) also on suicide psychological warfare 1980-2003 found out that most of the attacks were due to religious reasons. Attacks motivated by religious reasons have more death tolls than those attacks committed for other reasons other than religion. They maintain that religion van single handedly instigate suicide attacks and other forms of warfare. We likewise bolster these propelled components of religion are utilized by both non-religious and religious people.

Religion helps these attackers to achieve their goals and for them to create an efficient and effective system for monitoring. The high association of religion and terror can be attributed to the media. Fear based oppressors, especially kamikaze, are regularly spoken of by the media as insane religious fanatics, miserable brains and detached with reality. In recent research a recent photo showing the kind of lives these terrorist lead is different from what is expected they are more educated and economically stable than the general public. Besides, poverty is not an indicator of participation in political life or bolster the savagery of fear mongering. What's more, there was no proof of psychopathology at a worldwide show of Muslim fear based oppressors. The pioneers of psychological militant associations are certain that enlisted people can't be depressed or suicidal. As a representative for Palestinian Islamic Jihad clarified, "To be a terrorist you must want to live" Just as suicide boomer's notes additionally have a great deal of expectation, else it is futile to kill. In the event that terrorist and suicide bombers when all is said in done and, specifically, are religious bigots not insane, at that point what is the connection between religion and psychological warfare? Different analysts have contended that psychological oppressors have political and non-religious objectives. Religion is not the main cause of the contention, but instead an instrument used by terrorist to achieve their objectives. In view of patterns, religious convictions, ceremonies, and foundations are quick components that encourage the execution consequences of another impossible way.

Here we take a look at four primary reasons why religion is a powerful component for radicals. A substantial example of suicide bombers (90%) assaults were gone for casualties of an alternate religion.

Spiritual and everlasting prizes. Religion is not just a Divine and good measurement of the morals fear monger exercises battling for prizes can reach. At that point Considering the reward aggressor stand to benefits, Erlenmeyer presumed that "the reward for these youngsters was the religious experience the same battle: In the sense, they were part of something greater than them notwithstanding that Awards of amazing quality, religion can likewise legitimately offer advantages the future life they would they be able to seldom coordinated in this world. 9/11 attack everyone thought they would "be in the most astounding of the skies we can help them to support their activities.

Religious myths and custom images. The most vital part of religion in psychological oppression can be yours joining components and sincerely suggestive activities. These are noteworthy myth and custom images which serve to propel separately and by and large unify the different people with common interest. All fear based oppressor groups confront the Commitment of the Group and individual sense of duty regarding common interest. Anthropologists believe that "the principal faith" components of Religion, at the end of the day, images, myths and customs, this sense of duty regarding the gathering superior to other social foundation. For religious psychological militants, Promotion through intense religious associations Symbols that "frequently" move towards involving religious contrast" And, obviously, a similar affliction Sacrifice their lives due to faith. Religion gives ceremonies and bot images H propel and praise these neighborhood legends,

In this way, it gives them a generally and the unattainable state that is endless. Pope takes note of that "Fear based oppressor associations generally developed" conciliatory myths, " Setting images and customs to mark an individual the aggressor's demise as a Contribution to the country"

Fear based opprcssion and transformative research on religion Scalable connected investigations. In addition to our apprehension these psychological militant elements give vital advantages from advanced Policies to battle psychological warfare. Shockingly, it is a major error among the numerous Social sciences credit Religious developmental examination on. For instance, Zuckerman contends that the current information is high in Secularism rates in many parts of the world due to improvements in Theories of Religion. Zuckerman wrongly compares evolution on belief and evolution of genes and this comparison is wrong because favors supernatural beliefs more which is wrong as many individual do not seem to be religious fanatics. Hypothesis of evolution favors genetic determinism.

Despite what might be expected, the hypothesis of evolution assumes that as changes in nature take place is it is fundamental for the articulation and versatile working of numerous attributes, including religious convictions. Without this commitment, hereditary inclination it stays pending. Such a gene for nature

The statement permits wide scope of versatile time to ensure ideal assignment of restricted resources. The improvement of religious convictions and behaviors are probably going to indicate Interactive and development process. In spite of the fact that, obviously, it cannot be the writing on development of advancement religion, we support intrigue read books. Religion can be better comprehended as a mind boggling characteristic has advanced by consolidating intellectual, passionate, behavioral and formative components. At the core of this area is four attributes of intermittent religion culture:

- The participation of society in a costly custom
- Faith in paranormal forces and nonsensical ideas
- The detachment of the consecrated and disrespect
- Adolescence as a basic period of life.

Religious transmission Beliefs and qualities

These attributes are from pre-human frameworks and ceremonies, from that point forward added to the capacity of individuals to overcome the biological difficulties still present. Advance collaboration correspondence and coordination of the connection amongst time and space.

These four components have Provide adaptive benefits and as a rule co-happen in "religion", however not all time. Subsequently, Western qualifications Enter and "lord" lay "Light "are frequently troublesome factions to recognize. For instance, use of Communal customs and starting finance rituals.

Popular terrorist groups, for example, LTTE it's practically definitive In Marxist-Leninist blubbery goals the distinction between the hundreds of years and what is religious. These gatherings are conferred religious components depicted above Adaptive accumulation and numerous adaptively focal points picked up by religion .If other rebel groups do not support the movement it is considered to be terrible. As a potential radical one does not disclose the places of shrouded schemers, mystery code Communication, and don't escape when to make a dangerous assault or suicide?

At first look, development Theories of religion are not promising. Religion is seen to fail questions on why there is terrorism. Next generation genes are preferred by natural selection additionally a radical needs to go out on a limb in his/her life is relinquished deliberately for his/her ideological beliefs. Such activities appear negating to the development goals. This confusion lies in the comprehension of religion.

As a propelled correspondence framework, it gives components that can advance the gathering's trust and Commitment to overcome Problems. Religion is used because of is its capacity to encourage collaboration and beat the issues of aggregate activity that people have confronted in evolution. The religious cost, specifically what is alluded to as the four "B" – religious convictions, Behavior (customs), unmistakable (natural product juice has religious articles of clothing) And Prohibitions (Taboos) - Serves the group dedication motions as dependable and legitimate. Just the individuals who are included in the gathering will be committed to devoting time, vitality and the open door expenses of religion and execution. At the end of the day, individuals pay for the chances of religious connection, through dedication and unwaveringness.

You can get a net benefit of the aggregate activity of achievement and the various conditions. Benefits are accessible to confide in reporting specialists. People all over the world are fascinated by terrorism and it is becoming expensive for society to cater it. Indeed, global terrorism has been done alongside the worldwide development of religious fundamentalism. By and large, alludes to fundamentalism in a religious belief system that incorporates composing the intervals and conventional religious esteems. Current fundamentalist inclinations, in any case, have set customary practices in question. For instance, the guidelines kashrut

In Jewish history, hypothesis recommends that flagging factors that can inspire either fundamentalist pattern to expand ritual prerequisites. Initial, an expansion in costs recording can be an immediate reaction to builds it is the apparent danger of disaffection religious gatherings; a sort of hazard with the quick change Media Technology, Expect a more extensive group of onlookers than what Grave mainstream esteems and culture. Furthermore, and a bit "conversely, the multicultural opening of USA genuine business, can likewise add to Fundamentalist propensities. While a multitude of individuals observe Lutheranism has not yet acknowledged the hostility

Fundamentalism in organizations where diverse gatherings tolerances are endured and furthermore encouraged, maintaining the union of the gathering requires It will expand its refinement with the point of maintaining its cost bans and identifications of past gathering. Along these lines, multiculturalism you can really begin moving towards fundament Talisman despite the fact that he rejects fervently the message of fundamentalism possess life Just the genuine way. Specifically, that one of the all-inclusive qualities of religious radicals are a solid dismissal of the West Multiculturalism. Third, flagging hypothesis gives costs as an asset flag has expanded raises rivalry. An exceedingly focused way Multicultural national states, higher costs Supported by religious fundamentalism can Compensated with monetary and political advantages Reachable in religious union and the association having a place with the gathering. Revealing Evolutionary Religion Theory accept a U-molded switched relationship among the expenses of religious action and participation in gatherings. Since the costly duty Requirements of the Group and are troublesome rather than ideal

Terrorist groups have negative impacts on society. Most gatherings want to force ideals, religious terrorists, obviously, utilize religiously costly and arduous reporting commitments for affirmation Saved, bringing about salvation GH levels in the gathering.

Associates and dedication to Leadership; and they have an arrangement of and start customs of the session Emphasizing the level of a man's participation in the Community "(2005: 8) Tingling, among a lot of fear monger's performed these ceremonies they additionally incorporated a video recording before an attack. These videos are not only for immortalizing suicide fear based oppression but for its motivation among the supporters; they likewise make certain agreements. Disappointment subsequent to announcing it, is reporting the goals it would convert into, be mental, social, and presumably other worldly expenses. The advancement of hypothesis estimates that fleeting expenses are a flag show to gain personal benefits.

This makes a test for understanding suicide Terrorism announcing theory in a perspective point of view why people are and, obviously, not. Like suicide terrorism is maybe exclusively versatile reaction. It appears like three other contender's general comments. To start with, while the individual is confronting a definitive yield, self-destructive fear based oppression is probably going to profit Pope's Group Analysis (2003, 2005) among the gatherings that conferred suicide bombers seem to achieve their goals. With this knowledge suicide attacks can give a promising case of solid specific weight the operation of fear based operations.

What do parents stand to gain?

Groups of Palestinian *kamikaze* get money incentives (up to$ 10 000) after the demise of their sons and daughters. Notwithstanding, the arrangement of wrecking Israel's suicide bombarding homes appear to remunerate these backhanded picks up and be solid Disincentive to give up for your family. According to Krueger and Malenkov (2002)

They observe that the Hezbollah suicide bombers have advanced level of education beyond expectation, **Azzam** (2005) contends Suicide terrorist can attack future eras of most noticeably awful relatives (they emphasize on the importance of education for future suicide bombers). Nonetheless, this puts a collective activity issue and it appears that the situation would be better. Activists and saints let another person do the speculation (for instance, relinquish their lives for who and what is to come). They believe that they will receive rewards in the other world but only a third of the possibility of receiving these rewards are known by the terrorist it is relevant during the time of execution of religious action.

Solis (2003) and **Bulbulia** (2004) were of the view that benefits in their models, including gain/benefit later. They have found that, paying little heed to the effect of aging can be awesome.. Additionally, we don't speculate just saints who are hoping to gather divine prizes, however likewise incorporate notoriety the advantages that you hope to get as a saint in their counts. Despite the fact that obviously, they are not around to exploit their new status. In the event that existence in the wake of death awards and stresses after death. Reputation is inspiring suicide bombers, because they want to be seen as saints such convictions may be deficient, if their parents do not consider saints to be important. Belief in extraordinary beings and nonsensical ideas is the second element of promoting religious complex (**Bering** 2005: 418). Likewise, the collection of Research demonstrates that people have faith in Omniscient heavenly social specialists. Decline shows up in early adolescence and adulthood. Intercultural Studies with kids in the vicinity of 3 and 12 years of age that youthful kids have an "instinctive belief in a higher power" It separates the omniscience social heavenly specialist's error prone information Natural social on-screen character what's more, now found in an ethical system. Distinctive improvements the analysts underlined the part Supernatural discipline plays in advancement Moral conduct characterized by the group, and the specific Partial gathering collaboration.

The current trial encounter the proof shows that "even unpretentious of the oblivious presentation to religious recognizable proof EAS can essentially decrease Fear monger convictions about eternal life. The accomplishment of progress can be accomplished by exposing kids and young people with elective models of convictions before they are presented to future prizes Promise by fear based oppressors.

The partition of the consecrated and debase Separate the hallowed and the dishonor and the enthusiastic energy of sacrosanct images they are fundamental to seeing how psychological militants utilize religion for advantage. Religious ritual generally used to characterize the sacrosanct and Layman Stand (**Durkheim**, 1995; **Eliade** 1959). A study in 1999 showed that the custom is not exclusively to distinguish what is sacrosanct consecrated clean water is not simply water. It was observed to be holy by people or this water has been exhibited in a normal way in every one of the qualities. That is, fairly, water changes over through the custom. For individuals who have taken an interest in SANC custom. Most vital practices, the importance of the holy person and disrespect water is altogether different. Furthermore, passionate importance what is the premise of the holy S "confidence" and that is the custom support contribute the sacrosanct with sensations. Wide research shows that Emotions are modifications that measure the choices and the activities seen to be advanced/new (**Damasio**1994). The capacity to accumulate religious ceremonies have positive and negative enthusiastic responses that give the substrate to participate and have inspired training.

Military images of the motivation procedure and CLA Social and relevant molding, objects, Places of religious convictions and customs are intrusive with passionate importance. The utilization of Community of ritual to contribute past Neutral and impartial boosts makes a passionate sense. Therefore, it shares typical individual choices which persuade conduct. Note that the consecrated might be the most they resemble physical space. In each nation, suicide fear mongering is something that has to be fought and eradicated; a possessing power must be expelled from the nation. These contentions are constantly open.

On the off chance that the breaking points can be equivocal and the story can be scrutinized, the nation is inconvenient. Be that as it may, for recollections, implications and feelings. "Religious customs that help recollections, among others, advance these feelings Religious psychological oppressors are not in view of reasonable political contentions for open endorsement; they utilize hallowed images infused with an enthusiastic energy to enroll supporters for their motivation in the wake of acquiring the aggregate solidarity of enlisted people.

Furthermore, it can enhance the negative impacts assign ceremonies. Neuropsychological research on negative specimen are both fortifying more paramount and spurring power than positive boosts (**Cacioppoe**t al.2002). After this "negative cynicism" Deny religion perceived items more dependable systems for the enthusiastic still millions of euros for subordination of Individuals promptly interested in the goals of the agreeable gathering. Research customs Terrorist cells they utilize are uncommon, however a conspicuous privation, as long fasts are normal. Immaturity is a basic period of life and the transmission of brain science .Beliefs and teenage rituals standout amongst the most vital elements of religions between various societies. Through stride ceremonies age starts to realize what things are they consecrated. Customs, measure was intentionally dedicated to oblivious feeling and cognizant subjective process mechanisms. The subjective example accomplished by these customs prompts the blessing of these images, spots, articles and convictions. Since these images are profoundly connected with feelings, rituals created have rousing power. At the point when these customs are both group of experienced individuals double, the accompanying service: A mix of feelings evoked a particular subjective plan makes a social culture a quality as far as inspiration and conviction.

Differential brain development models in life create sensitive circumstances for a few sorts of learning. Just as the progressions that happen in the cerebrum of adolescents. Generally, the delicate improvement with respect to the time of social, militants and saints, these emotional and typical jolts are the extremely sort of boosts.

Youth is likewise described by a unrivaled passionate response, and move cerebrum compensate circuits. Accordingly, a basic period for learning approved Symbolic Emotional System (Ems) and the mixture of these frameworks of reward circuits in the mind. People at puberty are not afraid of taking risks with this framework. Therefore, it is not astounding what most fear based oppressors begin with. Activist for life in youthfulness proposes that "commonplace improvement Terrorist sensitivities could take after a circular segment: Adolescents are buddies in their arrangements, orientation and open to teaching. Positions solidify later in youth ... [and] numerous retirees "The psychological oppressors" uncover a state of mind of development. Obviously, when the individuals who have been brought up in a culture of the affliction achieved youthfulness they will yield even without ice Irregularity.

Sprout takes note of that at six years old Palestinian youngsters the young ladies say they need to develop and progress toward becoming Isitshhadis (Martyrs). "At age 12, they have to completely take an interest in acknowledging what suffering means. Like the older folks, individuals from the al-Qassim Palestinian gathering, he said "It's anything but difficult to clear the roads for kids. They need to do a suffering operation. In any case, the profile of the individuals who truth be told, making a suicide assaults might be marginally bigger reports a progression of 18- 38 among the Palestinians), recommending the energy Young individuals must be adjusted with the arrangement and the advancement of trust to complete such a mission. Lyly fear mongering, further ore, the advancement of religion leverage developmental approach we offer here is that setting up the center of adaptive religion encourages collaboration.

In conclusion terrorism has most disadvantages and measures and should be put in place to deal with it. Research has to be done extensively on terrorism to discover its root and the best way to avoid or even eradicate it. The religious belief passed on to children are keys in determining who they will be because as we have seen religion is an important tool being used by terrorist to advance their goals as it tends to make the participants believe that their attacks are for a higher being who will reward their good work. It is therefore important for parents to be careful with how they teach their children various beliefs because they cannot tell if their own children will kill them one day as they harm other families.

One suggestions that has been made to eradicate terrorism is reducing inter-country conflicts –conflicts between countries are seen to encourage terrorism as people are patriotic they won't stand to see their country being destroyed. They will rise up to defend their country and in this way terrorist groups are created. Another suggestion is to reduce recruitments by terrorist groups to reduce the manpower of the groups hence, causing them to fail.

CONCLUSION

Religions are not necessarily linked to terrorism motivated attacks, however religion based attacks are in full swing and therefore very dangerous. Evolutionary approaches can fill important gaps because there is an overlap between the choice of evolution and rational approaches to terror.

It is not clarified by sound decision overwhelming worldview. The extent of the stretched out developmental rationale to the investigation of history, writing, craftsmanship and religion as of late, the usage of the thoughts of advancement has come to.

10 BRIEF HISTORIES OF TERRORIST GROUPS AND BIOGRAPHIES OF LEADERS OF GLOBAL TERRORIST GROUPS

INTRODUCTION

It has been claimed that terrorists have psychological problems which motivate their actions. However, research of terrorist profiles, in general, says that terrorists do not show exceptional individual psychological characteristics. The analysis provides a conclusion that bin Laden shows archaic narcissism and paranoia. Similarly, after having administered 90 psychological tests and 57 semi-structured interviews with Israeli terrorists and Palestinians, and compared to the control groups, Gottschalk and Gottschalk reported that terrorists were more than authoritarianism size controls and hate pathological (LaFree and Ackerman 2009).

Trauma, injustice and alienation

While it may be a unique set of personality traits common to all (or almost) the terrorists that would allow authorities to reliably distinguish between terrorism and the non - terrorist

Less of certain experiences, attitudes and behaviors can be over-represented among terrorists,

Compared to its appearance in the general population, a major trauma, especially linked to the suffering, it showed a significant precipitating behavior in a combatant suicide attacks.

State and reward

Terrorists are created by adverse circumstances; Terrorism researchers discussed a number of professional self - satisfaction or participating in terrorist acts, including the style of emotional life fighting a sense of power through violence and an increase in personal status those whose actions are supported by their community, or at least their fellow terrorists. For example, the examination of the social history of men 40 Nazi two case studies, Hamm concludes that their problems have sought fame in their sub - culture and so strong was the unquenchable need to be famous that it prevailed.

The media and its responsibility

The noteworthy literature and increasingly in the media and its tasks in crime is transmitted easily terrorism. From comics nineteenth-century anarchists in newspapers (and the pump stopped shaving), the media encourages September the belief that political violence Opposition authority was both criminal and Folle.Gli killers are widely described as isolated criminal acts whose disabilities are attributable to individual diseases, the consequences of life without love and frustrated ambitious (see Turk, 2002a). Suicide is represented in the same way as acts manifestly irrational or badly driven by despair or fanaticism. (Turk, 2004)

THE TERRORIST LEADER

Osama Bin Laden

Osama Ben Laden was born on March 10, 1957 in Riyadh, Saudi Arabia, was one of the best known of the militants and the world's most dangerous Muslim leader. (**Stevenson,** 2011) The father s death 'in a helicopter crash in 1967when Osama was 9 or 10 years old. (**Aboul-Enein** 2006) in1979, he graduated from King Abdul Aziz University in Jeddah. Here, he was **1979-1982** He was influenced by Sheikh Abdullah Azzam an Islamic religious footballer Palestinian. He took university courses. The Khalifa brochure is just on the mark of Osama Ben Laden influenced by Azzam. Palestinian militant clan established the Maktab al-Khidmat that (service offices for the *jihadist [*Arab]) *mujahideen* in Peshawar, Pakistan, which entonnerait tens of thousands of Arab volunteers to fight the *jihad* against the Soviets in Afghanistan.

1982 – Osama was among the first in Afghanistan to fight the Soviets directly. He also provided for thc financing and construction products and the 'expertise to Azzam group of other factions of the Afghan *mujahideen.* This includes a group of engineers built by Ben Laden.

1984 - Osama adopted Arab Al-Bait Afghanistan Ansar (House helper) as «aid» refers to those who helped the Prophet Muhammad in early Islam. This organization completed the Azzam group, while Ben Laden had no experience of the old Maktab al-Azzam Khadamat organization. Therefore, the Bin Laden organization has focused on the tactical formation and treatment of the Arabs who wanted to fight the Soviets. Maktab al-Khadamat focused on recruitment and collections. It is important to understand that when Azzam died, bin Laden became the leader of the two organizations, which had become the center of Al Qaeda. Improved training techniques of Al-Ansar bait to acclimate the Arabs in the fight against the Soviets and their Afghan allies in an unconventional way. Graduates have the reputation of being the impact forces of jealousy and most of these Arab volunteers Abdul Rasul Sayyaf and Gulbuddin went to Hekmetyar.

1986 - In this year, Bin Laden had expanded its activities to include six military training camps on the move to escape the ' Soviet military attack. In this period he had developed a more formal method to allocate the talent of Al Qaeda, most of the Arab fighters were high school and university students, with doctors, engineers and Arabic retired military officers Those with combat experience at thc scrvice of the Arab armies would be used as trainers and commanders in the field. The former chief operating officer of Al Qaeda (third command after Ben Laden and Zawahiri) until his death in 2001 was Mohammed Atef, a colonel who withdrew from the Egyptian police. Another member of Al - Qaeda in

Iran and considered an operational planner Saif al-Adel was a former Egyptian army. Since Egypt has applied a compulsory scheme for all men, it is reasonable to suppose that members of Al - Qaeda Egyptian have at least three or four years of basic military training. In late 1986, he saw the battle of Jaji where bin Laden and an Arab contingent formed in the Al-Ansar Bayt withstood several attacks by Soviet Spetsnaz (Special Forces). The assault took sever.al weeks, and Arab jihadists made Small Mountain and a network of tunnels and caves used to escape and surprised Soviet troops.

1986-1989 - These years were considered top Arab jihadi movement in Afghanistan the book covers not only the battle of *Jaji,* but also says the Arab jihadist contingent participating in five battles, clashes and ambushes tens of thousands. These 36 months have been the best time to funnel recruits, weapons and funds from the Middle - Middle of Afghanistan.

Osama strategic thinking has changed over time; his hatred for the United States was renewed by the sight of the perception that the Saudi royal family depended on America for its security against Saddam Hussein. Bin Laden was the overall evaluation of strategic enemy for the Saudis face of the Republican Guard divisions of Saddam Hussein. Arab Mujahedeen had invited an irregular war in Iraq would bring a whirlwind mainly Al Saoud, Arab governments knew they could not control. In 1996, the Declaration of Ben Laden and new movement was Al-Jihad Al-Jazeera Lee rain Kufar Ikhraj Al-Arab (jihad to expel the infidels from the Arabian Peninsula). From 1996 to 1998, the brochure explains how Bin Laden, the Taliban and the Egyptian Islamic Jihad considered the initial report of 1996, adding that she had the power of a desktop short comedy (fatwa). While the debate was going on, Ben Laden has taken several strategic decisions as the leader of Al Qaeda:

* His alliance with the Taliban had become strong that it broke its neutrality agreement between the various Afghan warlords. This increases frustration in his efforts to unite the Afghan tribes in peace. Bin Laden provided suicide forces to collide Arab support for Taliban factions.

* Designed a *fatwa* sanctioning the assassination of Ahmed Shah Massoud Taliban enemies.

As the Taliban have evolved as the dominant force in Afghanistan in 1998, bin Laden has won the support of 40 Pakistanis and Afghan religious endorse his statement in 1996 to eliminate the infidels (USA) in the Arabian Peninsula. The Egyptian Islamic Jihad composed of people were the strategic direction of Al Qaeda, and represented by Ayman al Zawahiri, and jihadist affiliations in Kashmir urged bin Laden to extend the fatwa included lever Americans aged kill anywhere at any time the Jews. These discussions led to the declaration of Bin Laden in 1996, becoming the famous Declaration of the global movement of Islam in February 1998 for the murder of the Crusaders and Jews. It is important to realize that the advertising did not make Mullah Omar the Taliban leader happy and more irritated by the bombings of embassies in Kenya and Tanzania in August 1998.Mais Mullah Omar has had to balance that with Ben helpful to the cause Laden, the Taliban. Meanwhile, the book explains how jihadist fanatics 50 Arabs resisted a little 'Ahmed Shah Massoud defended section Kaboul. The Taliban were overwhelmed and committed to the fight against Shiites and Uzbeks in and around Bamiyan. North of Kabul, has become an opportunity for the forces of Ahmed Shah Massoud to use and you should see the focus barehanded Arab Capital jihadist Ben Laden in 1998, as well as financing and intermarriage have made Ben Laden Mullah Omar urged symbiotic relationship with unbreakable. It 'was after the battle of Kabul in 1998 between the Arab contingent of Ben Laden and Ahmed Shah Massoud, the two became implacable enemies. Two days before the September 11, 2001, agents of Ben Laden posing as journalists with a camera crew left a bomb killed Ahmed Shah Massoud. We do not know how many times Ben Laden attempted to assassinate the "Lion of Panjshir" (a name of Massoud won their tactical skills against the Soviets) and vice versa.

Personal Ben Laden

Osama Ben Laden was a devout Muslim and practitioner. He shares food, clothing and shelter with his men and their children. Osama spent with their families. Despite the flattering image, Ben Laden was not decisive and preferred to take important decisions. This interpretation is questionable since these strategic decisions 11/09 and he declared war in Afghanistan which has been occupied by Ben Laden with little debate and discussion. While living in Saudi Arabia would be – there was one day a week with family and sometimes extended it because of Jeddah, a farm their family owned. Ben Laden's three women have advanced degrees, a doctorate. Finally, the booklet talks about Ben Laden's health, it says here is with a net worth of Ben Laden. The first, freezing was excellent, and its affinity for honey to cure diseases. And "economically, he had two great financial successes after Saudi Arabia revoked his citizenship in 1991 and the second is the government of Sudan not Tahedi projects like highway from Khartoum to Port Sudan was made -. Bin Laden was dependent on contributions to keep him and their causes.

Although the killing or capture of bin Laden, as the priority was seen as the US mission in Afghanistan, he managed to evade capture. Despite occasional sightings or delays of unhealthy items or where Ben Laden remains was unknown. It was said that living in the mountains of Pakistan may be gold in Iran. In July 2009, Bin Laden announced several postponements and then came the news that he died in a missile strike in Pakistan. Meanwhile, bin Laden issued a series of audio tapes which included global political events and comments have continued to embrace the ideals Islamists of Al Qaeda. The US government continued to offer a reward of $ 25 million for information on Bin Laden.

On 1 May 2011, President Barack Obama reported that bin Laden was killed by US forces in Pakistan. Explanation of President Obama of the American government has a potential advantage over the position of Ben Laden in August 2010. When the following intelligence work has confirmed the presence of Bin Laden in a compound in Abbottabad, Obama ordered a small military detachment and ended the international manhunt.

The news of Bin Laden's death was reported around the world. In the United States, groups of people gathered on the web site of the White House and the shape of the World Trade Center to celebrate the occasion and remember the victims of the terrorist attacks. Meanwhile, Ben Laden in fact was living in a crowded Pakistani well-developed district near a military base in Pakistan. He spent a decade as a fugitive. However, the death of Bin Laden was welcomed by the President of Pakistan, Asif Zardari, and President Obama praised the cooperation of Pakistani intelligence force in efforts to locate bin Laden. (Stevenson, 2011)

He said in an exclusive interview with Hamid Mir, director Ausaf, Alba and Ausaf in a secret place near Kabul. The interview with a journalist was the first that Osama had done after the September

11 attacks in New York and Washington. He said that he is opposing the member - states government, not the people in the country. He was trying to reach the goals and objectives of Prophet Muhammad (peace be upon him).

His mission was to ensure that the word of God had spread. He enjoyed killing people. There are the same targeted murder, destruction and committing all manners of atrocities. He is on the defensive side of *Jihad* because he wants to defend his people and his land.

He emphasized that if they do not get the security, then the Americans do not get any security. He said that even an American child can understand this simple formula. Live formula and let him live.

He claimed that the reason for the *Jiha*d was to protect their territory. When they are not in charge of their territory, they have nothing else but to launch the *Jihad*. When asked to confirm whether he was making attempts to procure chemical and nuclear weapons, he said that if America used chemical or nuclear weapons against them, they would react the same way. He however didn't reveal the source of his weapons.

When asked if he could find a way to stop the war, he said that he didn't start it. The proposition should have been made to those who started it. Their only role in the war was to defend themselves.

He went ahead to justify America's attacks against them. The US had no proof against them. They were acting on a supposition and it's unfair to begin launching attacks based on these assumptions.

He termed that as a campaign declared by the then president of USA George W. Bush but not a change of wisdom He lamented over the demise of Afghan brethren who fell to improve Pakistan's economy. He warned that the perpetrators would be punished for Pakistan, by the people and God.

In present days, a war of Islamic history that is great is fought in Afghanistan. All the great powers were united against Muslims. It is "Sawab" to be involved in this war.

It was rumored at some point that his kidneys had failed, but he dismissed the rumor .He also denied the allegation of having a daughter with Mullah Omar. He however admitted that they had a spiritual relationship. He emphasized that all his wives are Arabs and likewise all his daughters are married to Mujahideen Arabs. (**Mir**, 2001)

Mohamed Atta

Abdeen Mohamed Atta lived 1978-1990 (**Power and Dickey**, 2002) His family and friends lived in Egypt and they described him as a young shy and unassuming that had struggled to make his mark. They say they were subjected to a change of the difficult personality to be the fear based operator who took care September 11 the Nile Delta had a city called Kafr El Sheikh and he was born there, Atta's father was a lawyer. As a child, he fancied chess, and he did not like violent games. He was young and skinny -. Just 5 feet 7 inches and was very thin. (The father called him "Bolbol," the Arabic slang for a small songbird.) His two sisters seemed to overshadow Attat, because they had become a teacher and a medical zoologist. Atta went to Cairo University and graduated with a degree in engineering and architecture was an average student according to his colleagues..

Atta made some friends in school, but he was a lonely. His friends did not see him pray and remember his strong words for Islamic terrorists "- irresponsible people without brains."

That's why many of his fellow Egyptians classmates could not affirm his guilt in interviews over time. "I could never imagine a map threaten people, kill people," said Ahmed Khalifa, 33, his best friend at Cairo University. "He would be scared to death. He was not a leader. He had his own opinion, and wasl modest. His emotions remained stable, and had not been influenced or affected. Mohamed was loved because he never offended or annoyed everyone "Ismail said." It was great roots."

However he had some weird behavior that could be interpreted as some worrying trends. Atta could be exercised by the defects of the world, large and small. He spoke impulsively against injustice. He was so sensitive that it could become an emotional dead insect. "Pure E '," said Khaled Kattan, another partner. "If he thought I said or did something wrong, I would tell everyone."

The father of Atta could be very serious, according to friends. In the aftermath of the 11 September, Mohammed El Amir was interviewed, denied the fact that Atta was involved in the attacks. "E '" moderate in his adherence to his faith and his mother as I do, "Amir said. But politics suggests that Atta El Amir learned a few things on his father's world. In a press conference last week, Amir raged accusing Israel and the US "the cause of terrorism. " Cairo is one of the most populated cities in the world in 90s, Atta felt strong pressure on the Egyptian bourgeoisie will not slip on the social rank. Khalifa said his friend Atta became frustrated because he was not able to achieve his academic ambitions in his homeland. So, in the fall of 1992, Atta enrolled at the Technical University of Hamburg-Harburg, in a quiet area of Germany. He was hoping to get a degree and intended to return to Egypt. In 1993. He often traveled with his partner Volker Hauth. They studied together in the coming years. . "I knew Muhammad as a man seeking justice," Hauth told the Los Angeles Times. "I was offended by this branch; the world was wrong."

In the mid-90s, Atta began to skip school for long periods of times. He will tell his friend that he was in Aleppo, Syria, to work on his thesis. (The conflict between Islam and modernity are explored and reflected in the planning of the city). When completed in August of 1999 he had scored high marks. Atta was absenting from work for a consulting firm in Hamburg in 1995. But he also criticized Western influence - especially the rising skyscrapers rising - Arab cities.

Since mid-1997 to October 1998, it looked like Atta had vanished from Hamburg. He told his supervisor that he had left due to family reasons, but clearly he had undergone significant changes during this period. He went back to school with a beard liked a fundamentalist. It had been more serious At the end of 1995Hauth, who left the university and had lost touch with Atta, the observer said in London on his friend laughed at jokes about Arab dictators. But Chrilla Wendt, who saw Atta after his return, said he did not remember his smile.

Atta grew more pessimistic about their prospects. His old friend Khalifa met him on the street one day in Cairo in 1999. He found Atta not depressed and had career backup or a family home. Atta disclosed+ he had made some German friends. "I think he felt that he had studied all these years," said Khalifa. "When I said goodbye, I was sad."

The German authorities now estimated that at some point this year, he began playing based on various people linked to terrorism. Focus on their relation with a Syrian businessman, Mamoun Darkazanli, who has power over a German bank account in the name of a man regarded as the Osama bin Laden CFO. Darkazanli has denied any connection with terrorists last week.

When Atta went out of the public view, he had to publicly spread the Koran's message. In early 1999, the university authorities had found a group of Islamic students. (The researchers believed that they have finally met the hijackers Marwan al-Shehhi and Ziad Samir Jarrah in the group). 40 participants gathered to pray every day. Moderate individual from the outskirts of Cairo became devout, surrounded by fellow spirit.

During the year end 1999, Atta, al-Shehhi and Jarrah reported their passports stolen, possibly to erase all traces of path in Afghanistan. In a few weeks, Atta and Al-Shehhi went to the US for a visit. During this visit, Atta may have been working on plan to attack the USA. Sometimes in the spring of 2000, Atta - is now a cartoon version of a Tommy Hilfiger American Hairless Cologne and heavy - in an office of the Ministry of Agriculture in Miami, Florida, and called on the purchase aircraft loans fumigator's office. It does not offer this type of loan, and walked away from him.

Atta briefly returned to Europe, but came June 3, 2000 in Newark, New Jersey, Prague, with a tourist visa for six months. Within a month, Atta and Al-Shehhi applied for training in flight at Huffman Aviation International in Venice, Florida. When the two men were moving in a small pink house near Nokomis, rental agent brought candy. House in Venice, Dru Voss said that if Al-Shehhi was a good person, Atta was an ice cube that has never looked into the eyes.

Atta and Al-Shehhi were curious students. They paid together about $ 40,000 for Huffman for training for four months. Rudi Dekkers Huffman's owner disliked Atta, the smaller man immediately. Dekkers said Atta disclosed he had once lived in Germany. Dekkers then started in German, but Atta simply refused. Ni Atta, al-Shehhi had socialized with another 15 to 20 students.

Atta's tourist visa expired on December 3, 2000, but it was not noticed by anyone (a number of shortcomings in procedures in immigration that helped the hijackers). On 21 December, Atta and Al-Shehhi received their pilot license. After a week had passed, they were trained for three hours each in the simulator Boeing 727 Cementer Inc. Oarlock outside of Miami. At that time, the two men, who called themselves cousins, all had recorded about 300 flight hours. They were starters in flying aircrafts, but they had enough knowledge to operate an aircraft in flight.

During that period, Atta and other terrorists buy global positioning devices called GPS-3 Name Tropic-Aero, an air space magazine in Fort Lauderdale, Florida. These units of $ 475, the size of the boy's suit, are used by pilots to navigate. Jerry told Carbone, president of the Tropic-Aero "It 'so easy to use, you and your wife would be able to find your way around a 767 Sometimes it is sad when [the kidnappers] anything can happen using K Mart".

In January that year, Atta boarded a plane from Miami to Madrid. We do not know what it was, and when he flew back to Miami International Airport on January 10, he was accepted into the states and the expiry of his visa. The list is not disturbed by the flight or carrier, but sailed through immigration. Next month, in Flight school, Al-Shehhi and Atta rented a single-engine Piper Warrior Gwinnett County, Ga. Like many other drivers, who have been honing their skills Atta asked for clean towels - this period in Belle Glade, Florida, and a few men and himself, inquired on how much fuel and chemicals Yellow Air Tractor 502 can carry. On the 26 day of April, the deputy Josh Strambaugh Broward County pulled over Atta for a traffic offence. Atta had not carried his license and so he received a subpoena. He did not attend the hearing, and 4 June, an arrest warrant was issued against him. However, at that time it was very late, because Atta and his followers moved after every two months, from a rented house to another. The final stages have been coming his way, he had become very cautious. They followed and seem to have frequented a mosque. Only from time to time someone noticed. An observer by the name Jim Woolard, who owns World Gym in Delray Beach, Fla., He remembers Attat as "tracks" on the weight machines (maybe one of the reasons that people have difficulty recognizing the new solid images of Atta released Sept. 11).

On the 29th day of June, Atta went to Las Vegas, and he stayed at an in expensive motel. While there, the investigators told the Press, he had been in meetings with other hijackers, Salem Alhazmi and Hani Hanjour. Friends Hamburg al-Shehhi and Jarrah were present, which suggested that planning was taking place. Four out of the five hijackers were on different flights on 11 September and the assumption was that the different leaders of the four hijacked airplanes had to settle final details.

Once again Atta went to Madrid on the 9th day of July and spent 10 days in Spain 1250 miles by car. But in that week six men were arrested on a suspicion that they are affiliated with a group being financed by bin laden. Investigators are trying to look into the ways in which Atta met with them.

Atta returned to the US via business visa. Sources said that in the 10 days before the September 11, Atta received at least two electronic money transfers from a man whom investigators linked to bin Laden. The aim of these days is not all businesses. On September 7, Atta, al-Shehhi and another individual met Shuckum at Oyster Bar and Grill in Hollywood, Florida. Among the three Atta was the only non-drinker of alcohol. Gold '97 T who played for 3 1/2 hours - instead, cranberry juice overnight, pinball drank fresh fuel.

When he died in the flames and had its image circulating in the world, his friends in Egypt were surprised. They looked back at the pictures, trying to find the boy they once knew, "To fly a plane, what a joke! Mohamed could barely ride a bike," said Abul Enein Osama partners. "Muhammad could not have done," Ibrahim Salah Colegiado, 33, an engineer who knew him at Cairo University.

Power goal. How can you change so much? Experts say that Muslims in the number of years of increasingly extremist groups in the world have attracted recruits who grew up comfortably. In most cases terrorists are educated and travel but it does not mean that you can reach the organization, said Hala Mostafa, an authority militant groups were in al-Ahram Center for Political and Strategic Studies in Cairo. "Terrorists must be of primitive illiterate gold? It does not work."

That still does not explain what happened to Mohamed Atta. "This whole program to find their prey to kill," a song of the letter found in Atta's luggage is read. While he never met his sword, Atta is known.

Hamburg years

During his time in graduate school, Atta is secretive and rigid in their faith.

The last months

He was charting secretly and made frequent trips.

19 suspects

Many had aliases, and some of their identity can still be wrong. Noting that last week the FBI released the final list, men also believed to be kidnappers. The Office expects drawings help find potential customers

flight 93

Newark infiltrates; It crashed in Pennsylvania

Ziad Samir Jarrah

Missing in Germany on 11 September by the sticky Turkish girl, a medical student

Saeed Alghamdi

The FBI lists seven aliases that run under unknown nationality.

Ahmed Ibrahim A. Al Haznawi

Only 21 years old, if your birth time is real. It may be one, according to FBI Arabia.

Ahmed al-Nami

Ali Ahmed al-Nami uses an alias and Ahmed al-Nawi; Delray Beach, apparently remained in Florida.

flight 77

Party Dulles to Los Angeles; the Pentagon was hit at 09:40

Hani Hanjour

It was in Arizona for training flight in May 1996. He calls himself Hani Saleh, sometimes.

Khalid Almihdhar

It is now believed that a photo published earlier was to be someone else

Majed Moqed

had a driver's license guida Virginia Guide (date of birth: June 18, 1977), but probably never lived in the state

Nawaf Alhazmi

It is thought to be a Saudi citizen, I seem to have spent time in San Diego and New Jersey

Salem Alhazmi

It is also believed that Saudi Arabia; however it is not clear if he is related to Nawaf

American Airlines Flight 11

Boston Party in Los Angeles; it affects the North Tower at 08:45

Mohamed Atta

The FBI lists seven aliases for him, Atta Mohammad Mehan including Amir

Satam MA Al Suqami

Saudi Maybe, but his last known address is in the United Arab Emirates

Waleed M. Alshehri

He used seven different dates of birth, 13 September 1974-5 November 1979

Wail M. Alshehri

He and his brother Walid reported missing two games for kid's pictures of a Saudi family

Abdulaziz Alomari

An Arabia with the same name and date of birth says his passport was stolen in Denver

United Airlines Flight 175

Boston Party in Los Angeles; He hit the South Tower at 9:06

Marwan al-Shehhi

mate Atta and possibly cousin. Only 23, if the date of birth is correct

Ahmed Alghamdi

You may have lived in Pensacola, Fla., Until August One of the four hijackers who had a Virginia license

Fayez Rashid Ahmed Hassan Al Qadi Banihammad

Messi sale by the FBI as one Ahmed Fayez

Mohand Alshehri

The FBI has published two photos; the other is shaved, with long hair and a face a bit 'fuller

Hamza Alghamdi

A second photo shows a chubby face smiling without a mustache. I went to Delray Beach Final

E 'was found a five-page letter written by hand luggage Atta and another hijacker, car rental, and through the US remains 93. Excerpts, translated into Arabic:

"Purify your heart and forget what is called life, playing time is gone and it's time for the truth ... God fulfills their sins, and be sure it will be right at that moment, and we'll get to the final and greater reward.

"Check handbags, clothing, knives, tools, identity card, passport, any documents. Make sure all weapons before departure. Let each find his weapon down the dam.

"As soon as you put your feet before entering [the plan] start praying and realize that this is a battle for the love of God, and when you sit in place these prayers tell us mentioned above. When the plane begins to move, then you fly to God and blessing the journey. "(**Cloud et al**., 2001)

Timothy McVeigh

Timothy McVeigh**,** full name was Timothy James McVeigh was born on 23 April 23, 1968, Pendleton, New York, United States. He died on June 11, 2001, Terre Haute, Ind., The American activist who bombed Oklahoma City on 19th April, 1995. 168 people were killed in the bomb. It was the biggest attack by terrorist in the United States before September 11, 2001.

He was from a working class family and a middle child among his siblings. They lived in rural upstate New York, and he was interested in ammunitions from the time he was young. He finished high school in

June 1986 and graduated in the same year. Some of his time was spent at a local business school. The other part of his time he spent reading *The Turner Diaries* (1978), that contained writings against the government and neo-Nazi William traces of writing. The book, had details of the truck bomb in Washington, DC, office of the Federal Bureau of Investigation (FBI), McVeigh fear fueled the repeal of the conspiracy of the Second Amendment of the US Constitution Government That guarantees the right to "have and keep arms. " In 1988, he signed up to be in the army and became a good soldier and earned a bronze star for his bravery in the gulf war (1990-1991). At the end of 1991 he left the army.

McVeigh goes back home, and finds it difficult to get a stable job. He meets Terry Nichols and Michael Fortier, pals from his time in the army, where ammunition are sold at fairs in the United States. In 1993 March, he went to Waco, Texas, to watch the FBI during the siege of the Branch Davidian compound. He termed the actions of the US government illegal and in that period McVeigh, Nichols and Fortier contacted militia groups and individuals in the Midwest. From September 1994, McVeigh started planning the attack on the Alfred P. Murrah Federal Building in Oklahoma City. The next six months he was involved in planning the attack with his two friends.. The attack required a number of tons of ammonium nitrate fertilizer, which, when combined with oil, the pump provides the explosive power. During the second anniversary of the Branch Davidian, on April19, 1995, deadly fire ended the siege, caused by a bomb in a truck parked outside the Murrah building.

At 9:02 am, there was an explosion, that wrecked the front of the building and 168 people were killed and there were more than 500 casualties. After an hour or so McVeigh was seen driving a car. Nichols, his partner in crime had been arrested two days before the attack due to driving without a license. When the officer discovered that McVeigh was illegally carrying a concealed handgun, he was arrested and held in prison awaiting trial on charges of firearms. While in prison, McVeigh was identified as "John Doe 1", the prime suspect of the attack in Oklahoma City. Two days after the bombing, McVeigh was arrested and Federal Nichols confessed to authorities. They were charged in August 1995, the government would go for the death penalty against the two as per the Attorney General. McVeigh's h court process started in 1997 April, a testimony taken by the jury to reach a collective guilty verdict. He was sentenced to die on June 13, 1997. Also in 1997, Terry Nichols was convicted of eight counts of murder and conspiracy and a sentence was passed for imprisonment for life. From 1963 no federal prisoner had been executed until June 11, 2001 when McVeigh was executed. ("American militant Timothy McVeigh |") Timothy McVeigh chose the poem Invictus, which means "invincible" in Latin, as their last declaration. He presented a handwritten copy of William Ernest Henley poem to the warden, Harley Lappin, shortly before his death. ("The last McVeigh statement", 2001)

Guy Fawkes

Guy Fawkes came to life in 1570 April in New York. In London at that time Protestants was the religion that was being practiced and accepted and his immediate family was obedient but his grandparents were disobedient because they were staunch Catholics. Guy's father died when he was eight, and his widowed mother married a Catholic, Dionis Baynbrigge. These early influences were forged Fawkes What beliefs as an adult.

Fawkes and Spain

At 21 he sold the property he had inherited from his father and went to Europe to fight for Spain that was Catholic against Dutch Republic that was Protestant in the Eighty Years' War. His military career was well and since 1603 had been recommended by a captain. They also adopted the Italian version of his name, which became known as "Guido."

In the same year, he went to Spain to ask the King Philip III of support to encourage the rebellion against England James I. "heretic" in spite of the fact that Spain and Britain were technically, still in the, his request was denied.

"A highly trained man in war"

Personally, Fawkes was a great man. His former classmate Tesimond Oswald, who had become a Catholic Jesuit priest, described as "forms of pleasant and cheerful approach, which fights ... and conflicts oppose faithful to his friends." Tesimond also said Fawkes was "a man of great experience in matters of war, Antonia Fraser the historian describes him as "a great man, fat, with red thick hair, a mustache flowing in the long tradition and beard reddish brown thick ... ... "a person whi is ready to act at all time, good physical strength and intelligent thinking.

Fawkes is introduced into the frame

It was during the Spanish campaign in Flanders that Fawkes was approached by Thomas Wintour, one of the conspirators, and what has been asked to be to be known as the gun powder plot led by Robert Catesby Guide.

Its dust experience gave him a key shot - role in the conspiracy, the source and turn explosive - and very dangerous. But 18 months of careful planning has been frustrated with a few hours to go, I was arrested at midnight on November 4, 1605 the House of Lords. No results were found directly under where the king was sitting at the opening of Parliament the next day thirty-six barrels of gunpowder in the basement stacked.

The plot was foiled been cleverly designed by chef Jacques Ier spies, Robert Cecil. Fawkes was subjected to various tortures, including the frame. Torture was technically illegal, and Jacques Ier was personally obligated to give a license for Fawkes to have its toll.

Theodore John Kaczynski

Theodore John (Ted) Kaczynski was born on May 22, 1942), He is also known as the Unabomber. The FBI used the title "UNABOM" (UNiversity & Airline BOMber) which resulted in the media calling him the Unabomber long before his identity was known. He was an American mathematician, anarchist and domestic terrorist. A mathematical prodigy, he abandoned a promising academic career in 1969, then between 1978 and 1995 killed 3 people, and injured 23 others, in a nationwide mail bombing campaign that targeted people involved with modern technology. He was opposing industrialization and advancing a nature-centered form of anarchism.

He grew up in Evergreen Park, Illinois. He was an exceptional child and was accepted into Harvard University at the age of 16. He earned his B.A. from Harvard in 1962, then his M.A. and Ph.D in mathematics from the University of Michigan in 1965 and 1967, respectively. Upon obtaining his doctorate at age 25, he became an assistant professor at the University of California, Berkeley but resigned abruptly two years later. As an undergraduate at Harvard, Kaczynski's research subject was in an ethically questionable experiment conducted by psychology professor Henry Murray, which some analysts have suggested influenced Kaczynski›s later actions.

In 1971, he moved to a remote cabin without electricity or running water in Lincoln, Montana, where he lived alone while learning survival skills in his desire to become self-sufficient. In 1978, after witnessing the destruction of the wild land surrounding his cabin, he concluded that living in nature was unsustainable and began his bombing campaign. In 1995, Kaczynski sent a letter to *The New York Times* and promised to "desist from terrorism" if the *Times* or *The Washington Post* published his manifesto, *Industrial Society and Its Future*, in which he argued that his bombings were extreme but necessary to attract attention to the erosion of human freedom and dignity by modern technologies requiring large-scale organization. Kaczynski was the target of the Federal Bureau of Investigation›s (FBI) longest and costliest investigation to refer to his case, which resulted in the media calling him the Unabomber. The FBI with Attorney General Janet Reno pushed for the publication of Kaczynski›s manifesto, which led to his sister-in-law, and then his brother, recognizing Kaczynski›s style of writing and beliefs from the manifesto, and tipping off the FBI. After his arrest in 1996, Kaczynski tried unsuccessfully to dismiss his court-appointed lawyers because they wanted to plead insanity in order to avoid the death penalty, as Kaczynski did not believe he was insane. On January 22, 1998, when it became clear that his trial would entail national television exposure, the court entered a plea agreement, under which Kaczynski pleaded guilty to all charges and was sentenced to life in prison without the possibility of parole at ADX Florence, where he remains as of 2017.

Jeff Fort

Jeff Fort was born in Aberdeen, Mississippi. on February 20, 1947; also known as Abdul Malik Ka'bah) was an American former gang leader from Chicago, Illinois. Fort was the co-founder of the Black P. Stones gang and founder of its El Rukn faction. Fort is presently serving a total of 155 year prison sentence; 80 year prison sentence after being convicted of conspiracy and weapons charges in 1987 for plotting to commit attacks inside the U.S. in exchange for weapons and $2.5 million from Libya[1] and a 75 year sentence for ordering a murder in 1981. Fort was also convicted of drug trafficking in 1983 and sentenced to 13 years in prison.

He moved with his family to the Woodlawn neighborhood on the South Side of Chicago in 1955. He dropped out of Hyde Park High School when he was in Grade 9. Fort spent time at Cook County Temporary Juvenile Detention Center and at the Illinois State Training School for Boys in St. Charles, where he met Eugene «Bull» Hairston

In 1959, Fort and Hairston organizedthe Blackstone Rangers gang at St. Charles. The Blackstone Rangers started as a small youth gang in Blackstone Avenue in the Woodlawn area, grouped together to defend themselves against other gangs in the South Side. Hairston was the gang›s leader with Fort as second in command. The Rangers fought rival gangs, especially the Devil›s Disciples. During the early 1960s, Fort earned the nickname «Angel» for his ability to solve disputes and form alliances between the Rangers and other gangs. By the mid1960s, Fort assembled a coalition of 21 gangs with about 5,000 members. He organized the coalition under a governing body called the «Main 21», composed of 21 gang leaders or «generals.» As the Ranger organization grew, it became involved in community and political activism. The gang also had the support of the Presbyterian minister Reverend John Fry who advised Hairston and Fort how to manage their organization.

Under Rev. Fry›s guidance, In 1967, Fort obtained a charter from the State of Illinois to form a political organization, Grassroots Independent Voters of Illinois. Fort›s organization applied for and received a US$1 million federal grant from the now-defunct Office of Economic Opportunity to fund a program to teach job skills to gang members. The Rangers also received grants and loans from private foundations. Unlike many gangs, the Blackstone Rangers were not considered outsiders but had been largely accepted by Chicago society, with Jeff Fort even receiving an invitation from President Richard Nixon, following the 1968 election to attend the 1969 inaugural ball but he declined the invitation, sending his Mickey Cogwell, his «top man» and one of his «generals» in his place.

Anders Behring Breivik

Breivik was born in Oslo on 13 February 1979. He was the son of Wenche Behring (1946–2013), a nurse, and Jens David Breivik (born 1935), a civil economist, who worked as a diplomat for the Norwegian Embassy in London and later in Paris. He spent the first year of his life in London until his parents divorced when he was a year old. His father, who later married a diplomat, fought for, but he failed to achieve, custody. When Breivik was four, living in Fritzners gate in Oslo, two reports were filed expressing concern about his mental health, concluding that Anders ought to be removed from parental care. In one report, a psychologist made a note of the boy›s peculiar smile, suggesting it was not anchored in his emotions but was rather a deliberate response to his environment. In another report by psychologists from Norway›s center for child and youth psychiatry (SSBU) concerns were raised about how his mother treated him: «She ‹sexualized› the young Breivik, hit him, and frequently told him that she wished that he were dead.» In the report Wenche Behring was described as «a woman with an extremely difficult upbringing, borderline personality structure and an all-encompassing if only partially visible depression" who "projects her primitive aggressive and sexual fantasies onto him [Breivik. The psychologist who wrote the report was later forbidden from giving evidence in court by Behring, who herself was excused from testifying on health grounds. Breivik lived with his mother and his half- sister in the West End of Oslo and regularly visited his father and stepmother in France, until they divorced when he was 12. His mother also remarried, to an officer in the Norwegian Army. Breivik chose to be confirmed into the Lutheran Church of Norway at the age of 15. In his adolescence, Breivik›s behaviour was described as having become rebellious. In his early teen years he was a prolific graffiti artist, part of the hip hop community in Oslo West. He took his graffiti much more seriously than his comrades did and was caught by the police on several occasions; Child Welfare Services were notified once and he was fined on two occasions. According to Breivik›s mother, after he was caught spraying graffiti on walls in 1995, at the age of 16, and fined, his father stopped contact with him. They have not been in contact since then. The opposite view is claimed by Breivik›s father, that it was his son who broke off contact with him and that he would always have welcomed Anders despite his destructive activities. At this age he also broke off contact with the hip hop community after he fell out with his best friend. Since adolescence, Breivik had spent much time on weight training, and started using anabolic steroids. He cared a lot about his own looks and about appearing big and strong Breivik has criticized his parents for supporting the policies of the Norwegian Labour Party and his mother for being, in his opinion, a moderate feminist.

Breivik attended Smestad Grammar School, Ris Junior High, Hartvig Nissens Upper Secondary School and Oslo Commerce School (1995–98). A former classmate has recalled that he was an intelligent student, physically stronger than others of the same age, who often took care of people who were bullied.

Breivik was exempted from enlisting in military service in the Norwegian Army and had no military training. The Norwegian Defence Security Department, which conducts the vetting process, say he was deemed "unfit for service" at the mandatory conscript assessment. In 1997, at age 18, he lost 2 million kroner ($369,556)[59] in the stock market. After the age of 21 Breivik was in the customer service department of an unnamed company, working with «people from all countries» for he was «kind to everyone».[61] A former co-worker described him as an "exceptional colleague",[62] and a close friend of his said he usually had a big ego and would be easily irritated by those of Middle Eastern or South Asianorigin.

According to Mikhail Reshetnikov, Belarusian opposition figure Anders Breivik underwent paramilitary training in a camp organized by retired KGB colonel Valery Lunev. According to Reshetnikov, Breivik visited Belarus three times and had lasting connections with the country. Norwegian prosecuting authorities claim that Breivik visited Belarus to meet a woman he had met on a dating website. This woman later visited him in Oslo. In his early twenties he underwent cosmetic surgery, according to friends, for his chin, nose and forehead, and was very satisfied with the result.

Breivik claims that in 2002 (at the age of 23) he started a nine-year-plan to finance the 2011 attacks, founding his own computer programming business while working at the customer service company. He claimed that his company grew to six employees and "several offshore bank accounts", and that he made his first million kroner at the age of 24.] The company was later declared bankrupt and Breivik was reported for several breaches of the law. He then moved back to his mother's home, according to himself to save money. The first set of psychiatrists who evaluated him said in their report his mental health deteriorated at this stage and he went into a state of withdrawal and isolation.] His declared assets in 2007 were about NOK 630,000. (US$116,410]),according to Norwegian tax authority figures.] He claimed that by 2008 he had about NOK 2,000,000 (US$369,556[59]) and nine credit cards giving him access to €26,000 in credit. In May 2009, he founded a farming company under the name "Breivik Geofarm", described as a farming sole proprietorship set up to cultivate vegetables, melons, roots and tubers. In 2010, he went to Prague to buy illegal weapons. He was unable to get weapon there, and decided to have weapons through legal channels in Norway instead. He bought one semi-automatic 9 mm Glock 34 pistol legally by demonstrating his membership in a pistol club in the police application for a gun license, and the semi-automatic Ruger Mini-14 rifle by possessing a hunting license. In his writings he detailed how he played video games such as *World of Warcraft* to relax, and *Call of Duty: Modern Warfare 2* for "training-simulation". He told a court in April 2012 that he trained for shooting using a holographic device while playing *Call of Duty*. He claimed it helped him gain target skills. He states that in January 2010 his funds were "draining gradually". On 23 June 2011, a month before the attacks, he paid the outstanding amount on his nine credit cards so he could have access to funds during his preparations. In late June or early July 2011, he moved to a rural area south of Åsta in Åmot, Hedmark county, about 140 km (87 mi) north-east of Oslo, the site of his farm. As he admits in his manifesto he used the company as a cover to legally obtain large amounts of artificial fertilizer and other chemicals for the manufacturing of explosives. A farming supplier sold Breivik›s company six tons of fertilizer in May. The newspaper *Verdens Gang* reported that after Breivik bought a small quantity of an explosive primer from an online shop in Poland, his name was among 60 passed to the Police Security Service (PST) by the Norwegian Customs Service as having used the store to buy products. Speaking to the newspaper, Jon Fitje of PST said the information they found gave no indication of anything suspicious. He put out the cost of the preparations for the attacks at €317,000 – «130,000 out of pocket and 187,500 euros in lost profits over three years.

Faisal Shahzad

Faisal Shahzad made headlines on 1 May, 2010 when he tried to blow up a car in Times Square House in New York.

Synopsis

Faisal Shahzad was born on 30 June 1979 in Nowshera, Pakistan. He landed in America on January 16, 1999.A woman from Denver got married to him and he obtained citizenship in 2009. After marriage he moved to Pakistan shortly after he learned to make the devices arsonists. On the headlines on May 1, 2010,he tried to detonate a car bomb in Times Square House in New York.

Profile

He is an infamous person suspected of terrorism though the records are not clear, Shahzad is believed to be born in Nowshera, Pakistan, a a city famous for Afghan refugee camps IST June 30, however, a relationship that I have documents 1979. Later born in Karachi, Pakistan .

In 1998, the training program Shahzad has participated in Karachi affiliated with the University of Washington southeast. The same year, I'm a student visa for America and came to America 16 January 1999.

Shahzad signed up at Bridgeport in University in Connecticut, for the degree of computer science and engineering in 2000. In January 2002, a H1B visa Extract Shahzad, valid for three years, and possible extension obtained. Shahzad got a job as a clerk in the accounting department that was temporary at the Elizabeth Arden cosmetics company in 2001. He obtained in 2005 a master's degree in business administration later the following time period, Shahzad got a job as a group of junior financial analysts, Affinion in Norwalk, Connecticut.

Shahzad married Huma Mian a resident at Denvar Colorado but after the loss of the couple's home, at the end, in 2004, the couple intended to leave the country. After two children, Shahzad had obtained citizenship through marriage in 2009. His family head in Pakistan soon after. Once there, take the Shahzad practising in Waziristan, Pakistan, learn how to make devices that were incidentary.

Shahzad was news May 1, 2010 while trying to retrieve officials detonated a car bomb in Times Square in New York. Shortly after the car started smoking, followed Shahzad responsible for a flight to John F. Kennedy Airport to Dubai 's. Police have taken into custody Monday night. ("**Faisal Shahzad**" nd)

Khalid Sheikh Mohammed

Khalid Sheikh Mohammed is in Kuwait in 1964, 1965 and one or more brothers and sisters. He said he is fluent in Arabic, English and Urdu Baluchi.

Once in Kuwait, is a Pakistani national from a family originally from Baluchistan, a region that includes those borders Pakistan and Iran to Afghanistan.

The increase was Fahaheel oil sector in the southern regulation of occupied Kuwait City, on the way to Saudi Arabia.

According to local press reports he had two religious parent They were Pere, Sheikh Mohammed Ali Doustin Baluchi, whose deaths would be decades, summer describes a former imam of the mosque of each.

The mother of Mohammed, Halema say those cleaning ladies have the burial of the body. A few well-paid, considered a prestigious job is CELA in Islam.

Sheikh Mohammed attends school in a boys' school. Disability and age, the young Ontario says that as memories of him here, if they are scholars focus on science.

Sheikh Mohammed in the US in 1983 he moved, ostensibly to study engineering. He attended Chowan College, a small Baptist school in North Carolina before moving to agriculture and technology of the State University of North Carolina. 1986 obtained the diploma with a degree in mechanical engineering.

He was guilty of the summer 1997 the fear based attack of the World Trade Center in 1993.

Before experiencing the capture, Sheikh Mohammed with the declaration of Al Qaeda cells around the world by all mail, email, telephone conversations and coded shortwave radio. German intelligence Sami said when force a summer hiding in rural areas sent a message. The Trois reported to have tens of used aliases.

In September 2002, the Inter-Services Intelligence in Pakistan two of his son,7 and 9 years, in custody. Agency

Sheikh Mohammed est aussi be an alleged associate of Abu Zubaydah, a member of the Circle of bin Laden in and one of the biggest al-Qaeda is responsible.

He 'has been accused of terrorism in the District Court for the Southern District of New York in the United States in 1996 and then in January was held October 10, 2001 the terrorist list intial Twenty-two FBI investigations.

The US government has offered to pay a premium of $ 25 million SES leader alleys and places TOUTE information. It took Pakistan in the summer of 2003 and was set to US custody: Finally.

In the first kept a secret prison in September 2006. However, the US government report Sheikh Mohammed was transferred to Guantanamo.

"It ankle Workers Al - Qaeda," an assistant to the president of Pakistan after his arrest said. "It's 'a great success." ("**Khalid Sheikh Mohammed** Biography," 2007)

TERRORIST GROUPS

Al Qaeda

Soviet war in Afghanistan and the beginning of Al Qaeda: 1979-1989

Real roots of Al Qaeda auction - Oussama Ben Laden conflicting network here for ten years Sevi in Afghanistan from 1979 to 1989. After the summer, the Soviet Union invaded Afghanistan, Islamic extremists Afghans pay crying Ontario has found its young because Muslims around the world Venus in Afghanistan have to pay as a volunteer in what was a jihad or "Call holy war" against the Soviet invader. The offices of the United Nations "young Muslims was a former Saudi Ben Laden called" Osama "23 years.

The son of a magnate rich sermons construction Ben Laden had taken Abdullah Azzam religious and Palestinian scholar Sayyid Qutb. In Afghanistan he attended some real battles, bin Laden best known for his huge Finance contribution turned against the Soviet jihad.

However, the ambitions bin Laden extensions beyond the borders of Afghanistan and the beginning of the international organization in June Develop complex. in a bad place for a network for financial support known as "chain" O ", composed mainly of financial Saudi Arabia and the Gulf states. Again the use of huge funds by the EC, Bin Laden and Azzam to create a "Service Bureau", here is a support for channeling recruits pay jihad in Afghanistan. Saudi Arabia and billions of dollars of American aid pouring in secrete rebels in Afghanistan against the Soviet jihad movement steadily gained. ("Bill Moyers Journal Brief History of Al - Qaeda |. Sd" PBS) Golden Chain "mainly Saudi Arabia and the states of financial Gulf compounds in a huge new use of these funds, Bin Laden and Azzam to create. A" Service Office "here is a quick pour jihad recruitment channel in Afghanistan. Saudi Arabia and $ interiors of the US aid to the rebels secrete billion in Afghanistan, is the jihad against the Soviets constantly keeps the field (" Bill Moyers Journal brief historical al - Qaeda | Sd. "PBS) or chain" mainly Saudi Arabia and the states of the Gulf financial compound. In a huge new use of these funds, Bin Laden and Azzam to create a "Service Bureau" Here's a quick intake spruce of the jihad in Afghanistan. Saudi Arabia and $ internal aid to the rebels in Afghanistan secrete billion, is the jihad against the Soviets in constant Look wedge. ("Bill Moyers Journal Brief history of Al - Qaeda |. Sd" PBS) with Saudi Arabia and the United States pouring billions of dollars in aid to secrete the insurgents in Afghanistan, the holy war against the Soviet movement has won. Constantly, ("Bill Moyers Journal Brief History of Al - Qaeda |. Sd PBS) with Saudi Arabia and the billions of dollars in the United States are in a secrete aid to the rebels in Afghanistan against the Soviet Jihad movement consistently won (" De Bill Moyers Journal brief history of Al - Qaeda | Sd PBS).

August 11, 1988 forms of Al Qaeda and bin Laden, Zawahiri and Dr. Fadl attended a meeting in Peshawar, Pakistan. Creation Group the extraordinarily rich collection Arabia, Egyptian life experience based activist and philosophical Jihad pour Cairo in June intellectual (Wander, 2008)

1989-1996: the first attacks of Al Qaeda in Sudan

When the Soviets was to withdraw from Afghanistan are from 1989 Bin Laden and Azzam Ontario your organization decides which news you should not dissolve. It 'was founded in June in Ontario - based ionic liquids calls (al - Qaeda) in general, as long as the future potential of Jihad neighborhood. However, bin Laden, the emir Now Claire Al - Qaeda, Azzam and Preassure different location where the Millennium when the future organization. Azzam al favored continued fighting in Afghanistan Up What is a true Islamic government Osama Bin Laden had wanted to prepare in this way - Qaeda part out poured into the world struggle. When Azzam died in 1989, Osama bin Laden instructed to take a complete control of the well-known group Al - Qaeda.

After leaving Afghanistan, and after he had been exiled in Saudi Arabia and Sudan, he moved bin Laden and his Al even with the basic payment operations - Qaeda. Sanctuary Sudan, Bin Laden synchronization groups start part out in North and Middle East Africa and the foundations are beginning the Jeter jihad against 'the West. in

in June against the fatwa calling deployment in Somalia, bin Laden was planning to help continuously and attacking the United States against them. Al - Qaeda helped both coaches swallow Black Hawk helicopter in 1993. Bin Laden and Al - Qaeda in Ontario aussi pour attack took credit against the World Trade Center in 1993. In 1995, Associate of "Al - Qaeda are loaded before June 1 trapped car explodes before installing joint UN -US Arabia Saudi Arabia continued here for the former national Guard IN Somalia, bin Laden and the attacks in view of the constant help us against the trainers of al Qaeda help swallow two Black Hawk helicopters in 1993. Bin Laden and al - Qaeda in Ontario aussi pour the attack brought against a loan from the World Trade Center in 1993. in 1995, the expenses associated with car are- Qaeda trapped here before it explodes install the Saudi Arabia -US joint UN here was followed for the former national Guard IN Somalia, bin Laden would help plan and continually atta ccato the United States against them. Al-Qaeda trainers help swallow two Black Hawk helicopters in 1993. Bin Laden and Al - Qaeda in Ontario aussi pour led attack on a loan from the World Trade Center in 1993. In 1995, the fees associated with drive Al Qaeda are- here that uses a trap before installing a joint US-Saudi in Saudi Arabia has been used here for the national Guard saoudienne.associés former head of al Qaeda car are trapped by installing all danger of outside Saudi joint US explosion -Saudi Arabia has been used here for the national Guard saoudienne.associés former head of al Qaeda car was stuck here for each blow-US joint installation Saudi Arabia national Guard here has been used to pay old Arabia.

1996-2000: The rise of the Taliban risen Al Qaeda

Due to the growing international pressure on Sudan forced bin Laden in Afghanistan, where he fought in the reconstruction are terrorist network. Fallu expected the Taliban Climb Ben Ladens al - Qaeda works again, and sure enough to pay of known fatwa issued against 1,998 US and its citizens. At this time, Al - Qaeda Jihad had amalgamated with the Egyptian Islamist, led by Ayman al Zawahiri, number two to become Bin Laden Order. Al - Qaeda's headquarters was now international terrorism.

February 26, 1993 The ambition of clear organization when converting a daring attack in the NIT launch of the World Trade Center in New York - March 6 as a blessing bombs are detonated 500 kg in 1000

October 4, 1993 18 American soldiers are in March, the black hawk crash in Somalia falls. al Qaeda fighters Ontario these are the use of incense in 1994 after firing helicopters Dr. Fadl Zawahiri women are looking Compendium of divine knowledge. Zawahiri, the modified entries. Fadl rising anger. The two men fall, and Fadl "takes withdr.ew" from terrorism.The book was based intellectual return them murderous campaign of Al Qaeda

1996 Bin Laden returned to Afghanistan, during which forms a relationship with the new leader of the Strait Taliban, Mullah Omar - also. EC once hung, Zawahiri is dismayed that learning militants are imprisoned in Egypt renounce violence.

1997 The group of Women in violent officially Islamic campaigns. Derailing payment peace agreement, an attack against Egypt offers Zawahiri.

November 17, 1997 62 men with weapons killed Luxor in Egyp.t

February 22, 1998 Bin Laden fatwa declaring an all Emet US al-Qaida targets CITIZENS' legitimacy and Muslims seeking to exercise their "right" to kill them.

August 7, 1998 223 people died in the US When Kenya and Tanzania embassies were attacked. One of the signature of Al Qaeda operations;

August 20, 1998 The first US military action against the group was in the form of Greves against camps in Afghanistan and Sudan.

October 12, 2000 the USS Cole was a small positive success carrying explosives SHIP Aden

June 2001 Al - Qaeda group of Osama Bin Laden and Al-Zawahiri's Jihad officially merged

11th September, 2001 2,974 people die hijacked planes collide in America Buildings

October 2001 Companies in the American invasion of Afghanistan, the Taliban involved power;

In November 2001, the battle of Tora Bora in Afghanistan to try and capture bin Laden but he escaped;

April 11, 2002 The campaign hoped of terror attack by Al Qaeda against Termines A is a synagogue in Tunisia;

March 20, 2003 the United States invaded Iraq to pay Saddam Hussein and reverse empêcher the production of ammunition of mass demolition;

May 12, 2003 March 27 civilians in attacks tides are composed Riyadh Foreign In guideline;

May 16, 2003, suicide bombing killed 45 people in Casablanca.

December 20, 2003, the 27 people were killed through an attack on British interest. The attacks were the work of the successor of Al Qaeda groups, while the organizational structure of the group shows that the Afghanistan war may have been damaged, its "franchise" capability, a deadly mix Islam and violence;

March 11, 2004 Madrid was under attack - 191 people were killed and about 2,000 injured;
17 October 2004 Giordano Abu Musab al - Zarqawi, has wreaked havoc Having those activities in Iraq, loyalty was pledged to the group - Qaeda in Iraq ;

7 JULY 2005 March 52, when transport networks were the most common attacks, the most important objectives to attack the terrorist suicide United Kingdom was not engaged –Bombers assigned to attack the Kingdom were all Muslims of "English origin, who spends time here in" training camps "in remote areas of Pakistan

May 2007 Fadl Jihad streamlining the Public Lancee attack in the campaign of violence by al Qaeda from his cell in Cairo. As the man an intellectual justification for the acts provided the LORS Group, the revaluation was created stunned knows jihadists

March 2008 Zahawiri knows releasds a critical letter entitled Fadl 200 pages reaction exemption. Montrésor reply measuring standard proposes the Fadl intellectual threat removal;

2 JUNE 2008. A car explodds at the Danish Embassy in Pakistan and Al Qaeda claimed the responsibility (**Wander**, 200 ed)

ISIS

Chronology: the rise and spread of the terrorist group. Also known as ISIS or ISIL acronym Daesh - created from the remnants of al-Qaeda in Iraq (AQI) a local rejection of Al Qaeda founded in 2004by Abu Musab al-Zarqawi. S'svenuto in the dark for several years following the onset of US troops in Iraq in 2007. In 2011 to strengthen their ranks and carry out their attacks they took advantage of the instability in Iraq and Syria that had been going on for years.

In 2013 they changed the group's name to the Islamic State of Iraq and Syria (ISIS) ISIS and set off an attack against Mosul and Tikrit in June 2014. On 29 June, the leader Abu Bakr al – Baghdadi of ISIS announced their area of jurisdiction starting from Aleppo to Syria to Diyala in Iraq and renamed the Islamic State.

On **7 August 2014** ISIS in Iraq were attacked through airstrikes by US led coalition and has expanded the campaign to Syria the following month. The United States on October 15

defined the campaign "Intrinsic Operation Resolve". During the next year in Iraq and Syria the USA launched mare than 8000 airstrikes to eradicate the terrorist groups. ISIS had suffered significant losses along the border of Syria and Turkey and by the end of 2015, Iraqi forces have made progress in the recovery of Ramadi. However, in Syria, ISIS has made progress near Aleppo, and has always remained Raqqa and other strengths.

In 2015, ISIS has developed a network of branches in at more than eight other countries. His branches, his supporters, and his affiliates made attacks more and more beyond the limits of his call to Caliphate. In October, Egyptian subsidiary ISIS bombed a Russian airliner, killing 224 people. They launched a series of coordinated attacks in Paris resulting in more than 300 casualties and 130 people died. In June 2016,in Orlando, Florida at least four dozen people were killed at a disco by a weapon that promised support for ISIS.

Here is a program outlining the main events of 2016.

2004-2012-2004 Abu Musab al Zarqaoui established by Al - Qaeda in Iraq (AQI).

June 7, 2006: Zarqawi was killed in a US attack .Abu Ayyub al-Masri is taking place.

October 15, 2006: Masri announced Abu Omar al Baghdadi the leader that of the created Islamic State of Iraq (ISI),.

2007: After the rise of US military in Iraq, ISI is expelled from Baghdad and Mosul to Diyala Salahideen. The organization retains only a fraction of their leaders, their cells and their abilities, which are concentrated in Mosul.

2008: ISI membership decreases considerably. At the beginning of 2008, 2,400 members of the ISI were killed and capturing 8,800, the membership being over 15,000. The flow of foreign fighters in Iraq is reduced by 120 per month five or six per month for 2009.

2009: Iraqi Prime Minister Maliki attacks Sunni leaders, stepped up sectarian tensions. ISI support begun to increase in Sunni tribal areas, and the hundreds of ISIs responsible for suicide bombings that have killed in Baghdad have been attributed.

April 2010: Abu Bakr al Baghdad becomes the new leader of ISIS following the deaths of Abu Omar al - Baghdadi and Abu Ayyub al Masri after US and Iraqi joint operations killed them.

July 2011: Abu Bakr to Baghdadi sends agents to Syria. One of them, Abu Muhammad al Julani, becomes Nusra's leader in January 2012.

July 2012-July 2013: ISI launches the campaign "Breaking the Walls. "He did 24 incursions and leak eight prisoners, the release of jihadists who participated in the AQI attacks in 2006 and 2007.

2013

March 4: Raqqa fell for Syrian opposition and secular opposition groups, the Nusra Front and ISI all work in Raqqa .ISI begins the transfer of military assets to consolidate control and enter new battlefields in Syria.

April 11: Baghdadi goes to Iraq for Syria, and disclosed that the Islamic State of Iraq (ISI) joined with Nusra in Syria to become Ma Julani rejects alliance and loyalty "The Islamic State in Iraq and the Syria."He told Al Qaeda.

July 21: To reduce the Iraqi security forces and captured territory ISIS launched "Harvest Soldier.

August: Liwa Al Tawhid, Ahrar al Sham, and Nusra Front at Raqqa and Aleppo were rebellious to ISIS so ISIS began to attack them;

December 30: ISIS militants in Iraq took control of Fallujah and Ramadi parts.

2014-January: ISIS takes Raqqa and declared the capital of the emirate ISIS.

February 3: Al - Qaeda officially cut ties with ISIS;.

June 10: Once again ISIS Mosul, launching its biggest offensive for the date. 600 Shiite prisoners and Badoush were killed during the attack by the militants.

June 11: Tikrit was taken over by ISIS militants.

June 12: Iran expanded forces against ISIS in Iraq and helped Iraqi troops take back most of Tikrit.

June 18: Iraq called on Member States to conduct air strikes against ISIS.

July 17: ISIS gas stormed Shaer, killing 270 people.

June 21: ISIS seized the strategic border Deir Ezzor border crossing in Syria and Iraq, and three other Iraqi cities.

June 29: ISIS announced the creation of a Caliphate and changed its name as “Islamic State”.

2-3 August: ISIS surpassed Kurdish towns of Sinjar and Zumar, forcefully evacuated most of civilians.

August 3: ISIS acquisition of Mosul Dam.

Among allegations of ISIS, more control of Iraq dam could become life or death of upto500,000: http://t.co/MBmG2U3aZL pic.twitter.com/EhCwI4gZC2

- ABC News (@ABC) August 7, 2014

August 7: The launch of air strikes against ISIS in Iraq to defend the yazid citizens stuck in Sinjar was announced by President Obama..

August 19: ISIS kills journalist James Foley of.

August 24: ISIS militants seized Taqba air base of al-Raqqa, Syria.ISIS now controls the'whol province of Raqqa.

September 2: ISIS releasds video showing decapitation by journalist Steven Sotloff.

September 13: ISIS videod messages about the execution of British cofounder David Haines.

September 19-22: ISIS advanced to the border town of Kobanê of Syria and thousands of refugees flee to Turkey.

September 22: The Gate - Abu Muhammad at ISIS word Adnani called attacks on US citizens, other countries and France participating in the coalition to destroy the group.

September 23: The United States launched its first air attack against ISIS in Syria.

September 24: Activists aligned with ISIS chap a French tourist, Herve Gourdel, Algeria.

September 27: The United States started air strikes in Kobanê.

October 3: Majlis Shura Shabab al-Islam, or Islamic Shura says Young Derna of the Libyan city for ISIS.

October 3: ISIS published a video showing the decapitation of a British humanitarian worker Alan Henning.CNN

October 7-8 ramped US air strikes significantly around Kobanê to counter ISIS progress.

October 15: The Pentagon names of the campaign against ISIS "Operation Transaction Resolution."

For its military operation against ISIS the USA gets a new name for its Military operation #ISIL: "Resolve inherent operation".Http://t.co/wK-mX4nzqcx

- The Wilson Center (@TheWilsonCenter) on October 18, 2014

November 2: In Atareb ISIS leaders and jihadist rival Jabhat al Nusra met to discuss assembly forces. It no merger or formal agreement between the two groups has not been established, but ISIS have sent fighters to help attack the Nusra Front Front for Harakat Hazm, a western moderate-backed rebel group. Military

December 16: An armed man belonging to ISIS held 17 hostages in a cafe in Sydney, Australia.

December 30: A suicide attack during a funeral in northern Baghdad in which 16 people were killed and injured 34. ISIS took responsibility

January 7:Two armed men, Chérif Saïd Kouachi, attacked French Charlie Hebdo satirical magazine offices in Paris, killing 11 people. A third aggressor, Amedy Coulibaly, led a synchronized attack on a kosher supermarket, taking hostages and killing four people. Coulibaly was quoted of his loyalty to the Islamic state.

January 26 Kurdish fighters, with the help of the Member - States and coalition air strikes, on the ISIS militants in the town of Ayn al-Arab Syrian border after four-month battle.

January 28: Allied activists responsible for ISIS applications for an armed attack on a luxury hotel in Tripoli, Libya, where at least eight people were killed.

February 4: ISIS released a Moaz military pilot on Jordan's video at Kasasbeh being burned alive.

February 16-15: The decapitation of 21 Egyptian Christians who were kidnapped on January 12 in Egypt was shown through a video taken by ISIS Libyan militant allies. Egypt launches Libya's air strikes for retaliation.

25 to 26 February: ISIS militants abducted at least 200 Assyrian Christians in Syria - is North. The US-led coalition launched air strikes in the same area.

March 18: ISIS said an attack on the Bardo Museum in Tunisia, where 22 people died.

March 20: ISIS-linked militants bombed two mosques in Sana'a, Yemen, killing 137 people.

April 5: Yarmouk ISIS refugee camp activists entered Palestine in Damascus, where more than 18,000 people reside.

April 8: ISIS freed more than 200 Yazids in captivity, most of them were held captives in northern Iraq since mid-2014.

April 19: ISIS messages a video showing Libyan militant militia to run dozens of Christians in Ethiopia.

May 17: ISIS to take off Ramadi, Iraq.

May 20: The old Syrian city of Palmyra is captured by ISIS

May 21: ISIS militants took full control of Sirte, Libya - the birthplace of Muammar Qaddafi.

New foreign fighters #Tunisia, Palestine and Yemen # #ISIS joins Sirte, Libya #: Source https://t.co/Zr7CBih68S pic.twitter.com/TkhTK76WUS

- Alwasat (@alwasateng news) December 10, 2015

May 22: ISIS suicide bomb in which there were at least 100 casualties and 21dead people was set against a Shiite mosque in the eastern part of Saudi Arabia,.

May 29: ISIS helped another suicide bombing in eastern Saudi Arabia in a shiite mosque where 4 people were killed.

June 17: Yemen's branch claimed ISIS's responsibility for bombings that were carried out series in Yemen's capital, in which more than 30people died.

June 17: ISIS Kurdish fighters expelled strategic Syrian city of Tal Abyad on the Turkish border.

June 22: full control of a military base Ain Issa is taken by Kurdish, ISIS militias.

June 26: ISIS fighters have attacked Kobanê, Syria and 145 citizens wer killed .On the same day, an attack is launched on a Shiite Mosque and 127 people die and wound more than 200 people.

June 27: ISIS attacksed Tunisian Sousse station and 38 people died and 39 injured, mostly were foreigners;

July 1: ISIS fighters carried out simultaneous attacks on military posts in the north of the Sinai Peninsula in Egypt, killing dozens of soldiers.

July 20: A bomber linked to ISIS reaches a Turkish border town a center with cultural heritage in Suruc where 30 people died.

August 6: ISIS said a suicide bomber against a mosque in Saudi Arabia, where more than 15 people, and 12 Saudi police forces in the province of Asir, died near the southwestern border with Yemen.

August 12: ISIS releases 22 Assyrians kidnapped dozens of villages in northern Syria in the early 2015.

September 3: Yemenite branch ISIS kills 20 people in two bombing attacks in Sana'a.

September 24: ISIS claims the responsibility of two bombs in a mosque in Yemen led by Houthi - a rebel group from shiite that captured Sana'a in September 2014. More than 25 people were killed.

From 29-29 September 3. Armed men linked to ISIS killing an Italian and veterinary co-worker in Dhaka, Bangladesh.On October 3, ISIS's responsibility for the death of a Japanese in northern Bangladesh was attributed.

September 30: Russia begins air strikes in Syria.ISIS says target, but US authorities claim that many attacks against civilians and rebel groups supported bythe 'West.

6th October More than 25 people are killed in a series of bombs fro ISIS in the two largest cities of Yemen, Aden and Sana'a.

October 9: ISIS has made significant progress in northern Syria - west, taking six villages near Aleppo.

October 10-12: ISIS are accused for attacking during a peace rally where at least 95 people were reported dead by Turkish Prime Minister Ahmed Davutoglu.

October 15: The Baiji refinery forces Iraqi forces recovered the largest oil refinery in the country, ISIS.

October 16: ISIS-related Bahrain militants responsible for the deaths of five Shiite faithful in the Saudi city of Saihat have been attributed.

October 22: A member of a special forceof the US operation killed during a rescue mission of ISIS hostages in northern Iraq - the first American who died in combat on the ground with ISIS. Twenty ISIS fighters dead during the operation and six others are detained.

October 31: Sinai State, Egypt Subsidiary Isis, the bombing of a Russian plane is attributed to the Sinai Peninsula, killing everyone on board 224.

November 12: ISIS attacks Beirut via suicide bombings and 40 people die.

November 13: Kurdish forces entered Sinjar, Iraq ISIS.

November 13: In Paris coordinated attacks were conducted by ISIS and 130 people die.

November 15: ISIS were raided by airstrikes by France in Raqqa, Syria.

#CJTFOIR performed attacks to weaken #ISIL.Here was the latest report of damaged / destroyed targets since November 13th.Pic.twitter.com/y1wwj4WrkJ

- CJTF-OIR (@CJTFOIR) November 17, 2015

November 27: militants attacking a mosque in Bangladesh for shiites, killing a religious and injuring three more ISIS-linked.

December 1: Ashton Carterthe Defense Secretary announced that United States Special Forces would be sent to Iraq to support Iraqi and Kurdish fighters and direct launch operations on Syria.

December 2: An apparently inspired marriage 14 people killed by ISIS in San Bernardino, California.

December 10: US officials announced that finance minister Abu Saleh and two senior executives in Tal Afar, Iraq are killed via airstrikes.

December 27: Iraqi military forces in Ramadi captured ISIS.

2016

January 12: An ISIS-related suicide bomber killed 10 people and injured another 15 - many of whom were German tourists - rather than Istanbul.

January 14: ISIS attacked Jakarta, Indonesia, where at least two people died and 19 injured;

March 18: Salah Abdeslam, the suspect's most wanted terrorist attack in Paris, was arrested in Brussels.

March 19: Suicide killed five people and dozens of injured in Istanbul. The Turkish Interior Ministry announced that the author had links with ISIS.

March 22: At the Zaventem Airport and the Brussels Underground three bombs exploded and 30 people died and dozens more injured. ISIS says the attacks.

April 11: Iraqi forces entered the town of Hit, which was under the control of ISIS from October 2014.On the same day, ISIS resumed Rai, a Syrian village on the border with Turkey, the Free Syrian Army.

May 5: Near Palmyra, gas field was captured by ISIS

May 12: On May 11 a lot of bombings took place and more than 100 people died. ISIS took responsibility.

May 19: Iraqi forces resumed the western city of Rutbah.

May 23: Iraqi forces backed by US air strikes - the United States and the coalition advancing to Fallujah, ISIS has occupied since 2014.

May 24: US-backed Kurdish forces launched an offensive in the northern territory of Raqqa, Syria.

June 12: A gunman attacked a gay nightclub that was popular in Orlando, Florida, and more than four dozen people died and at least 53 injured. The attacker Omar Mateen, would later call the police. ISIS took responsibility for the attack later.

June 26: The Iraqi army at Falluja ISIS resumes.

June 27: ISIS said a suicide attack with a car bomb in Mukalla, Yemen, where at least 42 people died.

June 28: At least 40 people died due to three suicide bombers at Ataturk Airport in Istanbul. ISIS is suspected to have instigated the attack by the Turkish government..

July 1: More than 20 people died in a restaurant in Dhaka, Bangladesh, most of them foreigners due to ISIS militants.

July 3: ISIS militants committed suicide attacks where more than 200 people died on a busy shopping street in Baghdad. The attack, which took place during the sacred month of Ramadhan, was the biggest bombing of ISIS against citizens to date.

July 4: suicide attacks against three sites in Saudi Arabia, including the Prophet Mosque in Medina, a Shiite mosque of Qatif and close to the American Consulate in Jeddah. Medina attack at least four people died and another five injured. The aggressors were suspected of having links with ISIS.

July 14: A 31-year-old man from Tunisia drove a truck through a crowd in Nice, France, killing 84 people. ISIS took the responsibility for the attack, but it is unclear whether the attacker had formal links with the group.

July 18: An Afghan boy carrying an ax in a German train and injuring at least five people. It was motivated by ISIS.(Glenn, 2016)

10.1.3: Alshabaab

The organization known as Al Shabaab originated from the Islamic Courts movement (ICU) in Somalia. The UCI was due to a loose group of Islamic Courts, and by 2006 had become a powerful Islamic militia, which controlled most of southern Somalia. Al Shabaab (literally "young") was the hard - line faction of young radicals in intensive care. The peak of its influence was reached after the Battle of Mogadishu in 2006, beating the US Alliance - peace and reconciliation backed Restoration (ARPCT) and the recovery control sun during the war in Somalia torn capital. The victory was important so that it was a major concern for the government of neighboring Ethiopia, which supported the Somali Transitional Federal Government (GFT). Ethiopian troops, with US air support, invaded Somalia to attack the UCI and seek to establish the authority of the federal transition government. The UCI's remains, in also Al-Shabaab, were evacuated out of Mogadishu and severe leaks in the south. Among the most moderate UCI reconciled with the federal transition government and became an alliance with elements of government. Survivors of Al-Shabaab in Kenya scattered survivors or HID.

The total defeat of Islamist Al Shabaab never destroyed, but as 2007 began, the circumstances looked very much from the group. Imperfectly, movement followers began to rearrange and re-orient their goals, avoiding any regular combat. Now limited by the need to cram the more intimate voices in intensive care, Al-Shabaab's leaders became more radicalized. They are efforts to overcome the static clan loyalty factors often undermined by a national movement in Somalia, and focus instead placed on a religious ideology as a unifying force. Suicidal attacks and high media activity is well known Somali, helping to enter the ranks of its followers. The rebirth of Al Shabaab has been greatly aided by the occupation of Somalia by Ethiopia, which creates a suitable environment for recruiting Al-shabaab members. Al-Shabaab was a viable alternative for some Somalis compared to foreign occupants, who were supported by the civilian US and often attacked without discrimination. In late

2007, the Somali government main opposition was the AL shabaab who are armed an lead a revolution by guerrilla attacks and suicide tactics. Al Shabaab has gained a good level of international help and finances, in particular through Its powerful Internet and media profiles. Themselves and other terrorist groups affiliated to al Qaeda and in part are fighting in Somalia as a form of rebellion to the West. [IV]

In 2009, Ethiopian forces were withdrawn from Somalia and replaced with several thousand Burundi and Uganda men distributed as part of the African Union Mission in Somalia (AIMSOM). Especially the AIMSOM forces were committed to GFP in Mogadishu Al Shabaab to continue to provide a vacuum of power in other regions of the country for development. The capture of Baidoa, the provisional capital TFG seems to be the greatest success so far. This also marked the tensions inherent to Shabaab. A key figure Ahmed Abdi Mohamud Godane, in leadership, has ordered the arrest of federal transition of political leadership in the city, however his commands have been questioned by other personalities, Abu Mansoor-Muktar Robow, ensuring a safe passage of several TFG policies His clan.

Al Shabaab proceeded with the fight against Tfg and AIMSOM throughout 2010, having more success by fighting the forces when the government. Local support for the organization has continued to grow, partly helped by the application system and justice in the field of law relative success the controlled introduction of Al-Shabaab. In accordance with the new ambitions of being involved an international jihad movement, Al Shabaab has expanded its attention beyond the borders of Somalia. The group in July 2010 released its first outbreak outside of Kampala, Somalia, Uganda, with coordinated suicide attacks, killing 74. [The attack was seen to be a retaliation for Uganda to provide Troops AIMSOM.

Internal and external challenges

Encouraged by Al-Shabaab's success and without the consent of Robow and others, Godane instigated an attack on Mogadishu to try to defeat AIMSOM forces. The effect was disastrous. After a month's battle for capital controls, a quarter of Shabaab fighters were killed, wounded or captured. [Xi] Attacks of large amounts of money also costing the Shabaab and the tensions in the Garde guard direction. intensive mediation made by Al Qaeda needed to resolve some disagreements within al-Shabaab, while Godane, Robow and speculation again denied is still divided into groups.

The southern invasion of Kenya in southern Somalia, in October 2011Operation Linda Nchi began. The Kenya government became concerned about the crisis of refugees and instability along the border with the intention of creating A north bearing area to prevent the spread of the conflict in Kenya. [habaab increased pressure on Kenya's participation in troops and AIMSOM TFGs to attack the group. This mixture challenged Al-Shabaab's positions in the south and led the Islamists from the port city of Kismayo important.suffered hunger in Somalia in 2011, weakening the Shabaab. In spite of increased challenges, al Shabaab was still able to perform marvellous attacks that attracted international attention. 2013 September, few armed men went to the Westgate mall in Nairobi and attacked it, killing 67 people and wound more than 200 people. [XIV] A spokesman for Al Shabaab said the operation was retaliated for the invasion of Kenya] He tried to AIMSOM fiscal consolidation in 2012, but a series of attacks by Al Shabaab has convinced the leadership of the mission to carry out a new attack in mid-2013, Ethiopia has accepted to give troops to increase AIMSOM with bringing Total strength of 22,000 missions with the support of Kenya's defense forces, which have reduced the increase in territorial. Internal strength conflicts within al Shabaab Shabaab and cook cook for years, finally, in June 2013. Godane appeared to have power over the handling of a violent purge, the use of some high-level commanders and the evacuation of others, including Robow. Although the Godane coup eliminates most disagreements in the group, few of its most important and respected leaders are also eliminated. Since then, al-Shabaab has reduced in terms of territory and its international profile. But, they are still a powerful force in Somalia and have over the years repeatedly demonstrated their ability to attack easy targets in Kenya. The coast of Kenya and the northern regions experienced Shabaab violence in various ways, mass murders in Mpeketoni and the University of Garissa. Kenya police responded with an aggressive campaign Designed for Somalis in Kenya, a slightly hypothesized move providing elements for Al Shabaab recruiting. It is clear that, in spite of current losses suffered by Al-Shabaab, the organization remains one of the largest in East Africa for the faction in time to come.

The Boko Haram

this year, April Boko Haram appeared for the first time in Westerners' consciousness However the group ain't a newcomer to the scene. For more than 10 years in Nigeria there has been a force growing in Nigeria which has deep roots in social development that goes far behind. Its origin is therefore not accidental and is a sign of a dangerous, movement of religious activist emergence that threatens the survival of Nigerians state of nations .

The Boko Haram history begins with Mohammed Marwa, a preacher who was born in 1927. He relocated to Kano currently known as northern Nigeria at the age of eighteen where he began his preaching career. His sermons were often extreme and strange. He said the popularity of Western culture in Nigeria made him angry also called Maitatsine, which means "Who curses." He said it was paganism sign and a sin to read any other book apart from Koran. This included the prohibition of reading Hadith or Sunnah, an equivalen doctrinal of a Catholic priest, he also said that parishioners did not read the testimonials of Saint Augustine, as they are not in the Biblical when he was almost dying he almost dangerously pointed out that he was a true prophet of God and not Muhammad.

Maitatsine was not recognized by political leaders in Nigeria, but his sermons that opposed the government became more and more in 1970, the government has acted. this force from the government in 1980 led their uprising, where Maitatsine's supporters at Kano began opposing government. The city fell into this scientist Elizabeth Isichei described as "practically civil war". The balance of the victims of the disorder in 1982 and the military repression that followed was more than 4,000 and Maitatsine Among the victims.

His movement, however, has lived. In 1982, 3,300 people died in Bulumkutu as a result of Maitatsine supporters' opposing the government again., Maitatsine followers grew all over the state in Gongola Two years later. This violence killed almost 1,000 people. Hundreds of others died one year later in a riot in the state of Bauchi.

After independence, Nigeria has experienced ethnic and religious conflicts. However, this tension has resulted to various communities that compete for power and resources. the northern population consiss mostly of Muslims Fulani and ethnic Hausa. The southern population consists of Christians who are mainly ethnic Yoruba and Igbo. The countrys reputation is divided almost equally between Muslims and Christians, and this division almost matches country's linguistic and ethnical one of the factors that contributes to political instability. But religious fundamentalism was not a feature of this struggle. The Maitatsine movement was dynamics changes signal, and the fundamentalism of Islams that is growing in Middle East in 1970 was becoming adopted by the Nigerians.

In the 19th and the beginning of twentieth century, in the north of Nigeria the law the country of is sharia. The judges were still Cadiz, Islamic scholars' Islamic scholars who served as jurists and an application of religious law, traditional Islamic practices. In 1960 Nigeria began its transformation to independence, the Sharia has been almost eliminated in the 1960 settlement Muslims in Nigeria under 1960 regulation, changed the right to imposition of Sharia in all areas in return for concessions in other fields such as' independent publishing where the first Nigerian constitution began. Sharia is only valid today for personal or family relationships in the north. Most Muslim leaders supported the resolution, saying that the Shari'a rejection was essential to moving towards modernity.

He started turning the opinion of Muslims in the 1970s, when the movement was rally support Maitatsine. According to **Sati Fwatshak and Philip Ostien** in his book on Sharia in Nigeria, "... in the mid-1980s, the idea that the Muslim Transactional Agreement in 1960 had been a terrible mistake ... is widespread and firmly anchored to the North."

The continuous growth of opposition in 1999, to the 1960s law manifests itself in tremendous attempts to impose sharia in northern states. Nigeria has adopted a new federal constitution this year as the fourth attempt was opened by the independence of the military dictatorship and build a lasting democracy. The 1999 Constitution has opened the door for the imposition of Islamic law by granting significant states of Nigeria and the establishment of a court appeals system to know about the sharia court's trial appeals. Over the next few years, the states of the North could seize the opportunity to impose sharia on its territory. Today, nine of the twelve states in the north are completely Shari'a and the other three are in sharia civil, non-criminal, case cases.

The abandonment of the extensions of the 1960s transformed north of Nigeria. Nigeria has always been a disunited country accompanied by mismanagement and ethnic divisions, but currently, the south and north are like two completely different countries. It is in this perspective that religious fervor that grows in northern Muslim and manifests with violent riots like Maitatsine is what led to the rise of Boko Haram.

Boko Haram was formed by Islamic religious group in Borno, Nigeria in 2002. Mohammed Yusuf, its founder, was a comittited fundamentalist whose thought was strongly influenced by Wahhabite theology. Their aim was to transform Nigeria into a real Islamic state in the dictation of Sharia law all over the country, including taxation of southern Christians.

Initially, Boko Haram was thorough but not violent. That however changed in 2009, when its members decided to refuse to obey all things, a law requiring motorcyclists to put on helmets for the fact that it was a non-Islamic way. The arrest of many mutilated members where Boko Haram first had his major confrontation with the police in Nigeria clashes that left 800 amazing deaths.

Yusuf Mohammed was arrested by the security forces in Nigeria and interrogated. His interrogations insulted him by possessing the equipment after years of denouncing science and Western learning. After the interrogation was executed without trial in which the government described it as a "battle of firearms."

After the 2009 disorder, Boko Haram was terribly violent. Abubakar Shekau, their new leader, is a persuasive supporter who used terrorist tricks to advance their radical Boko Haram embarks on a global systems of terrorist organizations such as the Al Qaeda agenda. Over the last two years,

Boko Haram has been trained by al-Qaida agents for the use of explosives and wounded terrorist attacks. The growing link between Al Qaeda and Boko Haram is disturbing to the region's observers who are afraid that Boko Haram will start knocking off Nigeria.

After every year from 2009, Boko Haram has become more violent. For example, to increase their useless violence, Boko Haram began terrorizing northern motorists and used chainsaws to remove the heads of truck drivers passing through regions where Boko Haram is strong.

The goal seems to be to bring the economy to a standstill in these regions, so it is life threatening to ship goods.

To fund its movement, Boko Haram began stealing from banks, taking enough money to buy heavy ammunition. It is not possible to replace this entry with piracy off the coast of Nigeria and drug trafficking. For the first time last year Boko Haram could not manage to buy weapons. They used heavy arms to start launching attacks against police stations and military. Often execute Nigerian soldiers to guard block posts When approaching Boko Haram fighters. When the president of Nigeria has offered pardon to all members of Boko Haram, if they surrender arms, the Boko Haram leaders have reacted by rejecting the agreement and the offer of amnesty, instead of government leaders they had The Boko Haram.

Boko Haram is increasing, it is becoming increasingly evident that the Nigerian state can not control the uprising Boko Haram. The news of the western countries about Africa gives the impression that violence due to politics is casual seeming like Nigeria is face with an earthquake rather than military insurrection. However Boko Haram is not a random occurrence. Its appearance is a directly related to the growth of fundamentalism in the country. The threat posed to the country now for decades. Unfortunately, it took the elimination of about 300 students to get strangers to read.(Ford, 2014)

10.1.5: Bodu Bala Sena

1975 (March 4): Galagoda Atte Gnanasara was born.

1992 (January 2). Vier Kirama Wimalajothi opened the Buddhist cultural center in Dehiwala, South Colombo.

In 2004 the first political party in the world made up of Buddhist monks Jathika Hela Urumaya called (National Heritage Party) was formed. The BBS is a branch of the party.

2012 (May 7): The Bodu Bala Sena was launched.

2011 (May 15): Buddhist Center Cultural was inaugurated by President Mahinda Rajapaksa in new posts in the city of Colombo, in the Sambuddha Jayanthi Mandira complex. This is also the home of the BBS are.

2012 (June24): BBS attacked Sirivardhana Buddha, famous and controversial Buddhist preacher Vanduramba, Galle District.

2012 (July28): The BBs had the first national convention at the Memorial

Band International Bandaranaike Conference.

2012 (October 14): The BBS has entered a "domestic church" in Homagama, allegations that a gospel group known as the name of the Lord Jesus were trying to convert the Buddhist Sinhalese.

2012-2013: The BBS has been accused of attacking several Muslim and Christian sites, as it has the role of the police in itself. In 2012, this was mainly oriented towards Buddhist "heretical" vigilantism and Buddhism hotels declared commercialized, but in the campaigns of 2013 against Muslims they learned their activities.

2013 (February 17): During a rally on the outskirts of Colombo, Maharagama, BBS made public its "Maharagama Declaration," a statement by ten points opposing certain Muslim customes such as Hala-certification, and clad women, such as the hijab and abaya.

2014 (June 15 and 16): Muslims in the town of Aluthgama, town of Dharga and Beruwela Valipanna were shown violence by the crowd after a BBS meeting (often called "Aluthgama Riots").

2014: for them to discredit the organization of BBS met with accusations that its monks were supported by Western powers, including Norway.

2014 (20 June): The Norwegian Embassy in Colombo issued a press release refusing any link between the state of Bodu Bala Sena Norway.

2015 : Vier Kirama Wimalajothi resigned BBS, the BBS participation of two parties in violence Aluthgama. We publicly proclaim that the actions of the BBS monks was against the teachings of the Buddha.

2015 (June): The BBS record, and Eksath Lanka Maha Sabha, as a political party under the name of Jana Bodu Peramuna Sri Lanka (BJP) and stand for election in August

Founder of the group / HISTORY

Post-Independent, Sri Lanka has active accounts of Buddhist advocacy groups in life for the public, which was the 'objective to "restore Buddhism" for his "place" in society. In general, we can say that, despite internal changes, these groups belong to the wider political tradition of

Buddhism. This "political Buddhism" refers to a series of ideologies that hold that Buddhism should give guidance for social and political life, and that it is a State's part to protect and promote Buddhism. "Political Buddhism" in Sri Lanka specifically refers to current ideas developed in the second half of the nineteenth century against the colonial removal of Buddhism from formal politics, and since 1930 as a democratic political ideology accepted. The policy is articulated and Buddhism both lay Buddhists and members AGI monastic order, the Sangha (Frydenlund 2016).

The most fanatics (and so far most militant) Bodu Bala Sena is the group (the Buddhist power of the army), or BBS, created in 2012 by few of Buddhist and lay monks. The highest figures (monastic now opted out of the group) was Ven. Kirama Wimalajothi, monaco expert who stayed long in Malaysia. [Right Picture] On his return to Sri Lanka, Wimalajothi began in 1992 at the Buddhist Cultural Center south of Colombo, which in 2000 had become a well-stocked library Buddhist center and publication. In 2011, the Buddhist Cultural Center had moved to the city center and has become a modern millionaire. The Center was inaugurated on 15 May 2011 by President Mahinda Rajapaksa and the Center BBS and generally considered to be operating under the protection of President Rajapaksa.

The main goal of Wimalajothi longs to improve the state of Buddhism in society. also to the Buddhist Cultural Center, a center of secular activities, temporary ordination for common men of the monastic order (which, unlike Myanmar and Thailand are not practiced in Sri Lanka) and the full ordination of women has been established In Control (bhikkhuni coordination). In addition, Wimalajothi expressed concern about the cultural heritage of Sri Lanka, as traditional medicines and food as well as the long - term migration from the Middle East to the Sinhalese families. We shall see, these concerns come back in BBS ideology.

While Wimalajothi era (2015), the executive and philanthropist BBS was the junior monk, Ven. Atte Galagoda Gnanasara (BBS General Secretary) has become the public figure and shaker in the public area. [Right Picture] Gnanasara participated in Buddhist activist groups in the 2000s, and also ran for Parliament Jathika Hela Urumaya, a Buddhist monastic political party formed in 2004. After the sudden demise of a charismatic Buddhist monk Soma Thero died in December, a monk group of " Patriots "were formed in 2004, the first political party made up of Buddhist monks in the world of 2003, Jathika Hela called Urumaya (National Property Party), BBS is a branch.

Another crucial aspect in the foundation of the BBS was Dilanthe Withanage, a layman who took the title of "chief executive". Withanage was also the spokesman and BBS has appeared in many discussions and interviews, including international media such as Al Jazeera, where the discussion in 2014 defended the need to "protect Buddhism" from "conversions to Islam."

In May 2015, Wimalajothi publicly shared his withdrawal from the participation of two parties Aluthgama BBS violence, BBS. 2015 June, the Grand Council Lanka States (Eksath Lanka Maha Sabha) BBS to be registered as a political party, the Bodu Jana Peramuna Sri Lanka (BJP), thus increasing the competition with JHU for "Buddhist vote" in the general election Sri Lanka this year. The BJP in six rounds in question, but only 0.18 percent of the national vote obtained.

Doctrines / CREDENTS

The overall objective of BBS is to ensure the protect Buddhism and Sinhalese, especially what they consider as invasion by foreigners. The movement joins Buddhist concerns about "fundamentalist" secularization of society, the differentiation and the supposed disintegration of Buddhism is the globalization with the specific concerns of Singal nationalism and the culture of the Singalans and the heritage. The emphasis is on the mastery of Singalian language and culture during present and past international criticism and the multicultural paradigm of human rights on the island, and in particular the rights of minorities. She is particularly worried about Islam.

In its first gathering in Colombo in 2012 July, BBS stated its objective to continue on five goals: 1) to ensure the increase of the birth rate of the Buddhist Singalese population to question the government and birth control planning policy familiar; 2) legal act/laws to better ensure protection of the rights of island Buddhists, remove legal pluralism and the implementation of a civil code (thus removing the right of the Muslim family); 3) restructure of the education system in accordance with Buddhist interests; 4) the creation of a government - sponsored organization to ensure Buddhist "orthodoxy" in books and media; and 5) acting on a series of recommendations to reform Buddhism has already been proposed in 1950. This "resolution" five times also suggests the government's ban on female labor migration in Sri Lanka Middle East. Workers mistreatment Sri - Lanka in the Middle - Middle has long been a controversial problem in Sri Lanka, and has been increasingly seen as a religious problem by Buddhist radical political groups, including the BBS.

A source close to the ideology of Islam construction BBS look shows that the discourse anti - Muslim work at different levels, serving different interests and issues: some interventions related to competition from local companies, while others are thc Muslims and the ' Islam as a threat to the security of the state. An important talk BBS deals with issues of cultural diversity, human rights and citizenship, which represents Buddhists as 'guests' and Muslims (and other religious minorities) as "guests" the rights of limited, accredited minorities. In public speech in Colombo in 2013, [right image] BBS argued that this was a general principle that minorities should live in a country [so] This does not threaten the career of majority and identity. Muslims were Buddhist singalic Buddhists their guests. In 2014 interview , With anage said that "[i] is Buddhist Singalesi are in danger We are those who live in fear our Buddhist Sinhalese leaders are incapable of two great powers of these so .. -. These minorities "In addition, during the BBS monks sermons said Muslims in Sri Lanka as" hungry ghosts "that threaten the careers of more and identity. Such rhetoric ignores peaceful coexistence one thousand years with Muslim communities Buddhist time Sinhalese ethnic diversity and Linguistics of Sri Lanka.

Although Buddhist and Muslim coexistence in Sri Lanka is necessary rather than an exception, BBS building local Muslims is a danger to national security. Local Muslim associations are seento be representatives of international terrorist networks and local agents of global Islamic imperialism by BBS monks. The BBS has published posters in Sri Lanka as a woman eye hijab red evil -dressed symbolically the hijab was identified as a state direct threat to security and territory. Radical Political Buddhism has unexpectedly supported local interlocking concerns with international alarms. The Global Discourse against Terrorism and New Kinds of Fuel of the Buddhist Media and intensifying the fears of Islam. Global demographic trends and the expected rise in the population of

Muslims in the world is another concern for the BBS. While challenging the number of population of Muslims in Sri Lanka, the alleged increase of the population of Muslims is of fundamental importance for both the BBS as an increase of the Muslim population is seen as a big threat to Buddhism as a social and cultural phenomenon around the world. BBS says that Buddhist societies ultimately convert Muslims, but no external pressures, but to change the relationship between Buddhists and Muslims in the population. To avoid "buddhist becoming a minority in their own country" (as the slogan says), Buddhists called radical groups to family planning policies, including legal regulation on women's reproductive health. In 2012 at the inauguration meeting, BBS leader BBS asked the government closed methods of family planning in the country of the Singhalese women could bear more children. Finally, the BBS was concerned that the decline of the Buddhist Sinhalese population implies a decrease in monastic recruits and small families are less likely to give up maybe two children from a small household in order.

The protection of Buddhism and the Cingalese race are familiar with the buddhist Singalian nationalism, so BBS's novelty is its strong rhetoric against Muslims, their fighting spirit in the public space and its proactive international network. This point is particularly noteworthy. In 2014, BBS has an official agreement with the 969 radical Buddhist group in Myanmar in an attempt to save Buddhism together what they see as the Muslim threat. As the 969 and BBS can be grouped as "Buddhist nationalism" has been questioned (Schontal and Walton 2016). However, it is quite possible that the ethnic-religious identity at local level is integrated with the more clearly defined Buddhist regional political identity, which permeates their anti-Muslim messages with greater urgency and importance (Frydenlund 2015). In many ways, the BBS 969 and incorporates the classic neo-radicalism (or fundamentalism) scheme is here defined as the will to work against institutional differentiation caused by colonial, modern, and secularization. According to the agreement signed in Colombo, "subtle raids that take place under the appearance of laity, multicultural, and other liberal notions ... Funded abroad ... Slightly conveyed in local situations."

Internal religious cleansing is another aspect, often overlooked, but often BBS ideology (**Deegalle** 2016). When Buddhist enemies not defined directly in the hymn BBS (bulletin board, but given the strong position against Muslims against Christians and generally not Buddhist in Sri Lanka is interpreted as a minority), the song also refers to false Buddha. On 24 August 2012, the BBS actually attacked Sirivardhana Buda, famous and controversial Buddhist spokeperson in the Galle district who claimed to be the next Buddha, Maitreya. A couple days later, the BBS has requested the intervention of the Department of Buddhist Affairs Sirivardhana against those who have felt insulted Buddhism.

RITUALS / practices

The BBS is another form of Buddhism, and its participants and followers belong to the 'traditional' learning institutions and the practice of Buddhism in Sri Lanka. BBS organizes meetings in spaces in the public that are open to the public. In these meetings, the BBS monks raise things to consider, as a Christian proselytizing or halal certification in Sri Lanka. [Image Right] meetings, according to Buddhist preaching (called bana Sinhalese) to Buddhist monks sitting on a CUI palladium in which they speak, sat wearing a lay white on the floor. Vier Gnanasara is a renowned poet and his verses BBS distributes protective singing the Pali Canon (eg Jaya Piritha) through its website. From a doctrinal point of view, the BBS is a particularly modernist strand of Buddhism, which focuses on reviving the practice of Buddhism for the housing needs of current society. For example, the major BBS monks support the temporary order for the laity to get into the monastic order (as practiced in Sri Lanka unlike Thailand and Myanmar) and support of the religious movement, which aims to reintroduce the order of nuns (Theravada Buddhism, which is not officially recognized by its disintegration in the eleventh century CE). The BBS is concerned about the presumed holiness of the Buddha 's teachings, and is hostile to form' popular 'of Buddhism, the worship of the deity and quick religious development, for example the indication will be indicated by its attack against the Sirivardhana preacher.

ORGANIZATION / LEADERSHIP

The BBS is monastic organization, but recognizes four groups as their electorate: monks, nuns, lay men and lay women, welcoming all who share their Buddhist, Islamic militant political agenda and anti-nationalist Sinhalese. [Image Right] Headquartered in Sri Sambuddha Jayanthi

Mandira, in Colombo, owned by the Buddhist Cultural Center. The BBS has used extensively of modern communication technologies, such as the 'Internet (eg web site (web Bodu Bala Sena 2015) and social platforms like Facebook. The hymn BBS is another important tool for BBS to send message. Played by famous singer Sunil Edirisinghe Sinhala Buddhist hymn called island to take steps to protect Buddhism (-to c. -structures that will destroy Buddhism) "ferocious forces of Mara" by launching a "war of dharma" pure (yuddhayak dharma). Anthem "BBS also made accessible for download as a ringtone in 2013 by Sri Lanka Telecom Mobitel. According to an advertisement display table, download the ringtone help fund the organization. Following the public issue Mobitel apologized, saying that BBS treated like any other ringtone content provider (based on a profit sharing method).

Although its mainly based is in Sri Lanka, the BBS is also a form of Buddhist activism and transnational ethnic and religious nationalism, which is supported by the Buddhist Sinhalese living outside the country in countries such as Australia, the United Kingdom and the United US. For example, in 2013 he led Gnanasara sing the opening of the Buddhist temple, Indiana in United States

Issues / Challenges

World discourse against terrorism and the policy of religious demographic changes are two key factors of Buddhist fear the rise of Islam. Another crucial aspect, but too often overlooked Buddhist anti - Muslim discourse, it refers to the economic sphere. In Sri Lanka in 2013, BBS has called for abolition of halal. Later this year, a BBS monaco was also sacrifice on the halal problem, being the first monaco in the history of Sri Lanka to participate in self-immolation. Animal rights are certainly high in the Buddhist calendar (not only among politicians Buddhist radicals), but a more detailed analysis of halal dispute analysis Sri Lanka demonstrates that the protecting animals, especially cows , is only part of the tale. At a press conference in Colombo in 2012, Ven. Gnanissara brought the specific question of commercial competition Buddhist Sinhalese, saying that the halal certification system involves unfair treatment Sinhalese and Muslim shopkeepers and boutique "boycott" without Halal certification. "This is a Buddhist Sinhalese country,» Fri Gnanissara argued, "since ancient times Sinhalese - dominated society and has helped the company to build and carry out their activities. Now these companies are frightened by Muslims with the symbol of halal certification and just make an issue out of it -. "On top of political agenda Buddhist Sri Lanka, therefore, we find the Sinhala-Muslim economic competition, particularly among manufacturers of halal food and non - halal, the location of products on supermarket shelves, and the extent to which it could offer halal food certification Buddhist monks in them. in fact, the BBS explicitly into account the concerns of the business Sinhalese community. in addition, it was observed that there should be several attacks sono stati Slaughter Muslims, supermarkets and shops.

The most serious charge against violent action against Muslims BBS refers directly to a variety of disorders often referred to as "The disturbances Aluthgama." [Photo right] on 15-16 June 2014, Muslims living in the southern town of Aluthgama, Dharga town, Valipanna Beruwela and were attacked by a mob, which made the three dead Muslims, burned hundreds of homes and shops to growth and thousands of displaced people, mainly affecting the Muslim community. Over the past two years of violence, hatred feeling cultivated by BBS has been through social media and through public events and media statements. There were sporadic acts of violence against the Muslim community in the country, in the same period, but riots Aluthgama shows unprecedented levels of organization and orchestration (Haniffa et al 2014). On 15 June 2014, BBS has organized a public event in Aluthgama, after an accident between a Buddhist monaco three young Muslims. In his speech, the secretary general of BBS Gnanasara concluded by saying that "the next time another yellow dress is even touched, without going to the authorities, the law of the jungle takes precedence" (quoted in Haniffa et al 2014: 19) . Later, the rally has formed a procession through the town, ending in massive riots. While the actual sequence of events (and the role played by the BBS or young Muslims in the region remains unclear and contested), it is clear that the riots have left damaged local Muslim communities far more than their neighbors Buddhist Sinhalese.

BBS and various small groups of similar type in Sri Lanka gave him STATES label are "militants" or adversaries "extreme" or through local and international media. Groups of them - would disagree with these labels because they are involved in military activities or forming militant wings. However, many contemporary Buddhists lobbyists involved in the military rhetoric, or the use of "force" (bullet) "army" (SENA) in their organization names, and are accused of being part of anti-Muslim violence. As noted above, this violence includes attacking the Christian churches, looting shops belonging to Muslims in Colombo and attacks that are widespread on the Muslim community in Aluthgama in 2014. The dictative regime of President Rajapaksa protected (2005-2015) encouraged, radical Buddhist movement through to get tacit support of the police (leaving work as security guards) and then by impunity. In addition, the president 's brother, Defense Secretary Gotabaya Rajapaksa then repeatedly publicly stated its support BBS monks. [Image Right] While the BBS him - although he was not armed, widely believed that mobilized the armed forces in support of the State.

The new Maithripala Sirisena (2015-) regime, facilitated decreased public support and the political space for such movements. Note, however, that the root pressure Buddhist groups are part of Sri Lanka's political life, and thus decreasing its current plan for the operation opposes a new importance in the coming years.("Bodu Bala Sena (Army of Buddhist Power) – WRSP," n.d.)

REFERENCES

1. Anghie, A. (2009). Rethinking Sovereignty in International Law. Annual Review of Law and Social Science, 5(1), 291–310. https://doi.org/10.1146/annurev.lawsocsci.4.110707.172355
2. Bodu Bala Sena (Army of Buddhist Power) – WRSP. (n.d.). Retrieved June 16, 2017, from https://wrldrels.org/2016/10/08/bodu-bala-sena/
3. Digest of Terrorist Cases. (2010). United Nations Office on Drugs and Crime. Retrieved from https://www.unodc.org/documents/terrorism/Publications/Digest_of_Terrorist_Cases/English.pdf
4. Ford, J. (2014, June 6). The Origins of Boko Haram [Text]. Retrieved June 16, 2017, from http://nationalinterest.org/feature/the-origins-boko-haram-10609
5. Glenn, C. (2016, July 5). Timeline: Rise and Spread of the Islamic State. Retrieved June 16, 2017, from https://www.wilsoncenter.org/article/timeline-rise-and-spread-the-islamic-state

6. Anghie, A. (2009). Rethinking Sovereignty in International Law. Annual Review of Law and Social Science, 5(1), 291–310. https://doi.org/10.1146/annurev.lawsocsci.4.110707.172355
7. Aboul-Enein, Y. (2006). Street Literature on Usama Bin Laden. Infantry, 95(3), 22.
8. Anders Behring Breivik. (n.d.). Retrieved June 16, 2017, from https://www.biography.com/people/anders-behring-breivik-20617893
9. Barrett, J. (2016, December 7). A Complete List of Radical Islamic Terror Attacks on U.S. Soil Under Obama. Retrieved June 16, 2017, from http://www.dailywire.com/news/11410/complete-list-radical-islamic-terror-attacks-us-james-barrett
10. Bianchi, A. (2011). Terrorism and Armed Conflict: Insights from a Law & Literature Perspective. Leiden Journal of International Law, 24(1), 1–21. https://doi.org/10.1017/S0922156510000567
11. Bill Moyers Journal . Brief History of al Qaeda | PBS. (n.d.). Retrieved June 16, 2017, from http://www.pbs.org/moyers/journal/07272007/alqaeda.html
12. Biography of Khalid Sheikh Mohammed. (2007, March 14). [Text. Article]. Retrieved June 16, 2017, from http://www.foxnews.com/story/2007/03/14/biography-khalid-sheikh-mohammed.html
13. Blumenau, B. (2014). The Other Battleground of the Cold War: The UN and the Struggle against International Terrorism in the 1970s. Journal of Cold War Studies, 16(1), 61–84.
14. Byman, D. (2005). Strategic Surprise and the September 11 Attacks. Annual Review of Political Science, 8(1), 145–170. https://doi.org/10.1146/annurev.polisci.8.082103.104927
15. Chapter 2. Country Reports: Middle East and North Africa Overview. (n.d.). Retrieved June 16, 2017, from http://www.state.gov/j/ct/rls/crt/2015/257517.htm
16. Charney, J. (2001). The Use of Force Against Terrorism and International Law, 95(4), 835–839. https://doi.org/https://doi.org/10.2307/2674628
17. Chaskalson, A. (2008). THE WIDENING GYRE: COUNTER-TERRORISM, 67(1), 69–91. https://doi.org/https://doi.org/10.1017/S0008197308000032

18. Chenoweth, E. (2013a). Terrorism and Democracy. Annual Review of Political Science, 16(1), 355–378. https://doi.org/10.1146/annurev-polisci-032211-221825
19. Chenoweth, E. (2013b). Terrorism and Democracy. Annual Review of Political Science, 16(1), 355–378. https://doi.org/10.1146/annurev-polisci-032211-221825
20. Cloud, J., MacLeod, S., Radwan, A., DeQuine, J., Klarreich, K., Liston, B., … Wosnitza, R. (2001). Atta's Odyssey. Time, 158(16), 64.
21. Colijn, K. (2003). Weapons of mass destruction A medium-power concern?
22. Faisal Shahzad. (n.d.). Retrieved June 16, 2017, from https://www.biography.com/people/faisal-shahzad-564894
23. Gialampoukidis, I., Kalpakis, G., Tsikrika, T., Vrochidis, S., & Kompatsiaris, I. (2016). Key Player Identification in Terrorism-Related Social Media Networks Using Centrality Measures. In 2016 European Intelligence and Security Informatics Conference (EISIC) (pp. 112–115). https://doi.org/10.1109/EISIC.2016.029
24. Hamed Tofangsaz. (2015). Rethinking terrorist financing; where does all this lead? Journal of Money Laundering Control, 18(1), 112–130. https://doi.org/10.1108/JMLC-12-2013-0049
25. Hegde, L. V., Sreelakshmi, N., & Mahesh, K. (2016). Visual Analytics of Terrorism Data. In 2016 IEEE International Conference on Cloud Computing in Emerging Markets (CCEM) (pp. 90–94). https://doi.org/10.1109/CCEM.2016.024
26. Heinze, E. A. (2011). The evolution of international law in light of the 'global War on Terror.' Review of International Studies, 37(3), 1069–1094. https://doi.org/10.1017/S0260210510001014
27. Henry W. Fischer. (1999). Dimensions of biological terrorism: to what must we mitigate and respond? Disaster Prevention and Management: An International Journal, 8(1), 27–32. https://doi.org/10.1108/09653569910258192
28. Jeff Fort. (n.d.). Retrieved June 16, 2017, from https://www.biography.com/people/jeff-fort-578620
29. Jin, S., Ge, J., & Peng, J. (2016). Terrorism risk assessment using

hierarchical bidirectional fuzzy rule interpolation. In 2016 IEEE 15th International Conference on Cognitive Informatics Cognitive Computing (ICCI*CC) (pp. 403–410). https://doi.org/10.1109/ICCI-CC.2016.7862068

30. LaFree, G., & Ackerman, G. (2009). The Empirical Study of Terrorism: Social and Legal Research. Annual Review of Law and Social Science, 5(1), 347–374. https://doi.org/10.1146/annurev.lawsocsci.093008.131517
31. Lister, C. (2014). Profiling the Islamic State. Brookings Doha Center Analysis Paper.
32. McCormick, G. H. (2003). Terrorist Decision Making. Annual Review of Political Science, 6(1), 473–507. https://doi.org/10.1146/annurev.polisci.6.121901.085601
33. McVeigh's final statement. (2001, June 11). The Guardian. Retrieved from https://www.theguardian.com/world/2001/jun/11/mcveigh.usa1
34. Mertz, E., & Rajah, J. (2014). Language-and-Law Scholarship: An Interdisciplinary Conversation and a Post-9/11 Example. Annual Review of Law and Social Science, 10(1), 169–183. https://doi.org/10.1146/annurev-lawsocsci-102612-133958
35. Mir, H. (2001, November 7). Osama claims he has nukes: If US uses N- arms it will get same response. Retrieved from https://thesis.haverford.edu/bitstream/handle/10066/4732/OBL20011107.pdf?sequence=3&isAllowed=y
36. Muga, W. (2016, March 26). Recent terrorists attacks in Africa. Retrieved June 16, 2017, from http://www.the-star.co.ke/news/2016/03/26/recent-terrorists-attacks-in-africa_c1320034
37. Patrick Hardouin, & Reiner Weichhardt. (2006). Terrorist fund raising through criminal activities. Journal of Money Laundering Control, 9(3), 303–308. https://doi.org/10.1108/13685200610681823
38. Power, C., & Dickey, C. (2002). Muhammad Atta's Neighborhood. Newsweek, 140(25), 36.
39. Recent Major Terror Attacks in Europe. (2017, May 23). Bloomberg.Com. Retrieved from https://www.bloomberg.com/news/articles/2017-05-23/recent-major-attacks-in-europe

40. Savelsberg, J. J., & McElrath, S. (2014). Crime, Law, and Regime Change. Annual Review of Law and Social Science, 10(1), 259–279. https://doi.org/10.1146/annurev-lawsocsci-110413-030555

41. Sosis, R., & Alcorta, C. (n.d.). Militants and Martyrs: Evolutionary Perspectives on Religion and Terrorism. Department of Anthroplogy, University of Connecticut.

42. Stevenson, K. (2011). Osama bin Laden. Osama Bin Laden, 1.

43. Ted Kaczynski. (n.d.). Retrieved June 16, 2017, from https://www.biography.com/people/ted-kaczynski-578450

44. Timothy McVeigh | American militant. (n.d.). Retrieved June 16, 2017, from https://www.britannica.com/biography/Timothy-McVeigh

45. Turk, A. T. (2004). Sociology of Terrorism. Annual Review of Sociology, 30(1), 271–286. https://doi.org/10.1146/annurev.soc.30.012703.110510

46. Vats, P. (2016). A comprehensive review of Cyber Terrorism in the current scenario. In 2016 Second International Innovative Applications of Computational Intelligence on Power, Energy and Controls with their Impact on Humanity (CIPECH) (pp. 277–281). https://doi.org/10.1109/CIPECH.2016.7918782

47. W.A. Tupman. (2009). Ten myths about terrorist financing. Journal of Money Laundering Control, 12(2), 189–205. https://doi.org/10.1108/13685200910951938

48. Wander, A. (2008, July 13). A history of terror: Al-Qaeda 1988-2008. The Guardian. Retrieved from https://www.theguardian.com/world/2008/jul/13/history.alqaida

INDEX

A

Afghanistan 102, 107, 108, 110, 112, 116, 118, 119, 120, 121, 122
Animal Liberation Front (ALF) 20
anti-globalization 127
atomic bombs 155

C

Ceccules Communists Combats(CCC) 128
CIA counter - terrorism (CTC) 112
criminal matters 81

D

Director of Central Intelligence (DCI) 106

E

economically 180
entitlements 67
Eumenydes cycle of tragedies 102

F

financial support 89
foreign direct investment (FDI) 39
frequently 165, 166

G

global community 141
global Terrorism Index (GTI) 61
Gross Domestic Product (GDP) 37

H

Hegghammer's triangle 22
Human rights prohibits 68

hypothesis 155

I

Ideology 18, 21, 24
illustrating 22
International Atomic Energy Agency (IAEA) 160
international Humanitarian law (IHL) 137
Irish republican Army (IRA) 52
Islamic imperialist 30
Islamic scholar 30

J

Japanese Red Army (JRA) 129
jihad 121
Jihad 28
Jihadism 122

L

Les Bienveillantes 102
Liberation Tigers of Tamil Eelam(LTTE) 129

M

Muslim brotherhood public 31

P

Palestine Liberation Organization (PLO) 53
paramilitary 89, 90, 91, 92, 93, 94, 97
psychological 175

S

Sawab 181
Security Council plays 141
spectacular 95, 99
staphylococcus 156
strategy 2, 21, 23, 25

T

terrorism 101, 102, 103, 104, 107, 108, 110, 111, 112, 113, 114, 115, 116, 117, 118, 119, 120, 121, 122
terrorist 81, 82, 83, 84, 86, 87, 88, 89, 95, 96, 98
Terrorist ambition 66
terrorizersas 128
the Wretched of the Earth' 125

U

United People's Front of Nepal (UPF) 129

W

Wal-Mart 161
weapon of mass destruction (WMD) 58